SHE-HULK   MEDUSA   DAZZLER   CAPTAIN MARVEL   ??

A-FORCE

WRITERS
**MARGUERITE BENNETT
& G. WILLOW WILSON**

PENCILER
JORGE MOLINA

INKERS
**JORGE MOLINA,
CRAIG YEUNG
& WALDEN WONG**

COLORISTS
LAURA MARTIN
WITH MATT MILLA (#1)

LETTERER
VC'S CORY PETIT

COVER ART
**JIM CHEUNG
& LAURA MARTIN**

ASSISTANT EDITOR
ALANNA SMITH

EDITOR
DANIEL KETCHUM

COLLECTION EDITOR
JENNIFER GRÜNWALD

ASSISTANT EDITOR
SARAH BRUNSTAD

ASSOCIATE MANAGING EDITOR
ALEX STARBUCK

EDITOR, SPECIAL PROJECTS
MARK D. BEAZLEY

SENIOR EDITOR, SPECIAL PROJECTS
JEFF YOUNGQUIST

SVP PRINT, SALES & MARKETING
DAVID GABRIEL

BOOK DESIGNER
JAY BOWEN

EDITOR IN CHIEF
AXEL ALONSO

CHIEF CREATIVE OFFICER
JOE QUESADA

PUBLISHER
DAN BUCKLEY

EXECUTIVE PRODUCER
ALAN FINE

A-FORCE VOL. 0: WARZONES! Contains material originally published in magazine form as A-FORCE #1-5. First printing 2015. ISBN# 978-0-7851-9861-1. Published by MARVEL WORLDWIDE, INC., a subsidiary of MARVEL ENTERTAINMENT, LLC. OFFICE OF PUBLICATION: 135 West 50th Street, New York, NY 10020. Copyright © 2015 MARVEL No similarity between any of the names, characters, persons, and/or institutions in this magazine with those of any living or dead person or institution is intended, and any such similarity which may exist is purely coincidental. **Printed in Canada.** ALAN FINE, President, Marvel Entertainment; DAN BUCKLEY, President, TV, Publishing and Brand Management; JOE QUESADA, Chief Creative Officer; TOM BREVOORT, SVP of Publishing; DAVID BOGART, SVP of Operations & Procurement, Publishing; C.B. CEBULSKI, VP of International Development & Brand Management; DAVID GABRIEL, SVP Print, Sales & Marketing; JIM O'KEEFE, VP of Operations & Logistics; DAN CARR, Executive Director of Publishing Technology; SUSAN CRESPI, Editorial Operations Manager; ALEX MORALES, Publishing Operations Manager; STAN LEE, Chairman Emeritus. For information regarding advertising in Marvel Comics or on Marvel.com, please contact Jonathan Rheingold, VP of Custom Solutions & Ad Sales, at jrheingold@marvel.com. For Marvel subscription inquiries, please call 800-217-9158. **Manufactured between 9/25/2015 and 11/2/2015 by SOLISCO PRINTERS, SCOTT, QC, CANADA.**

10 9 8 7 6 5 4 3 2 1

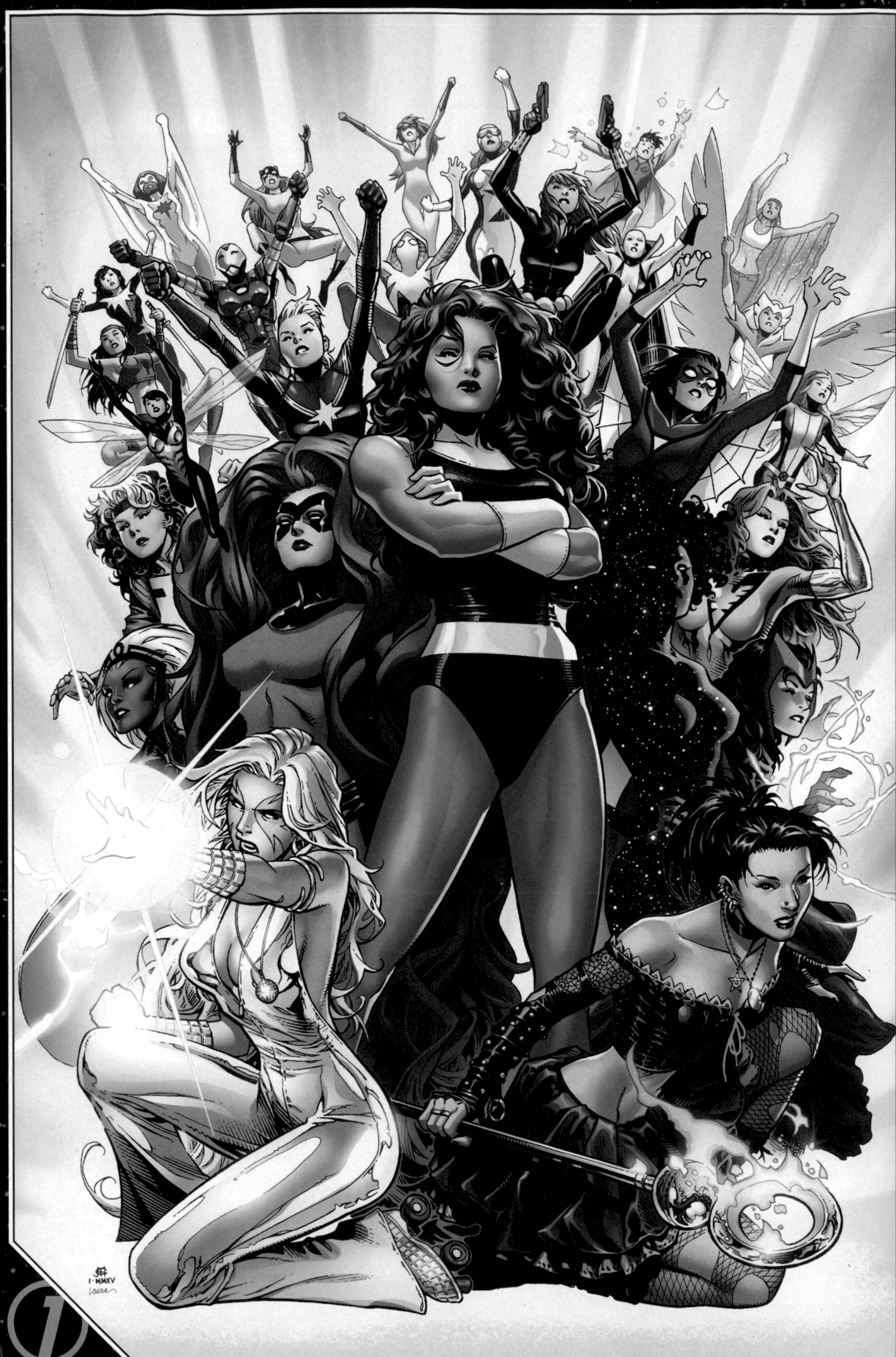
1·MMXV
Laura
1

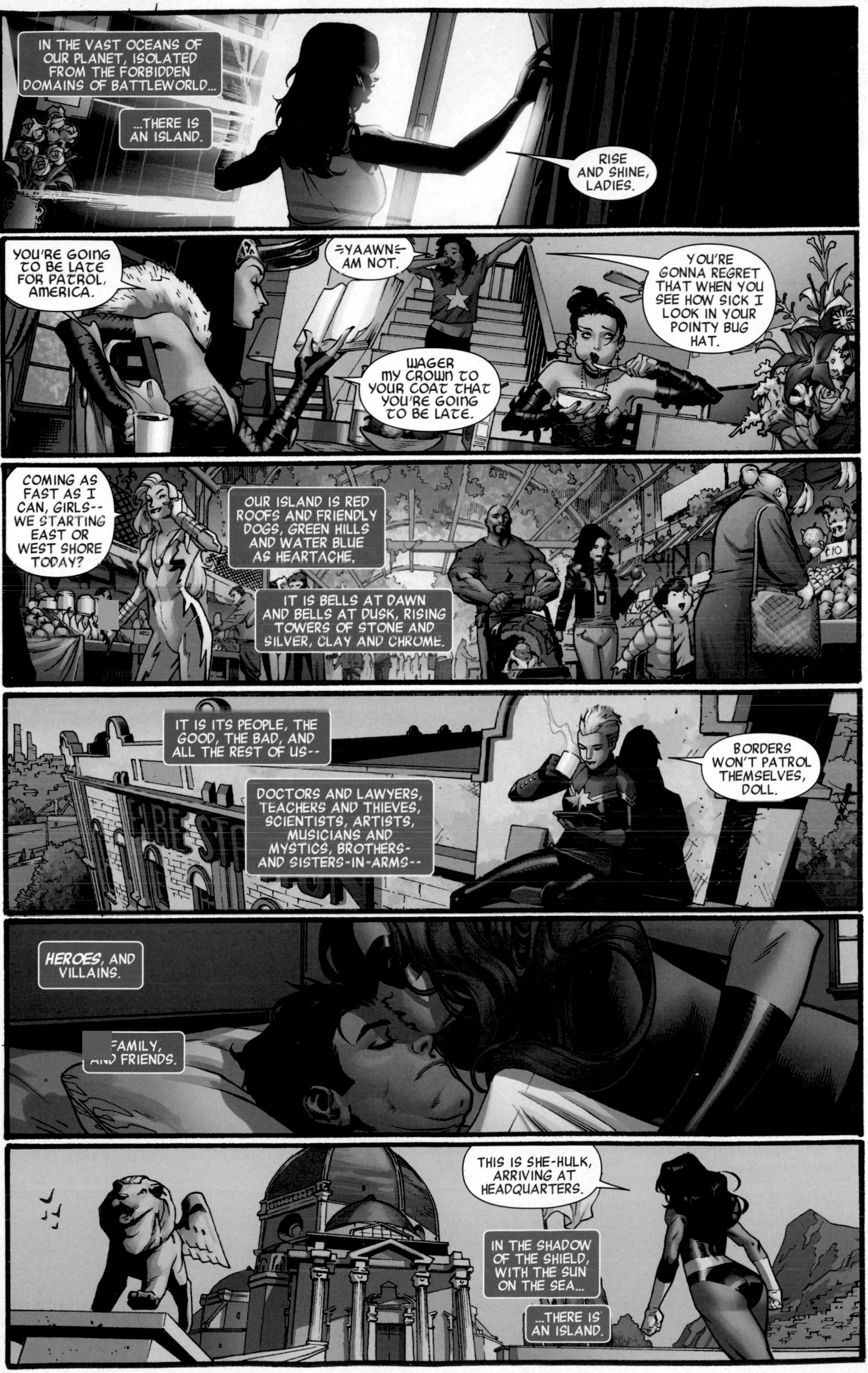
IN THE VAST OCEANS OF OUR PLANET, ISOLATED FROM THE FORBIDDEN DOMAINS OF BATTLEWORLD...
...THERE IS AN ISLAND.
RISE AND SHINE, LADIES.
YOU'RE GOING TO BE LATE FOR PATROL, AMERICA.
=YAAWN= AM NOT.
YOU'RE GONNA REGRET THAT WHEN YOU SEE HOW SICK I LOOK IN YOUR POINTY BUG HAT.
WAGER MY CROWN TO YOUR COAT THAT YOU'RE GOING TO BE LATE.
COMING AS FAST AS I CAN, GIRLS-- WE STARTING EAST OR WEST SHORE TODAY?
OUR ISLAND IS RED ROOFS AND FRIENDLY DOGS, GREEN HILLS AND WATER BLUE AS HEARTACHE.
IT IS BELLS AT DAWN AND BELLS AT DUSK, RISING TOWERS OF STONE AND SILVER, CLAY AND CHROME.
IT IS ITS PEOPLE, THE GOOD, THE BAD, AND ALL THE REST OF US--
DOCTORS AND LAWYERS, TEACHERS AND THIEVES, SCIENTISTS, ARTISTS, MUSICIANS AND MYSTICS, BROTHERS- AND SISTERS-IN-ARMS--
BORDERS WON'T PATROL THEMSELVES, DOLL.
HEROES, AND VILLAINS.
FAMILY, AND FRIENDS.
THIS IS SHE-HULK, ARRIVING AT HEADQUARTERS.
IN THE SHADOW OF THE SHIELD, WITH THE SUN ON THE SEA...
...THERE IS AN ISLAND.

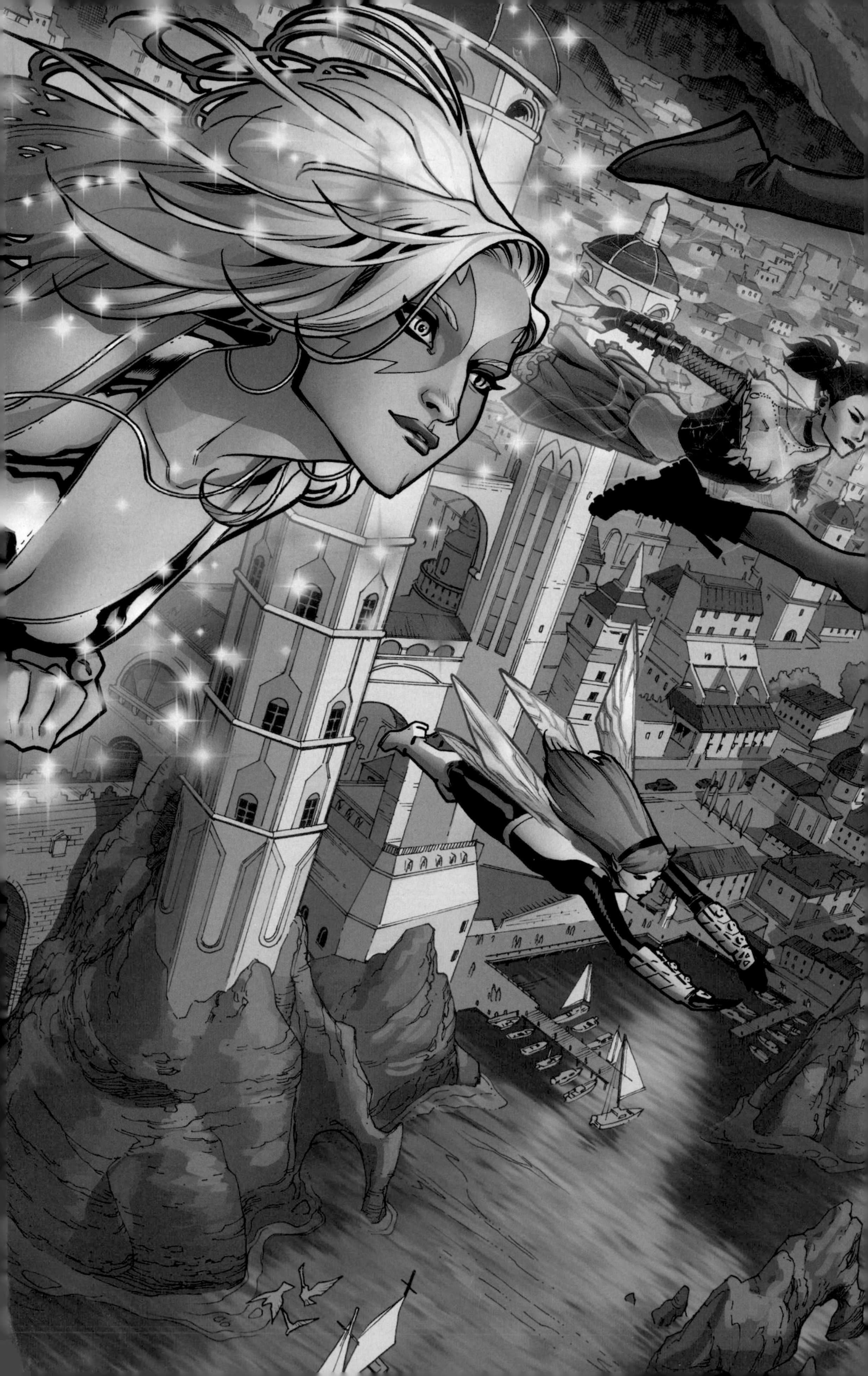

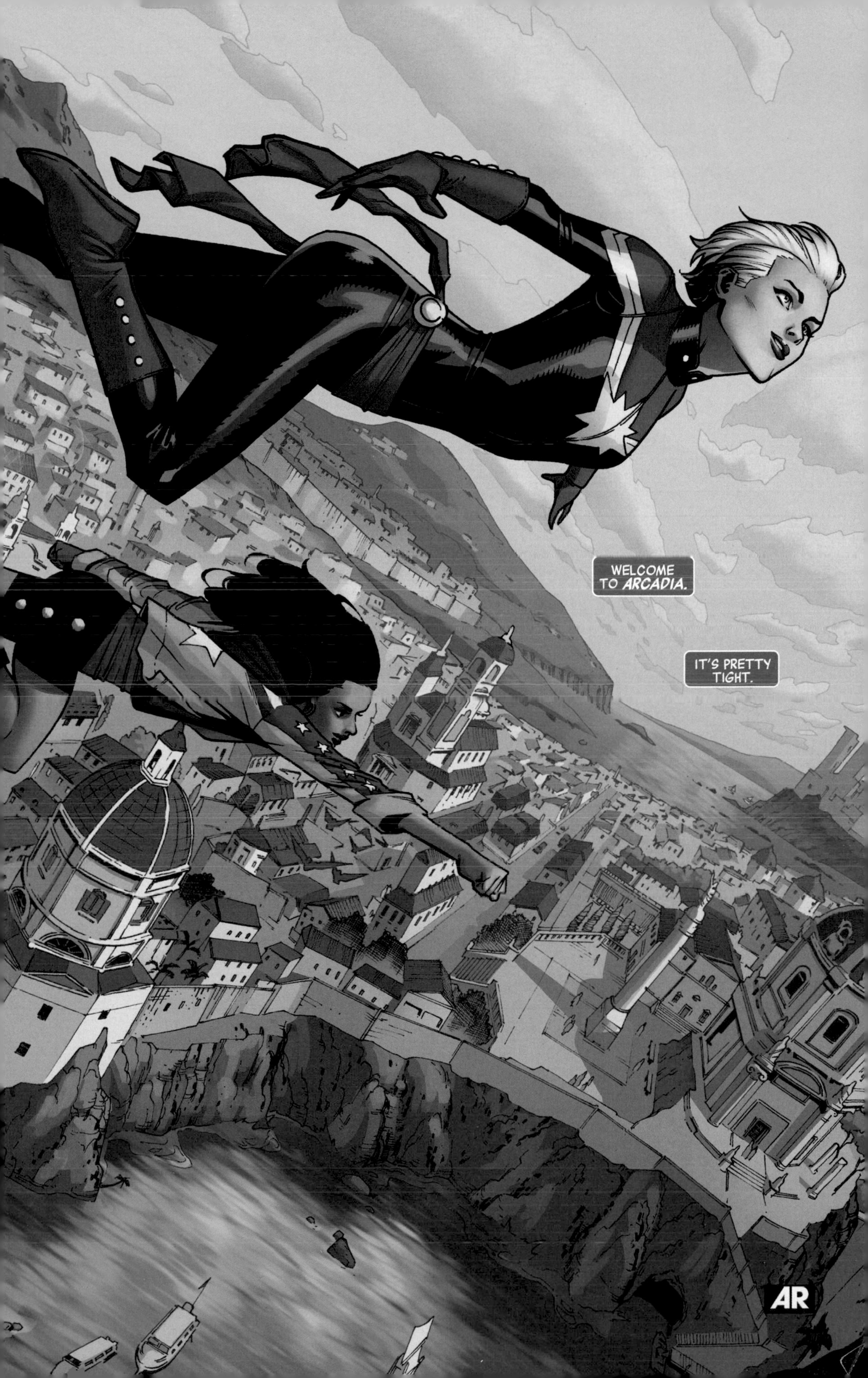
WELCOME TO ARCADIA.
IT'S PRETTY TIGHT.
AR

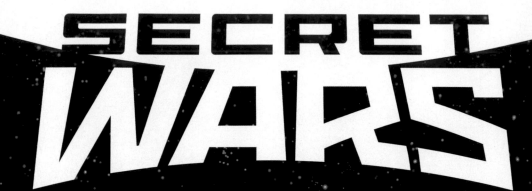

SECRET WARS

THE MULTIVERSE WAS DESTROYED!

THE HEROES OF EARTH-616 AND EARTH-1610
WERE POWERLESS TO SAVE IT!

NOW, ALL THAT REMAINS...IS **BATTLEWORLD**!

A MASSIVE, PATCHWORK PLANET COMPOSED OF THE FRAGMENTS OF WORLDS THAT NO LONGER EXIST, MAINTAINED BY THE IRON WILL OF ITS GOD AND MASTER, VICTOR VON DOOM!

EACH REGION IS A DOMAIN UNTO ITSELF!

THIS IS THE STORY OF...

A-FORCE

When you see this: **AR**, open up the MARVEL AR APP (available on applicable Apple ® iOS or Android ™ devices) and use your camera-enabled device to unlock extra-special exclusive features!

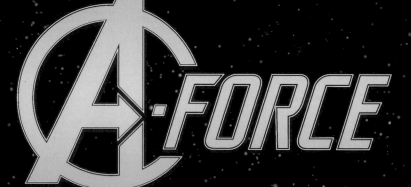

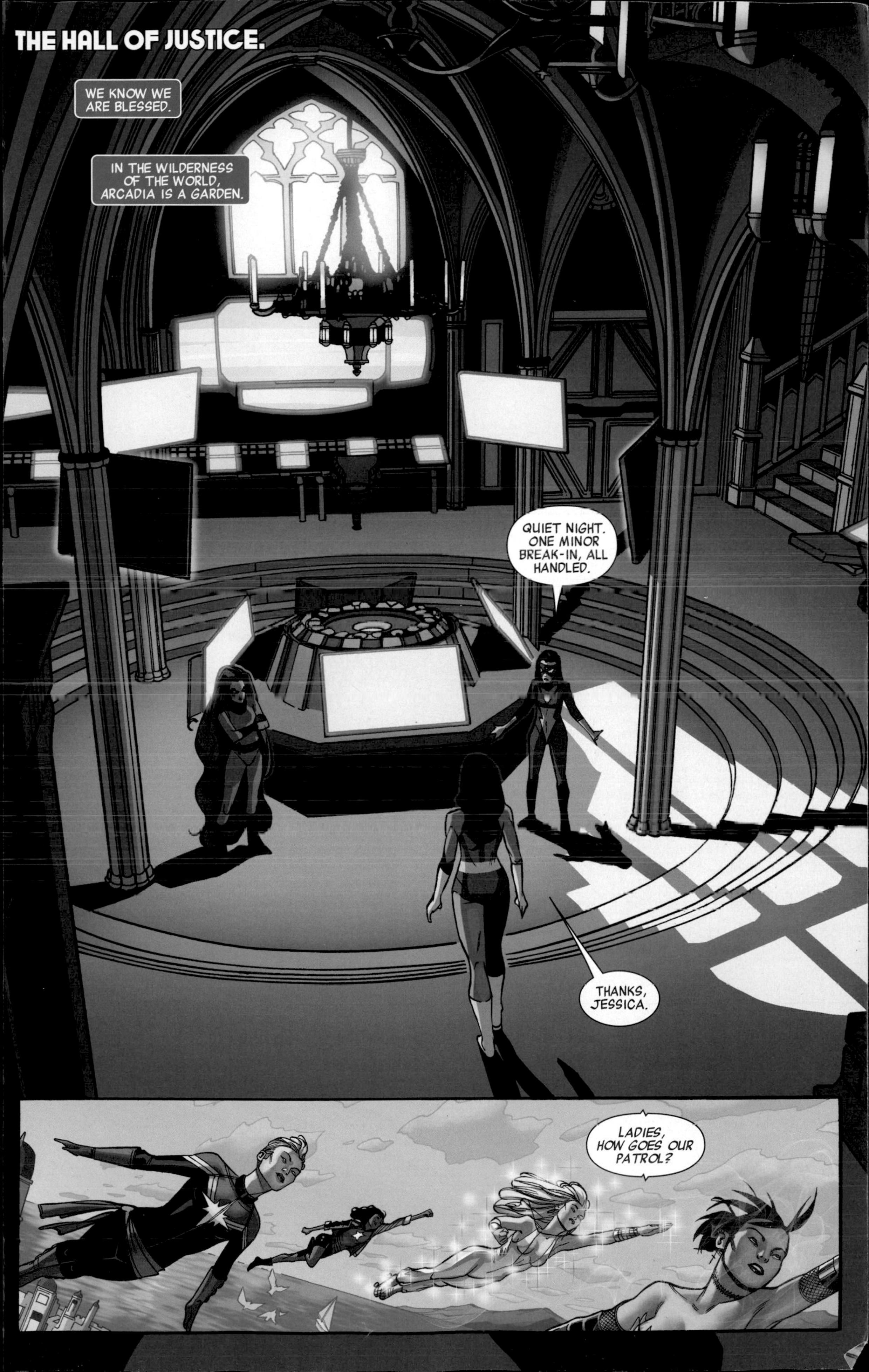
THE HALL OF JUSTICE.
WE KNOW WE ARE BLESSED.
IN THE WILDERNESS OF THE WORLD, ARCADIA IS A GARDEN.
QUIET NIGHT. ONE MINOR BREAK-IN, ALL HANDLED.
THANKS, JESSICA.
LADIES, HOW GOES OUR PATROL?

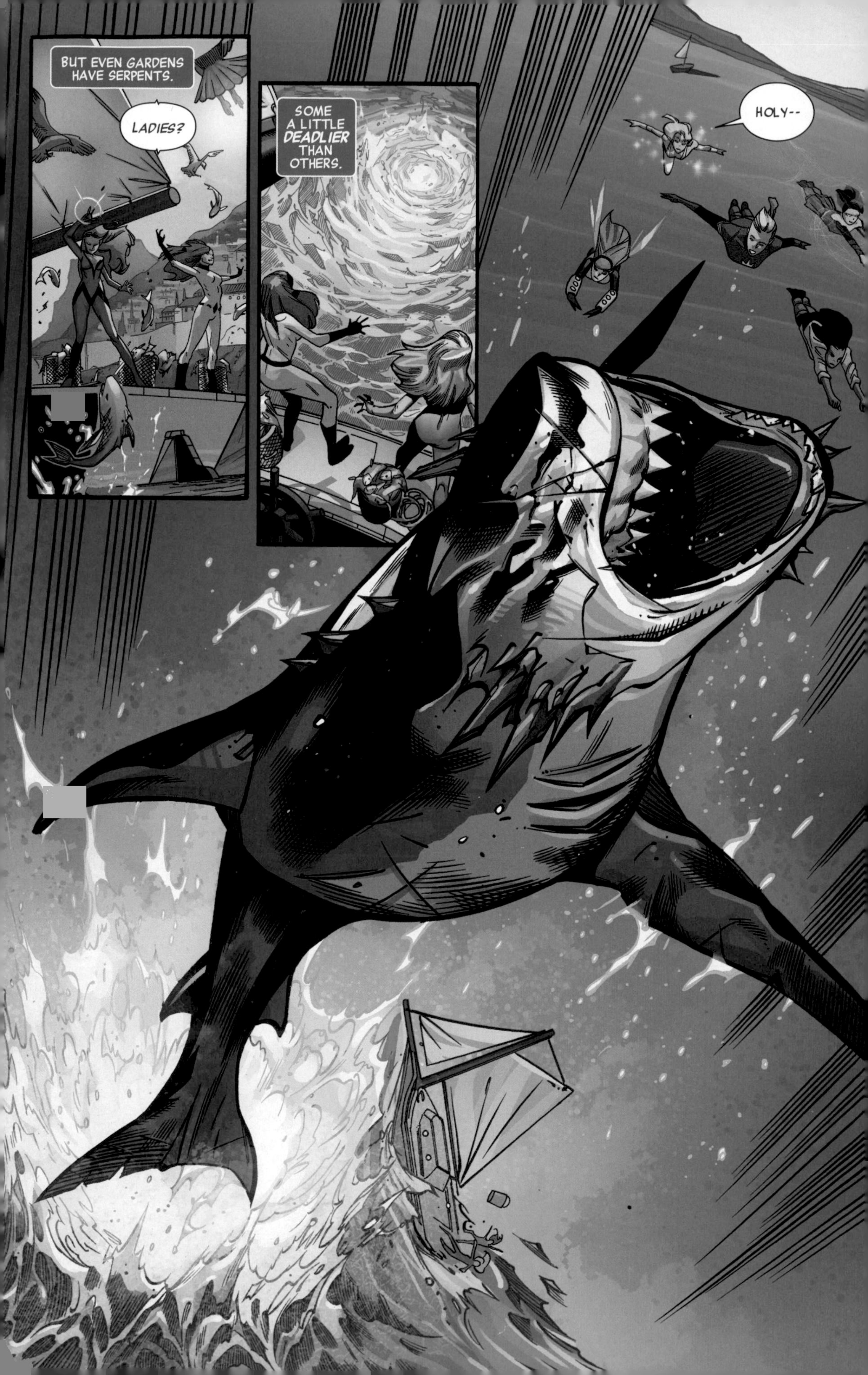
BUT EVEN GARDENS HAVE SERPENTS.
LADIES?
SOME A LITTLE DEADLIER THAN OTHERS.
HOLY--

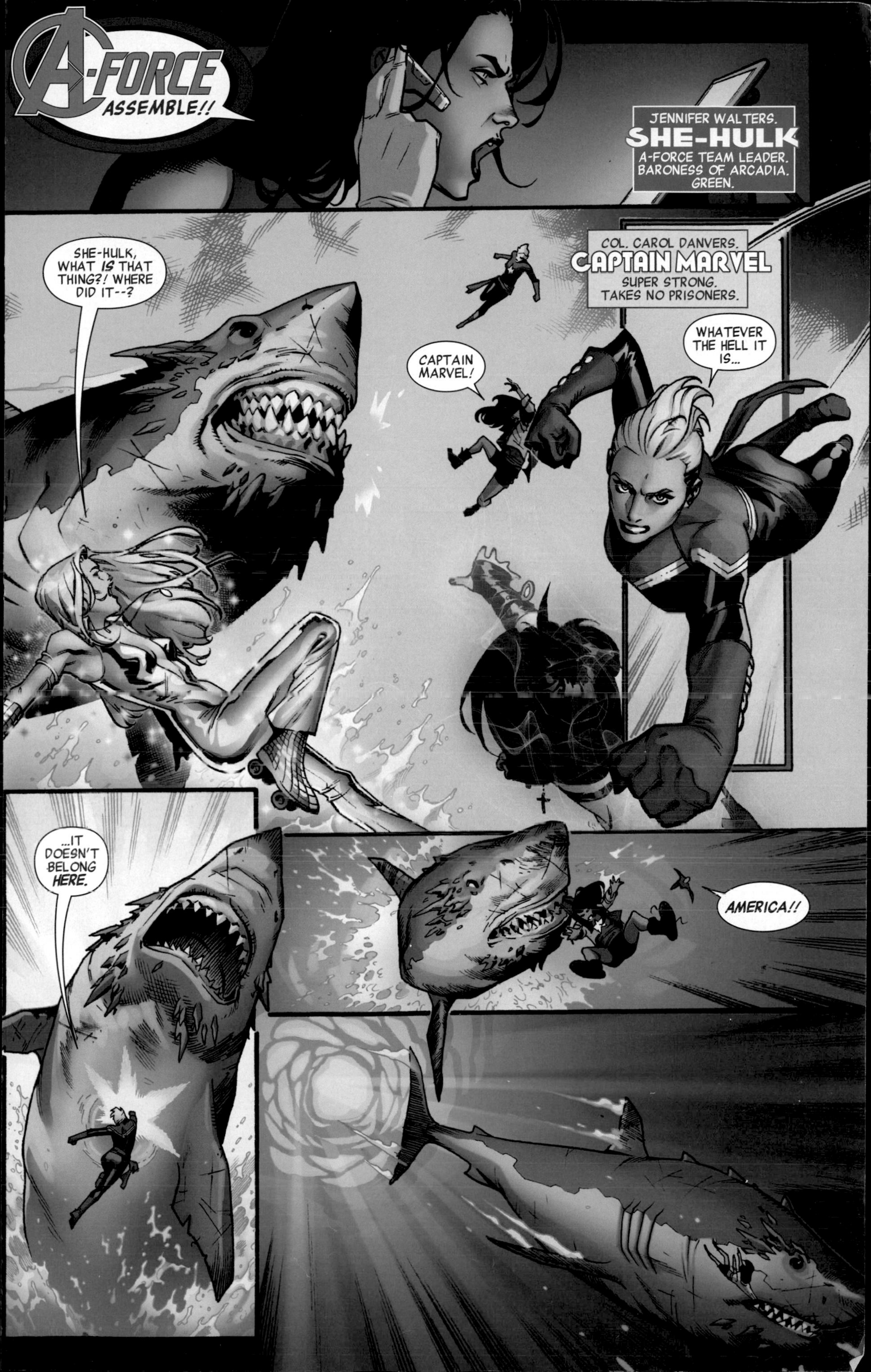
A-FORCE ASSEMBLE!!
JENNIFER WALTERS.
SHE-HULK
A-FORCE TEAM LEADER. BARONESS OF ARCADIA. GREEN.
SHE-HULK, WHAT IS THAT THING?! WHERE DID IT--?
COL. CAROL DANVERS.
CAPTAIN MARVEL
SUPER STRONG. TAKES NO PRISONERS.
CAPTAIN MARVEL!
WHATEVER THE HELL IT IS...
...IT DOESN'T BELONG HERE.
AMERICA!!

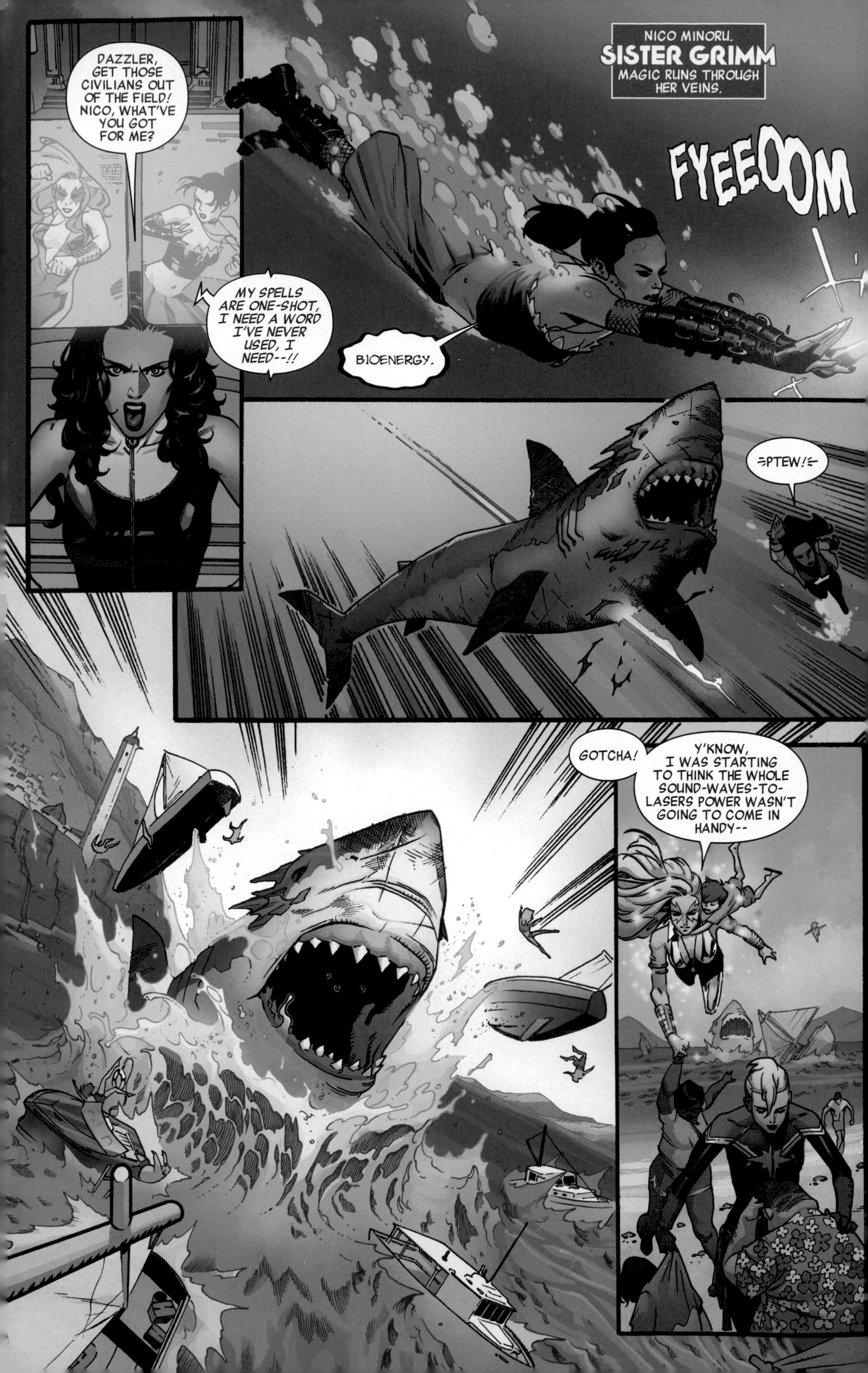

DAZZLER, GET THOSE CIVILIANS OUT OF THE FIELD! NICO, WHAT'VE YOU GOT FOR ME?
NICO MINORU. SISTER GRIMM MAGIC RUNS THROUGH HER VEINS.
MY SPELLS ARE ONE-SHOT, I NEED A WORD I'VE NEVER USED, I NEED--!!
BIOENERGY.
FYEEOOM
=PTEW!=
GOTCHA!
Y'KNOW, I WAS STARTING TO THINK THE WHOLE SOUND-WAVES-TO-LASERS POWER WASN'T GOING TO COME IN HANDY--

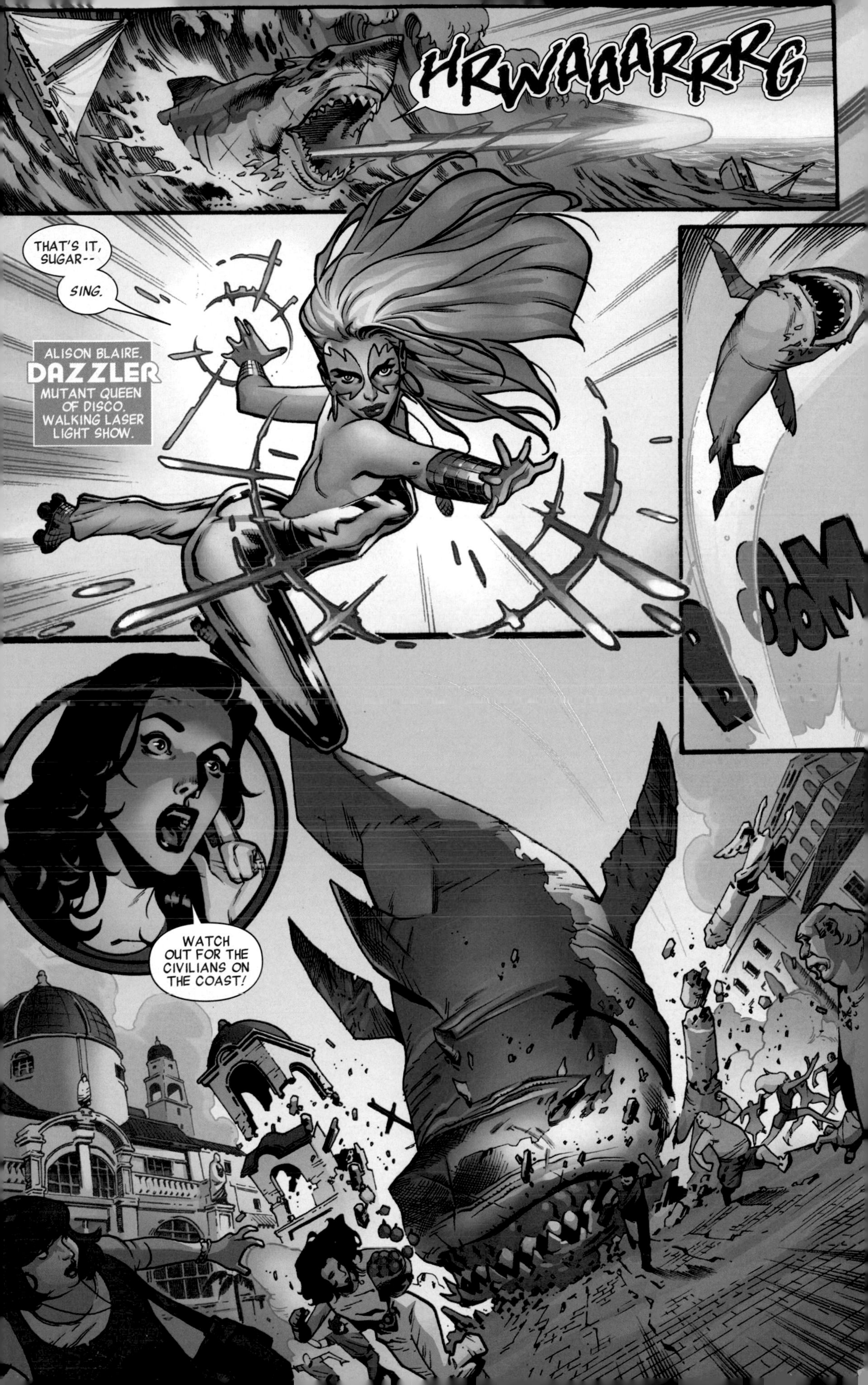
HRWAAARRRG
THAT'S IT, SUGAR--
SING.
ALISON BLAIRE.
DAZZLER
MUTANT QUEEN OF DISCO. WALKING LASER LIGHT SHOW.
BOOM
WATCH OUT FOR THE CIVILIANS ON THE COAST!

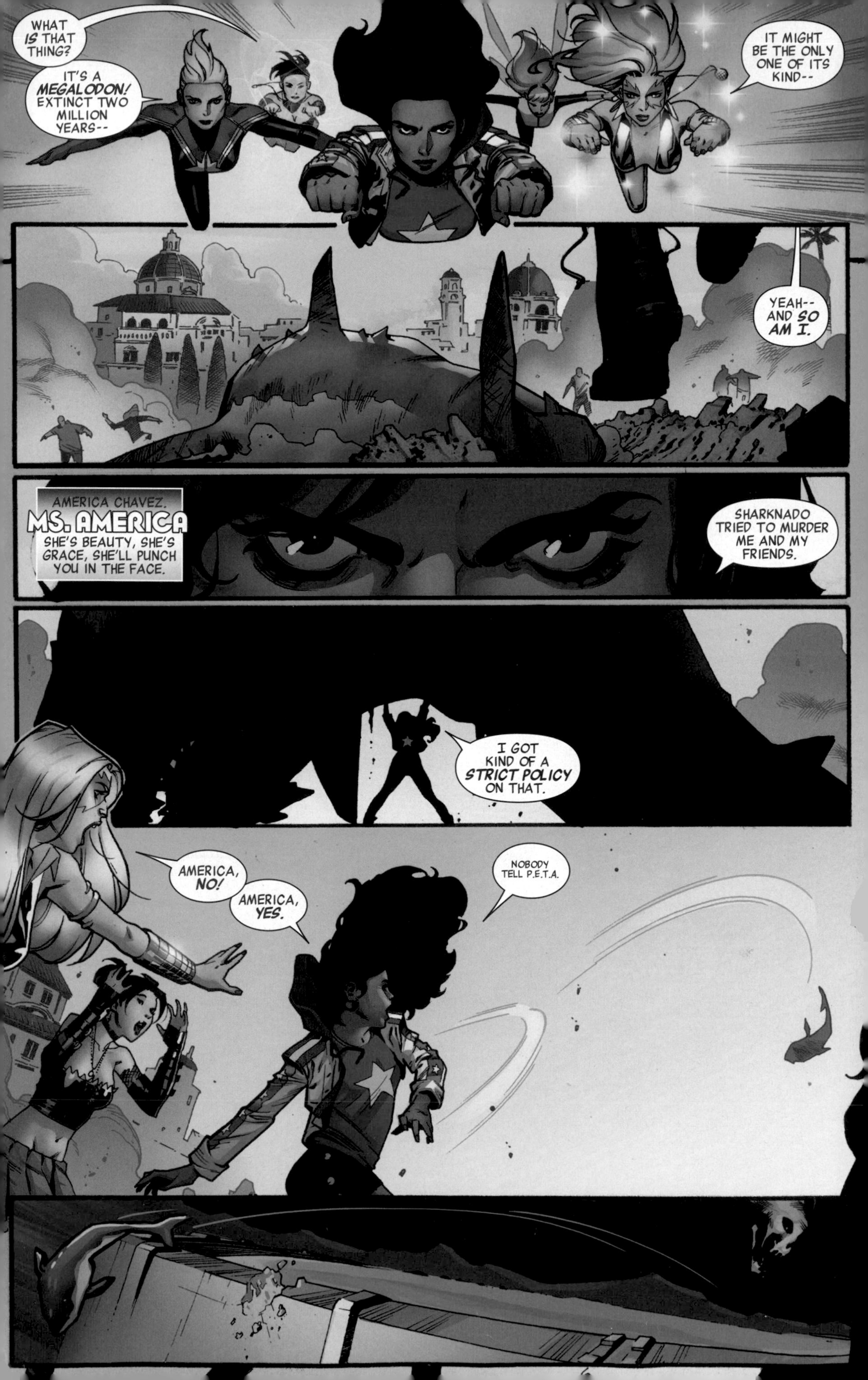
WHAT IS THAT THING?
IT'S A MEGALODON! EXTINCT TWO MILLION YEARS--
IT MIGHT BE THE ONLY ONE OF ITS KIND--
YEAH-- AND SO AM I.
AMERICA CHAVEZ.
MS. AMERICA
SHE'S BEAUTY, SHE'S GRACE, SHE'LL PUNCH YOU IN THE FACE.
SHARKNADO TRIED TO MURDER ME AND MY FRIENDS.
I GOT KIND OF A STRICT POLICY ON THAT.
AMERICA, NO!
AMERICA, YES.
NOBODY TELL P.E.T.A.

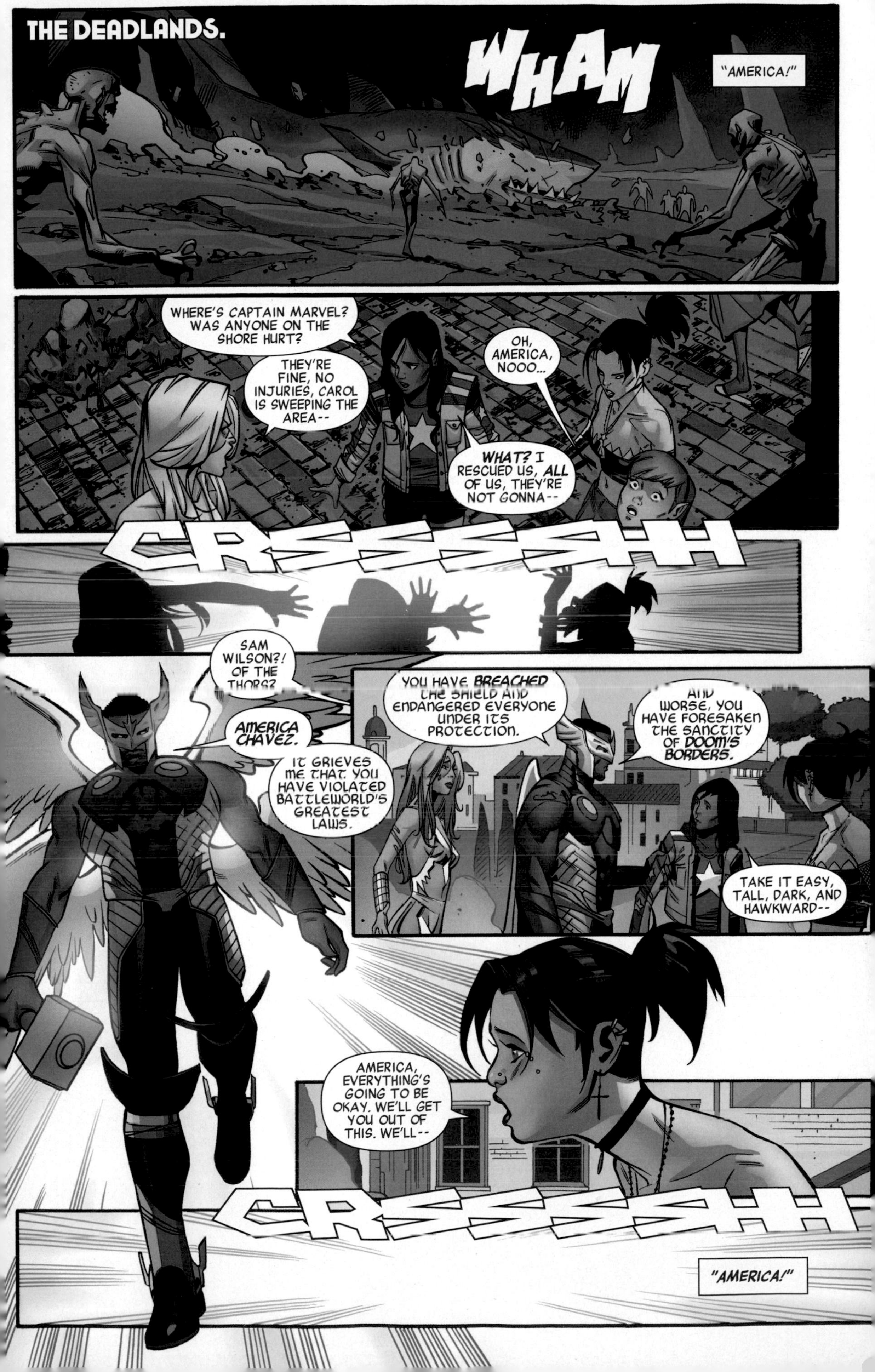
THE DEADLANDS.
WHAM
"AMERICA!"
WHERE'S CAPTAIN MARVEL? WAS ANYONE ON THE SHORE HURT?
THEY'RE FINE, NO INJURIES, CAROL IS SWEEPING THE AREA--
OH, AMERICA, NOOO...
WHAT? I RESCUED US, ALL OF US, THEY'RE NOT GONNA--
CRSSSSHH
SAM WILSON?! OF THE THORS?
AMERICA CHAVEZ.
IT GRIEVES ME THAT YOU HAVE VIOLATED BATTLEWORLD'S GREATEST LAWS.
YOU HAVE BREACHED THE SHIELD AND ENDANGERED EVERYONE UNDER ITS PROTECTION.
AND WORSE, YOU HAVE FORESAKEN THE SANCTITY OF DOOM'S BORDERS.
TAKE IT EASY, TALL, DARK, AND HAWKWARD--
AMERICA, EVERYTHING'S GOING TO BE OKAY. WE'LL GET YOU OUT OF THIS. WE'LL--
CRSSSSHH
"AMERICA!"

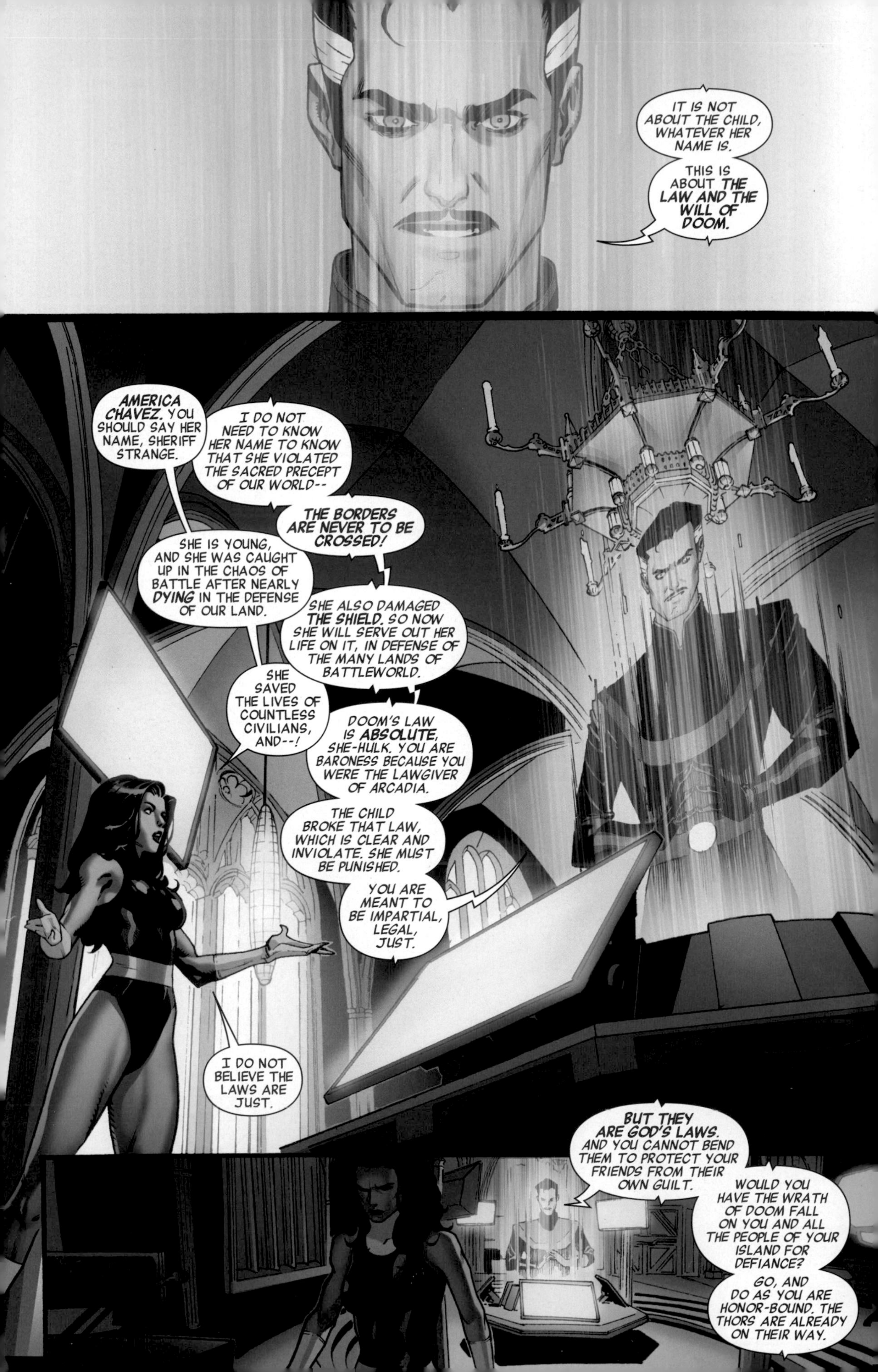

IT IS NOT ABOUT THE CHILD, WHATEVER HER NAME IS.
THIS IS ABOUT THE LAW AND THE WILL OF DOOM.
AMERICA CHAVEZ. YOU SHOULD SAY HER NAME, SHERIFF STRANGE.
I DO NOT NEED TO KNOW HER NAME TO KNOW THAT SHE VIOLATED THE SACRED PRECEPT OF OUR WORLD--
THE BORDERS ARE NEVER TO BE CROSSED!
SHE IS YOUNG, AND SHE WAS CAUGHT UP IN THE CHAOS OF BATTLE AFTER NEARLY DYING IN THE DEFENSE OF OUR LAND.
SHE ALSO DAMAGED THE SHIELD, SO NOW SHE WILL SERVE OUT HER LIFE ON IT, IN DEFENSE OF THE MANY LANDS OF BATTLEWORLD.
SHE SAVED THE LIVES OF COUNTLESS CIVILIANS, AND--!
DOOM'S LAW IS ABSOLUTE, SHE-HULK. YOU ARE BARONESS BECAUSE YOU WERE THE LAWGIVER OF ARCADIA.
THE CHILD BROKE THAT LAW, WHICH IS CLEAR AND INVIOLATE. SHE MUST BE PUNISHED.
YOU ARE MEANT TO BE IMPARTIAL, LEGAL, JUST.
I DO NOT BELIEVE THE LAWS ARE JUST.
BUT THEY ARE GOD'S LAWS. AND YOU CANNOT BEND THEM TO PROTECT YOUR FRIENDS FROM THEIR OWN GUILT.
WOULD YOU HAVE THE WRATH OF DOOM FALL ON YOU AND ALL THE PEOPLE OF YOUR ISLAND FOR DEFIANCE?
GO, AND DO AS YOU ARE HONOR-BOUND. THE THORS ARE ALREADY ON THEIR WAY.

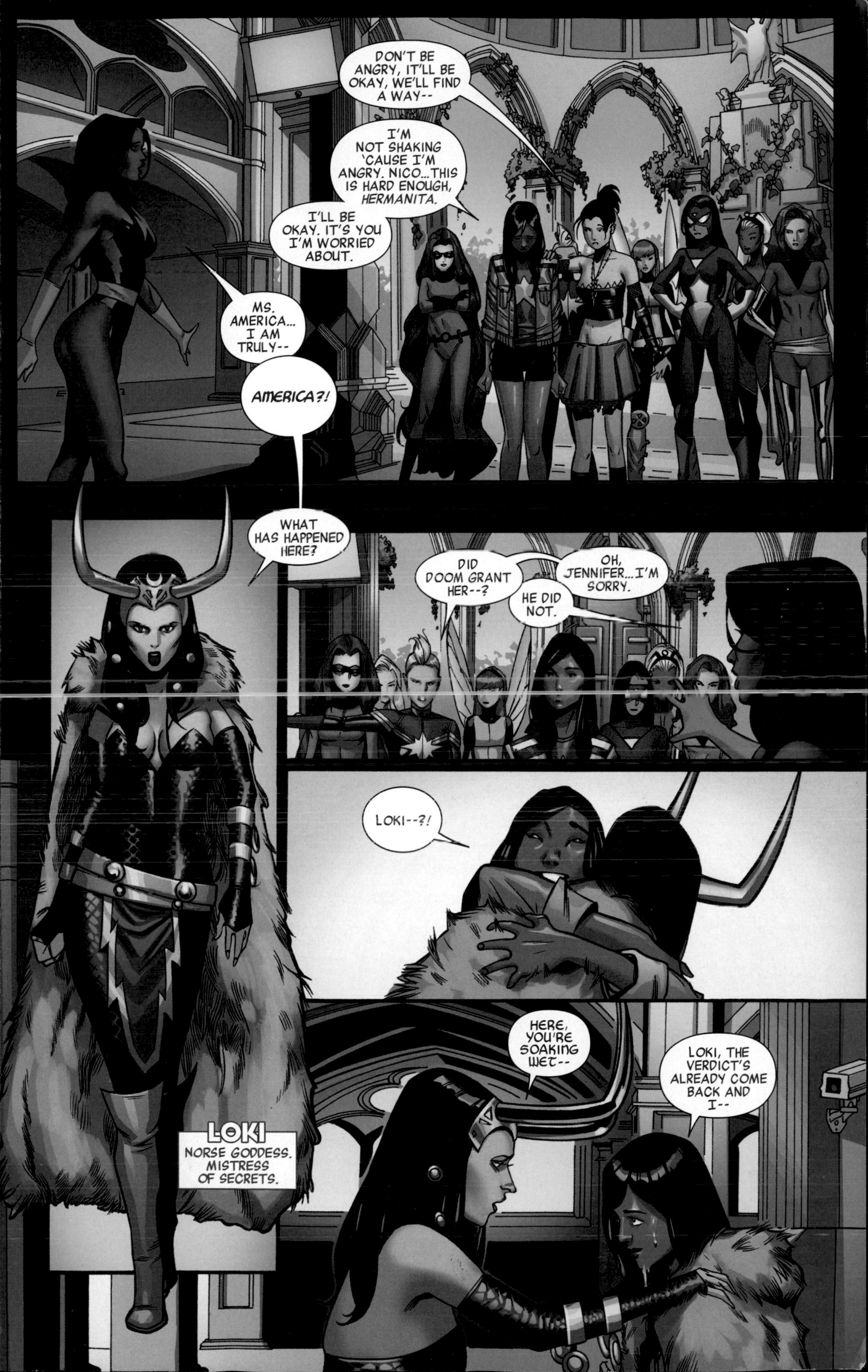
DON'T BE ANGRY, IT'LL BE OKAY, WE'LL FIND A WAY--
I'M NOT SHAKING 'CAUSE I'M ANGRY. NICO... THIS IS HARD ENOUGH, HERMANITA.
I'LL BE OKAY. IT'S YOU I'M WORRIED ABOUT.
MS. AMERICA... I AM TRULY--
AMERICA?!
WHAT HAS HAPPENED HERE?
DID DOOM GRANT HER--?
OH, JENNIFER... I'M SORRY.
HE DID NOT.
LOKI--?!
LOKI
NORSE GODDESS. MISTRESS OF SECRETS.
HERE, YOU'RE SOAKING WET--
LOKI, THE VERDICT'S ALREADY COME BACK AND I--

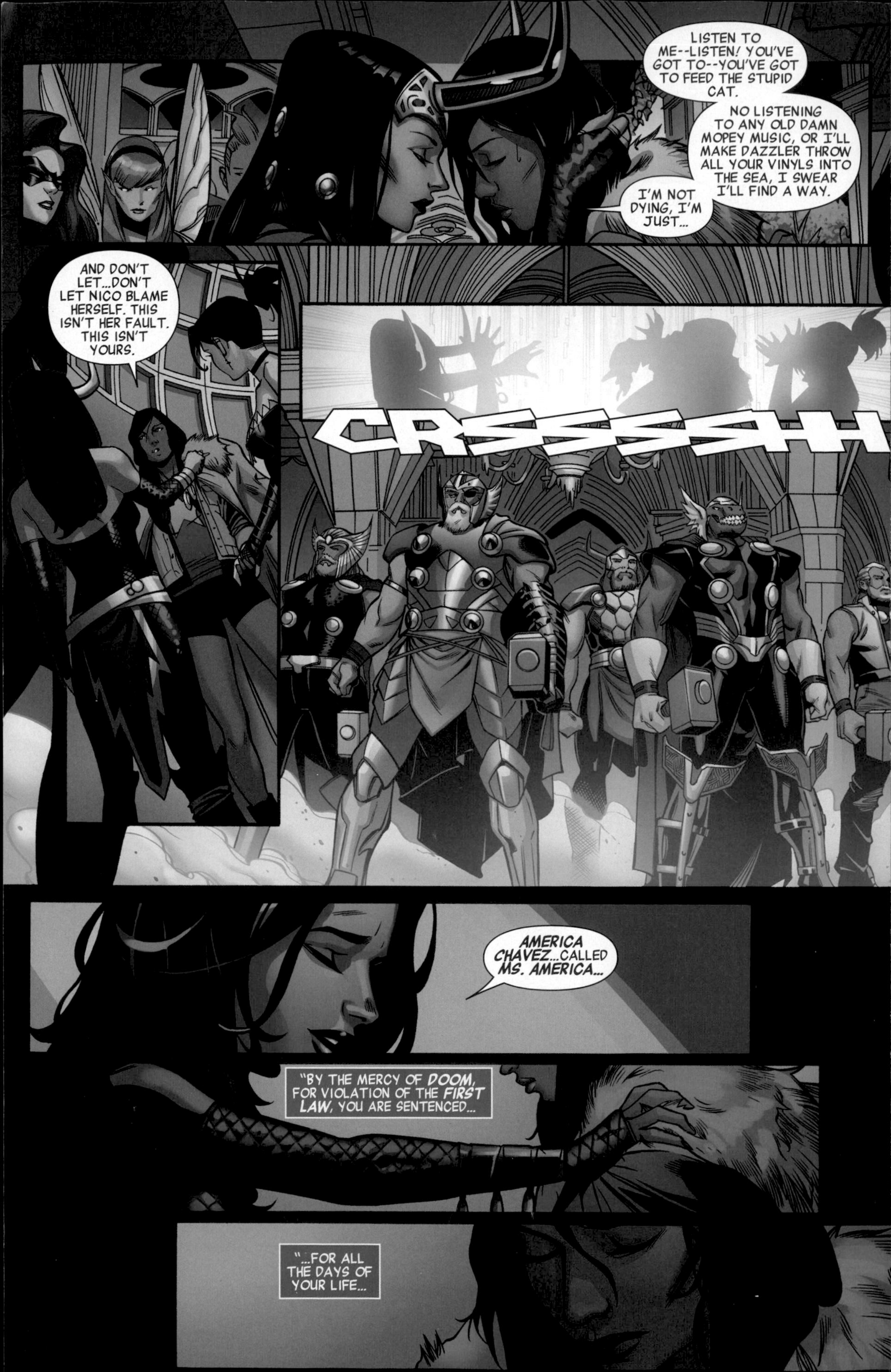
LISTEN TO ME--LISTEN! YOU'VE GOT TO--YOU'VE GOT TO FEED THE STUPID CAT.
NO LISTENING TO ANY OLD DAMN MOPEY MUSIC, OR I'LL MAKE DAZZLER THROW ALL YOUR VINYLS INTO THE SEA, I SWEAR I'LL FIND A WAY.
I'M NOT DYING, I'M JUST...
AND DON'T LET...DON'T LET NICO BLAME HERSELF. THIS ISN'T HER FAULT. THIS ISN'T YOURS.
CRSSSSHH
AMERICA CHAVEZ...CALLED MS. AMERICA...
"BY THE MERCY OF DOOM, FOR VIOLATION OF THE FIRST LAW, YOU ARE SENTENCED...
"...FOR ALL THE DAYS OF YOUR LIFE...

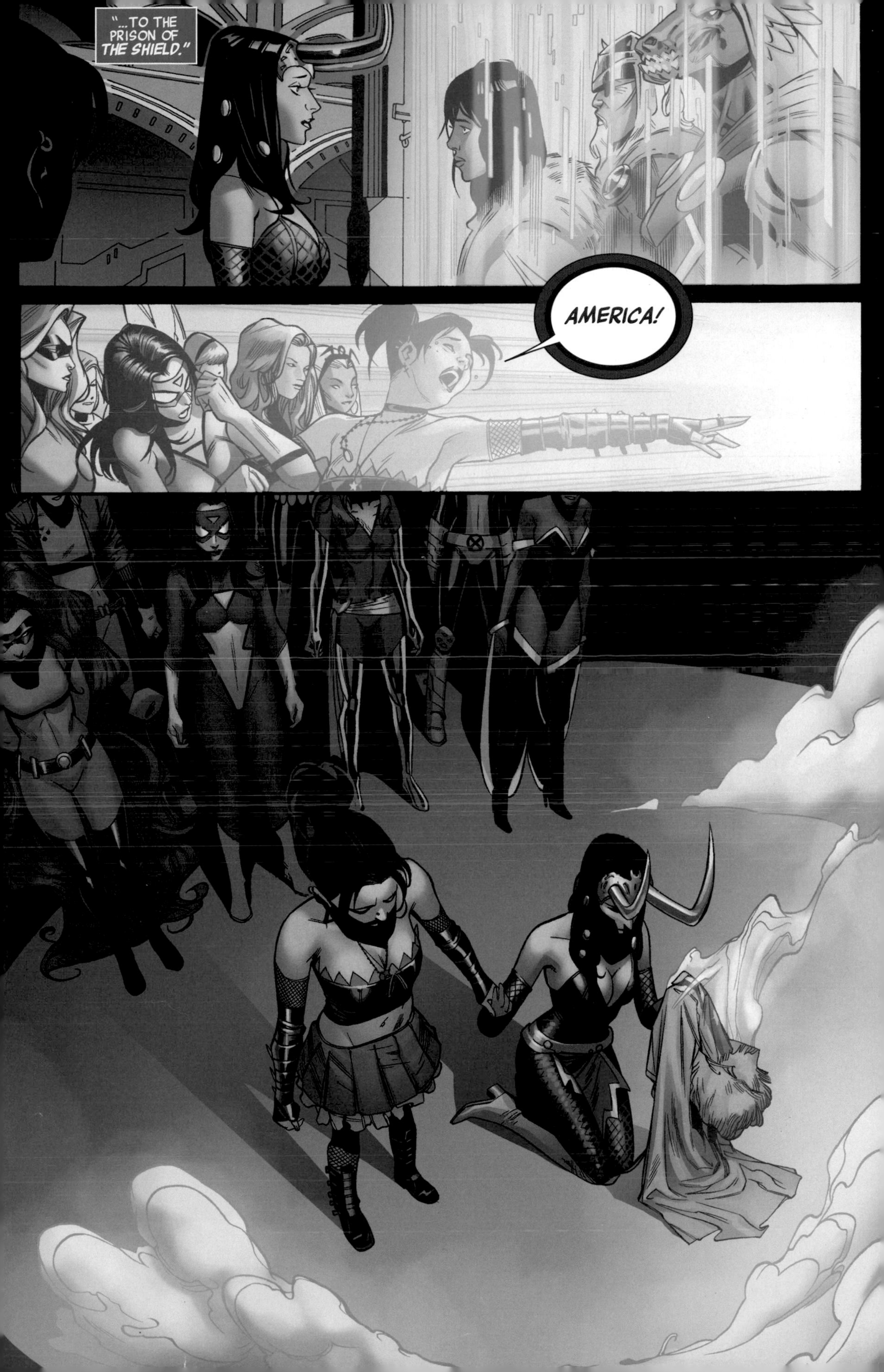
"...TO THE PRISON OF THE SHIELD."
AMERICA!

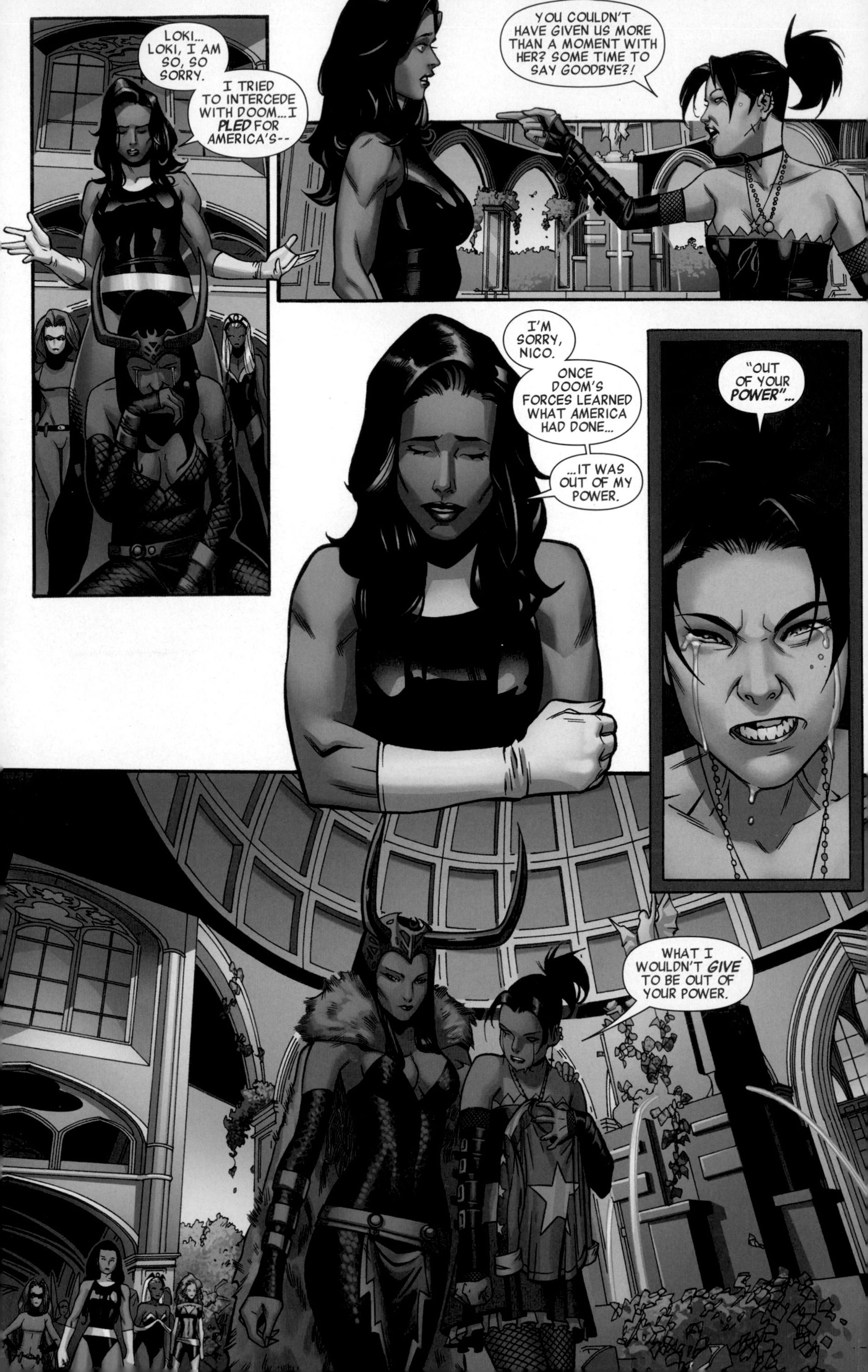
LOKI... LOKI, I AM SO, SO SORRY.
I TRIED TO INTERCEDE WITH DOOM...I PLED FOR AMERICA'S--
YOU COULDN'T HAVE GIVEN US MORE THAN A MOMENT WITH HER? SOME TIME TO SAY GOODBYE?!
I'M SORRY, NICO.
ONCE DOOM'S FORCES LEARNED WHAT AMERICA HAD DONE...
...IT WAS OUT OF MY POWER.
"OUT OF YOUR POWER"...
WHAT I WOULDN'T GIVE TO BE OUT OF YOUR POWER.

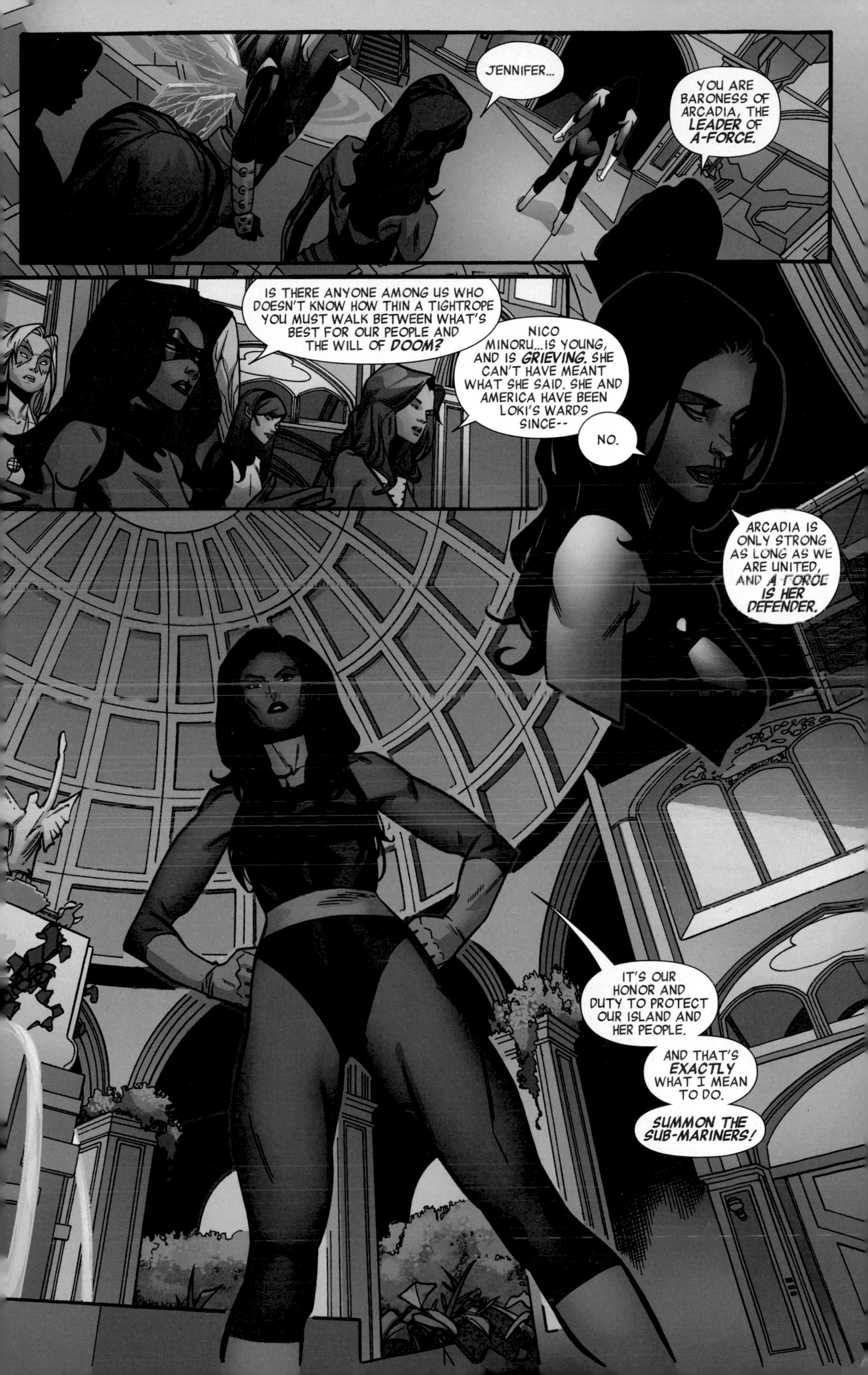
JENNIFER...
YOU ARE BARONESS OF ARCADIA, THE LEADER OF A-FORCE.
IS THERE ANYONE AMONG US WHO DOESN'T KNOW HOW THIN A TIGHTROPE YOU MUST WALK BETWEEN WHAT'S BEST FOR OUR PEOPLE AND THE WILL OF DOOM?
NICO MINORU...IS YOUNG, AND IS GRIEVING. SHE CAN'T HAVE MEANT WHAT SHE SAID. SHE AND AMERICA HAVE BEEN LOKI'S WARDS SINCE--
NO.
ARCADIA IS ONLY STRONG AS LONG AS WE ARE UNITED, AND A-FORCE IS HER DEFENDER.
IT'S OUR HONOR AND DUTY TO PROTECT OUR ISLAND AND HER PEOPLE.
AND THAT'S EXACTLY WHAT I MEAN TO DO.
SUMMON THE SUB-MARINERS!

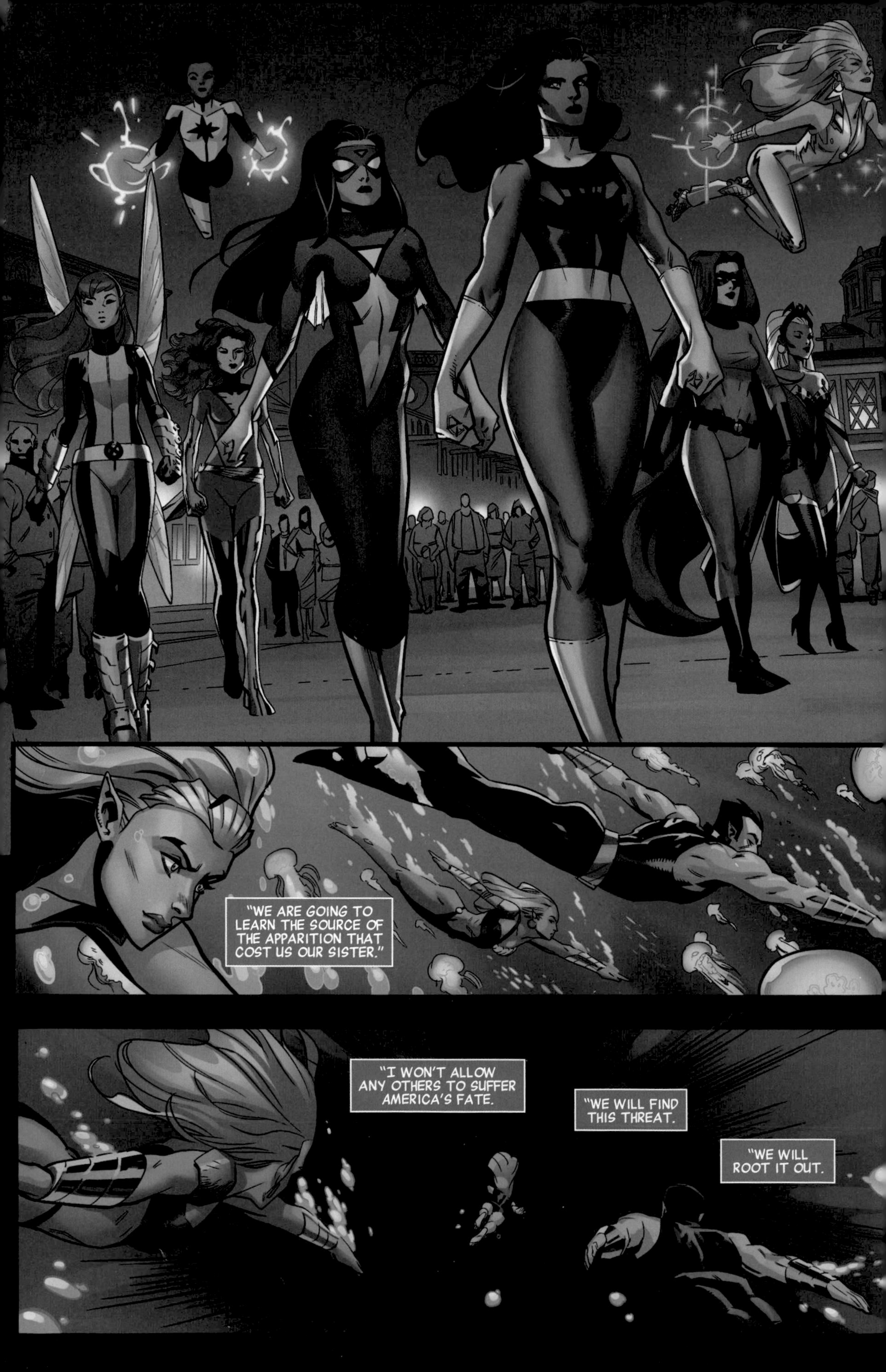
"WE ARE GOING TO LEARN THE SOURCE OF THE APPARITION THAT COST US OUR SISTER."
"I WON'T ALLOW ANY OTHERS TO SUFFER AMERICA'S FATE.
"WE WILL FIND THIS THREAT.
"WE WILL ROOT IT OUT.

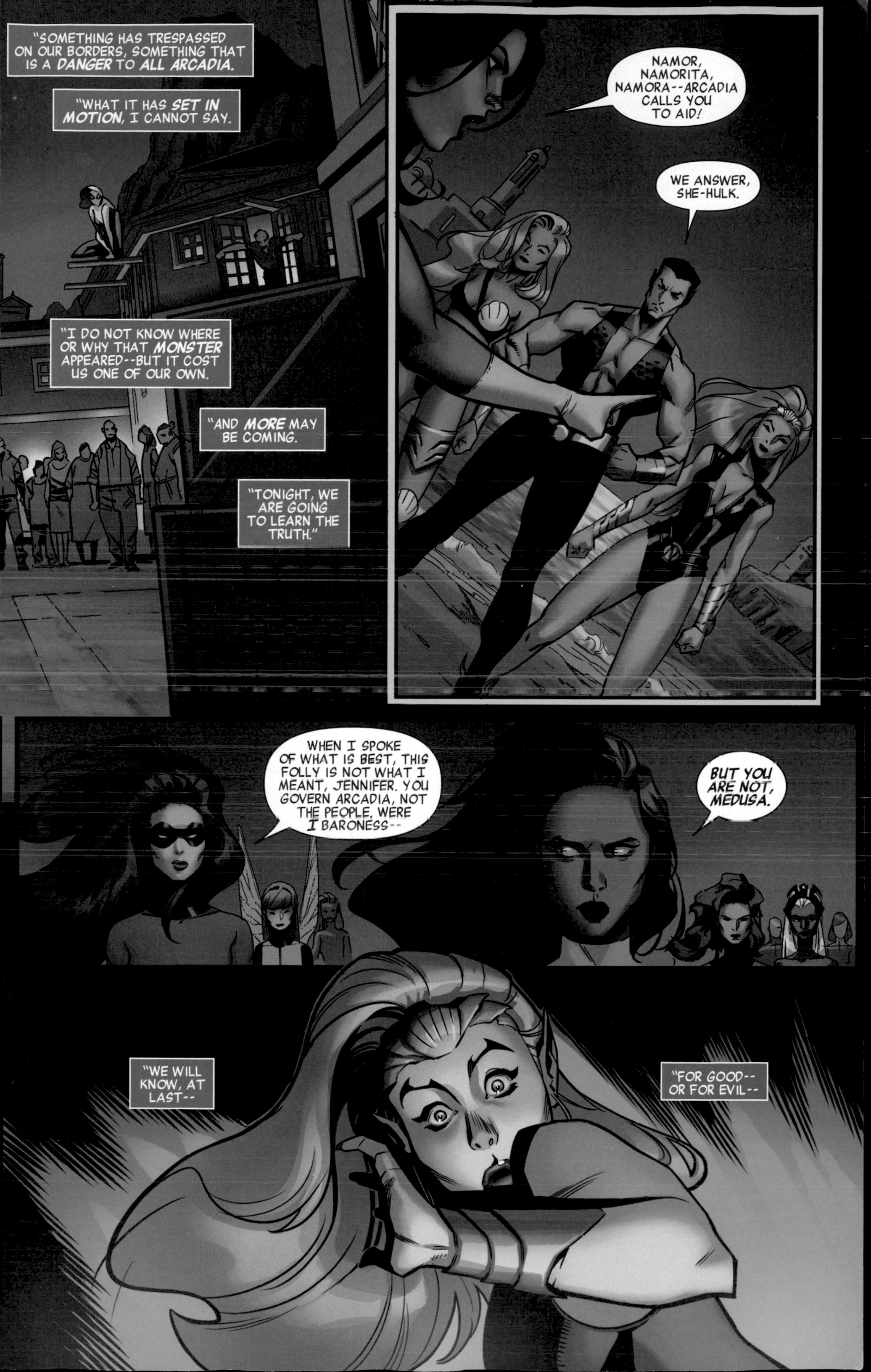
"SOMETHING HAS TRESPASSED ON OUR BORDERS, SOMETHING THAT IS A DANGER TO ALL ARCADIA.
"WHAT IT HAS SET IN MOTION, I CANNOT SAY.
"I DO NOT KNOW WHERE OR WHY THAT MONSTER APPEARED--BUT IT COST US ONE OF OUR OWN.
"AND MORE MAY BE COMING.
"TONIGHT, WE ARE GOING TO LEARN THE TRUTH."
NAMOR, NAMORITA, NAMORA--ARCADIA CALLS YOU TO AID!
WE ANSWER, SHE-HULK.
WHEN I SPOKE OF WHAT IS BEST, THIS FOLLY IS NOT WHAT I MEANT, JENNIFER. YOU GOVERN ARCADIA, NOT THE PEOPLE. WERE I BARONESS--
BUT YOU ARE NOT, MEDUSA.
"WE WILL KNOW, AT LAST--
"FOR GOOD--OR FOR EVIL--

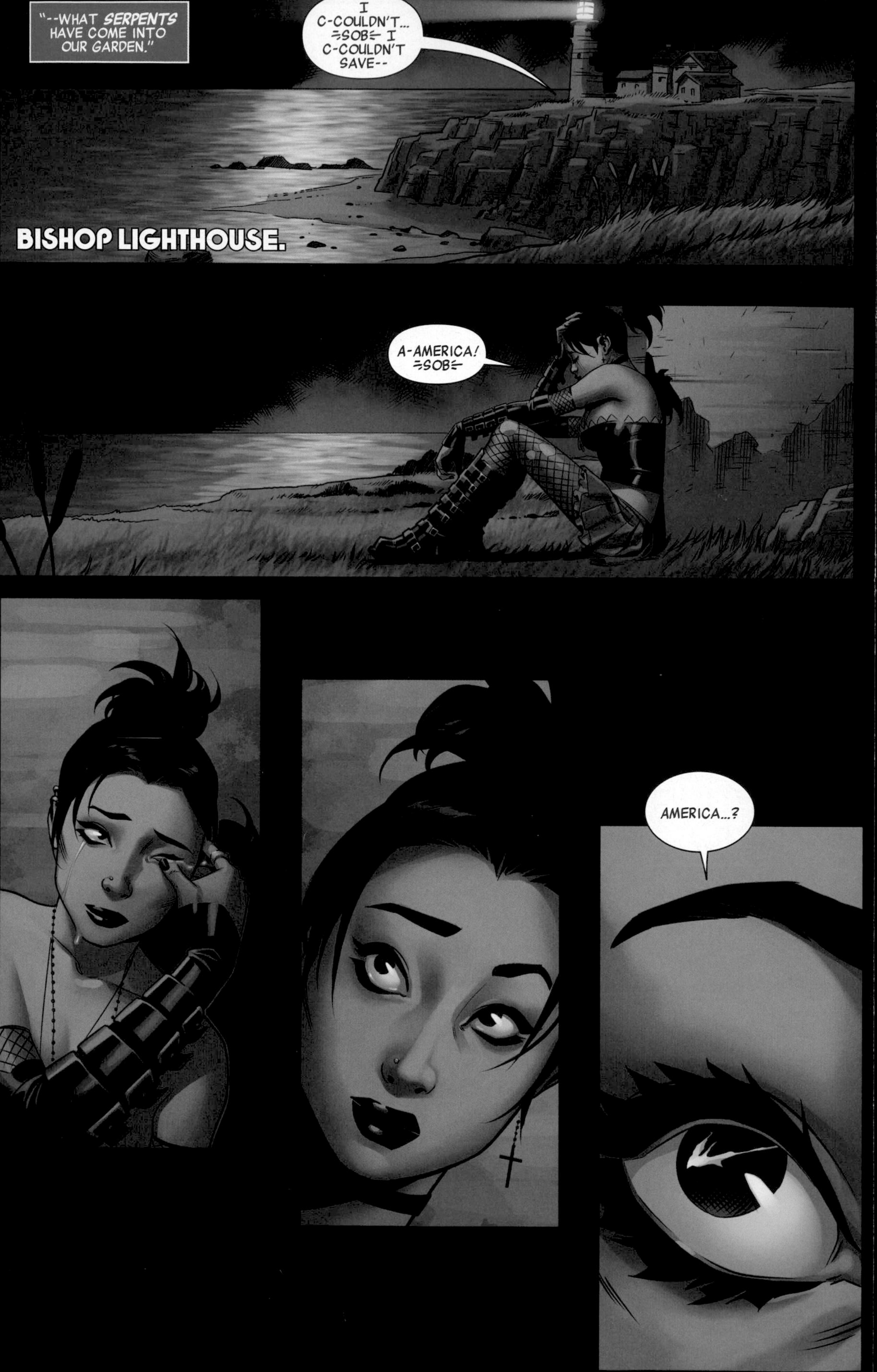
"--WHAT SERPENTS HAVE COME INTO OUR GARDEN."
I C-COULDN'T... =SOB= I C-COULDN'T SAVE--
BISHOP LIGHTHOUSE.
A-AMERICA! =SOB=
AMERICA...?

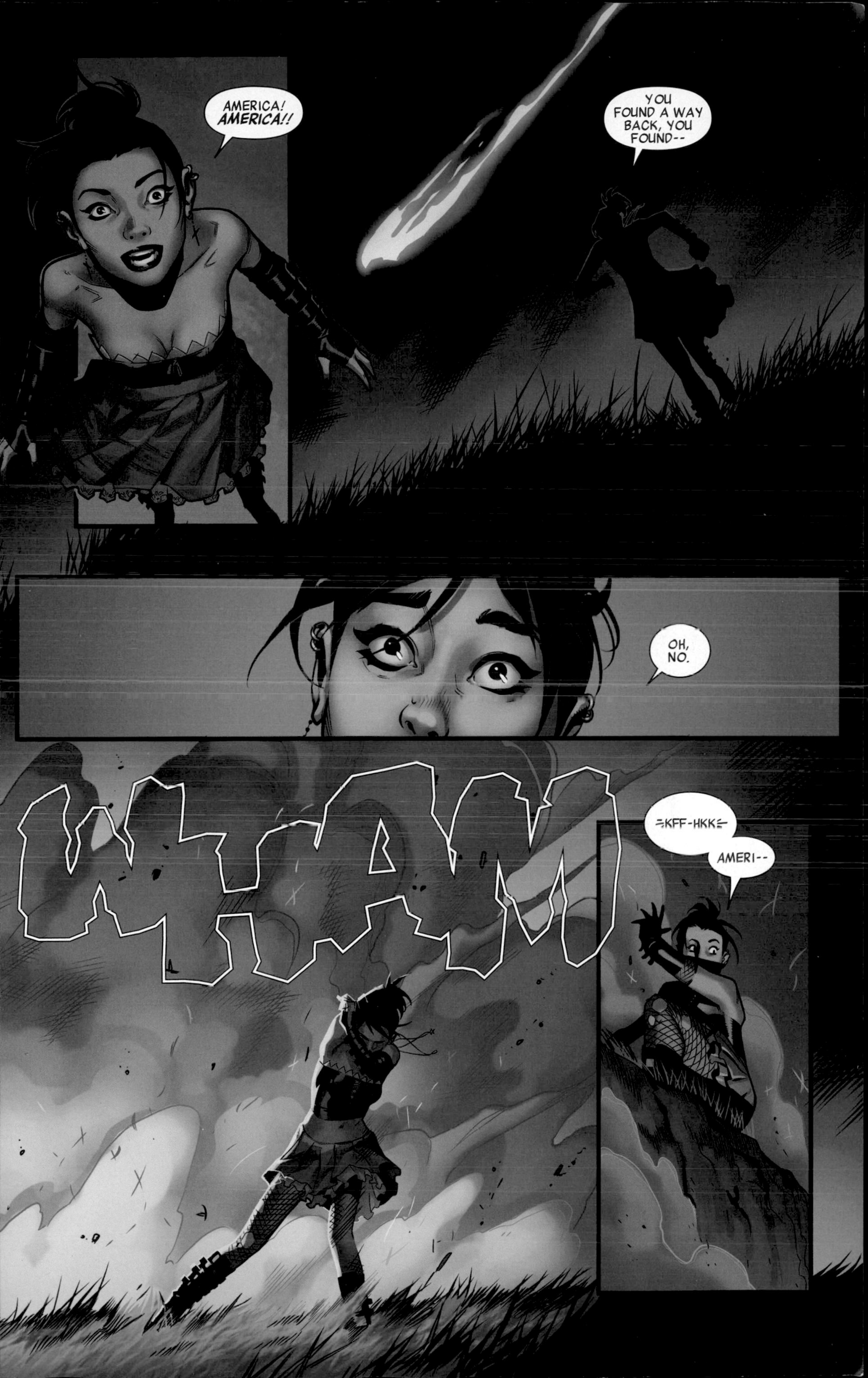
AMERICA!
AMERICA!!
YOU FOUND A WAY BACK, YOU FOUND--
OH, NO.
WHAM
=KFF-HKK=
AMERI--

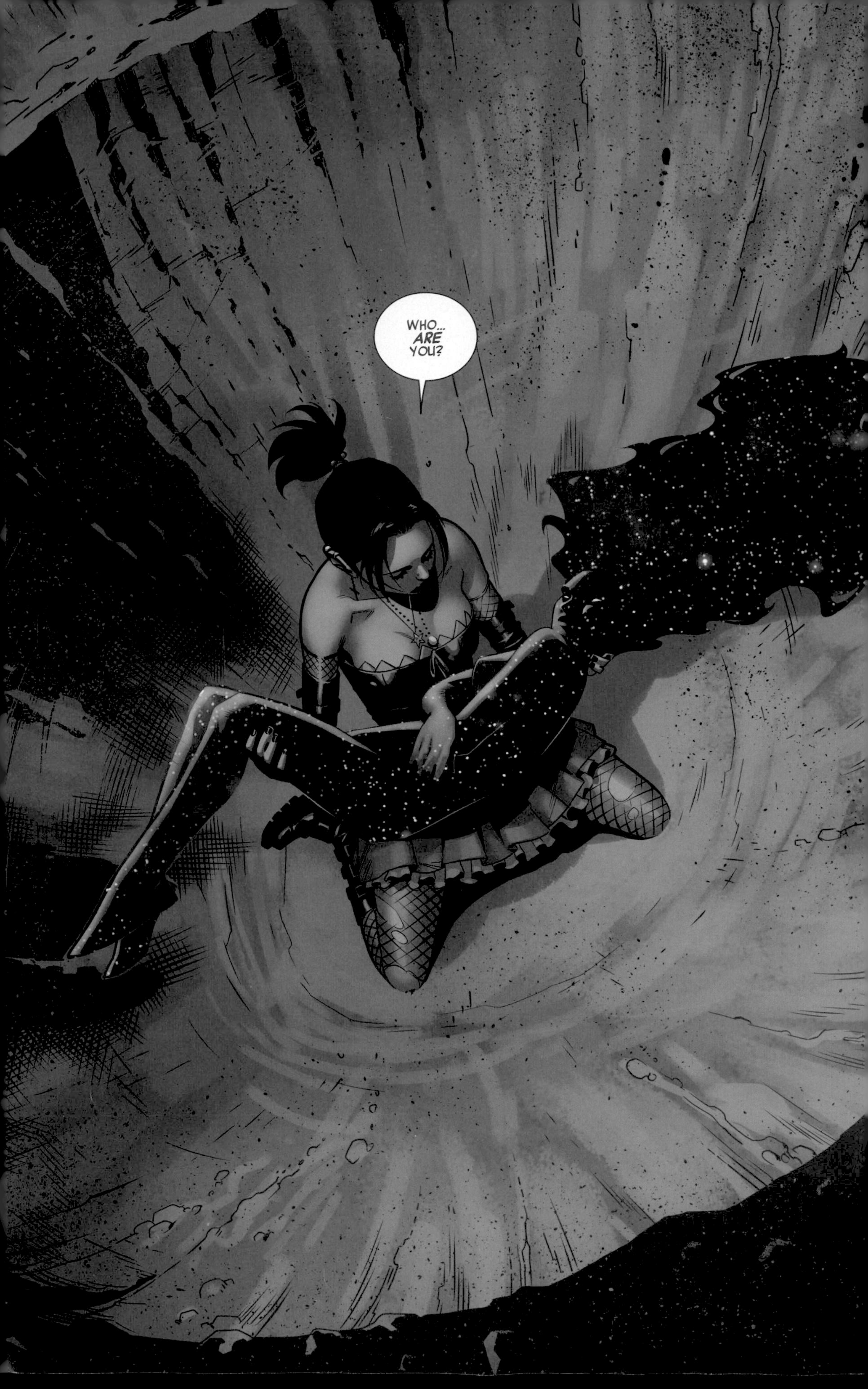
WHO... ARE YOU?

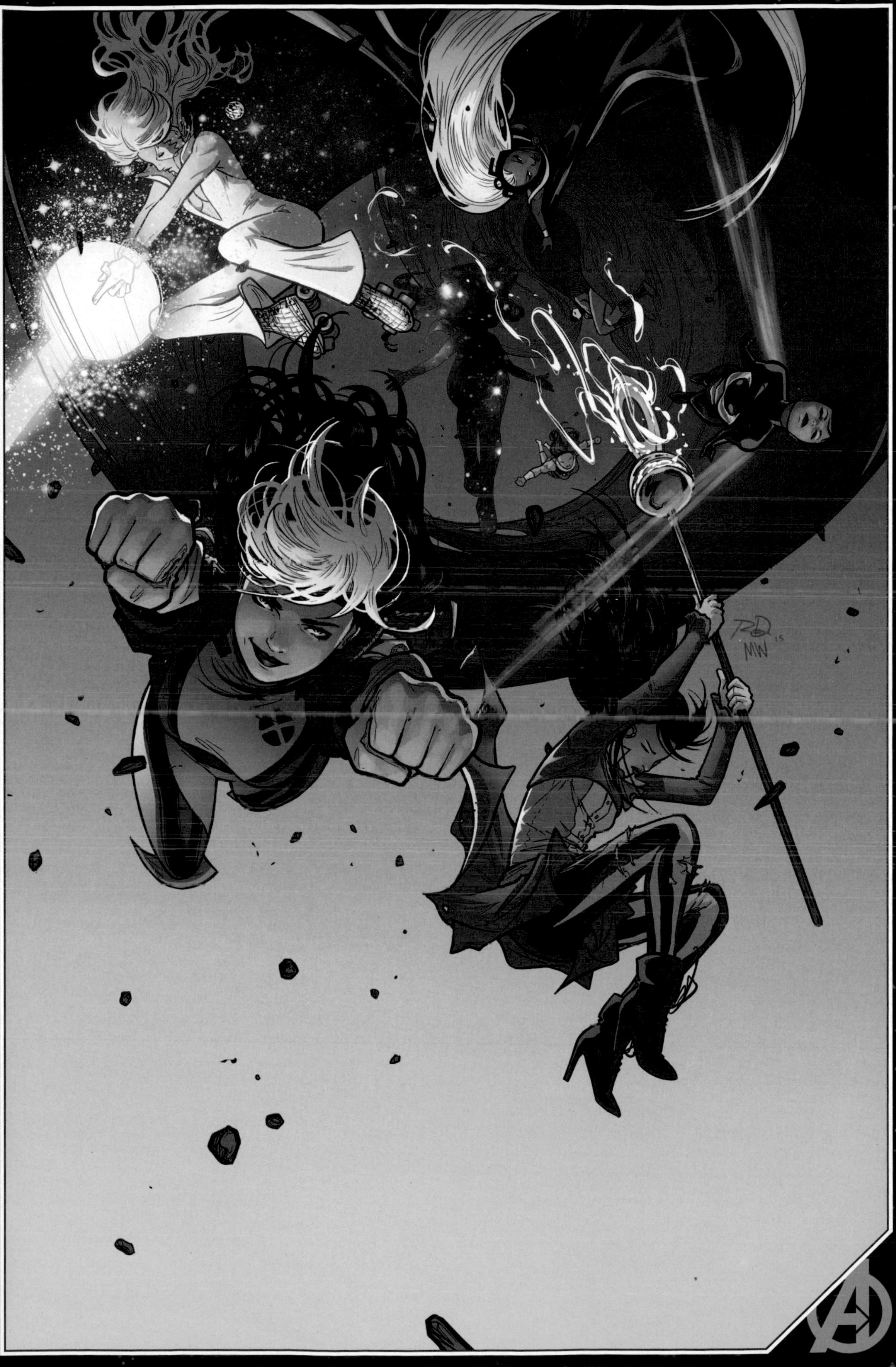
RD '15
MW

#1 VARIANT BY **RUSSELL DAUTERMAN** & **MATTHEW WILSON**

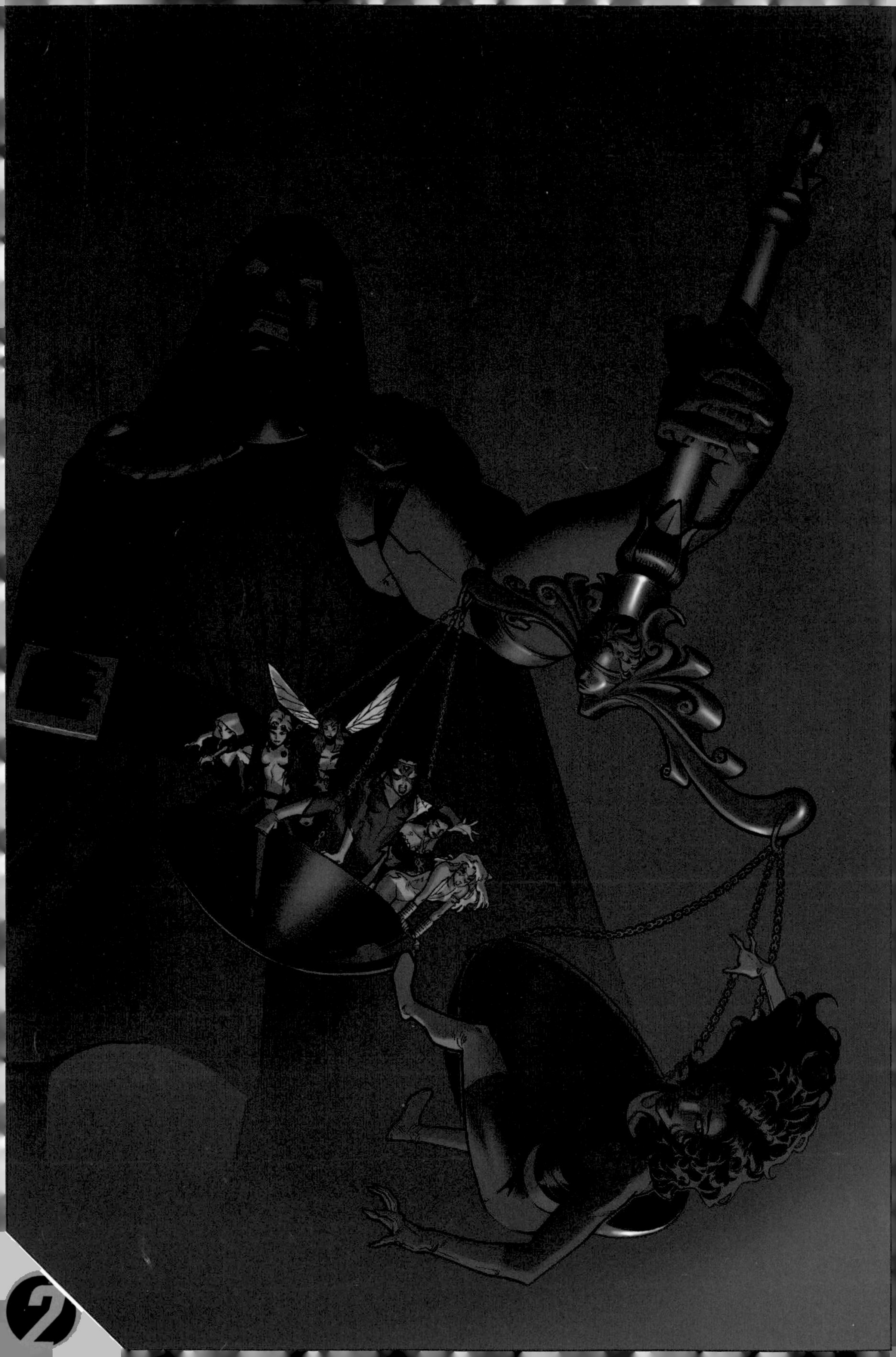
2

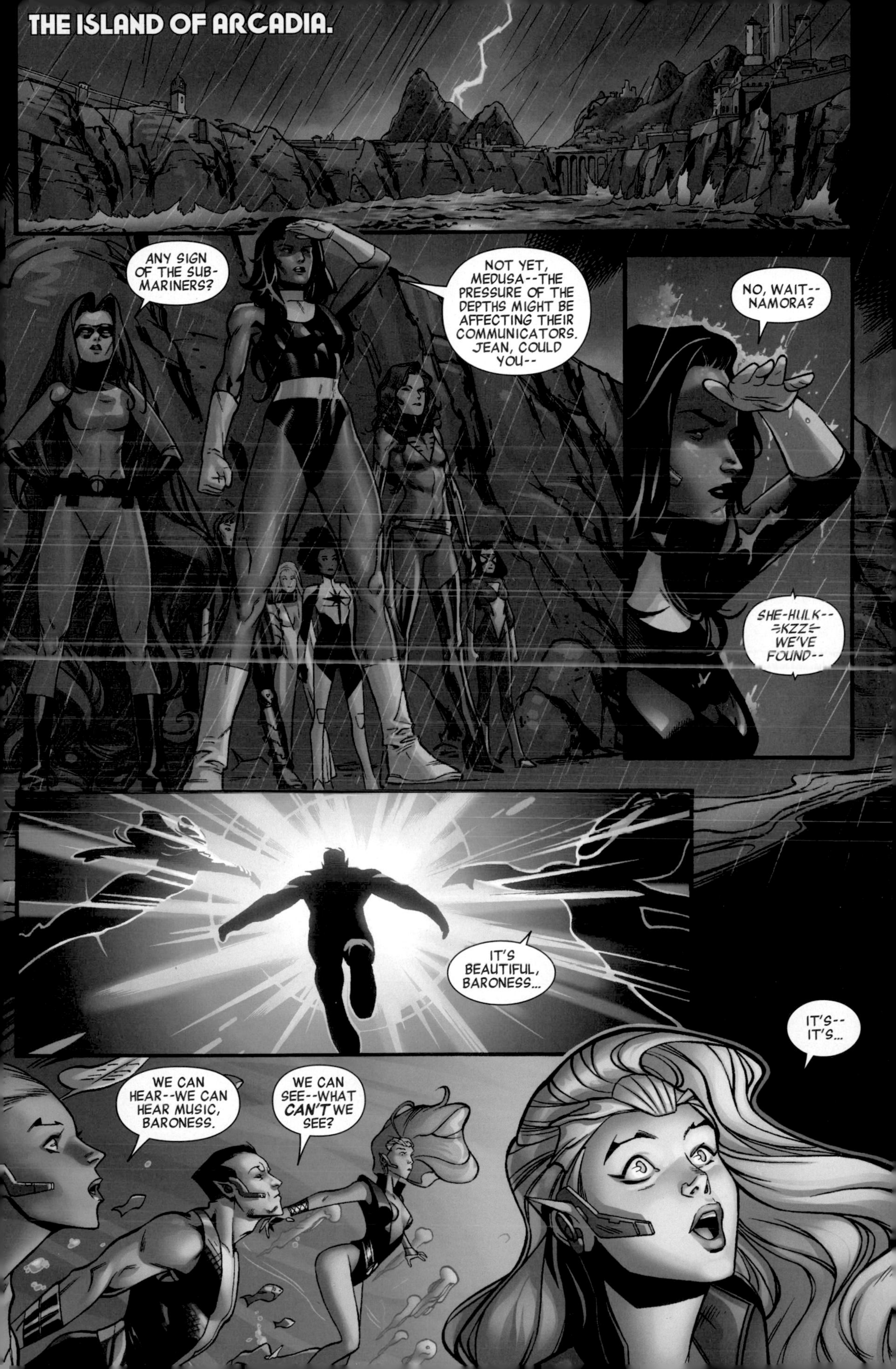
THE ISLAND OF ARCADIA.
ANY SIGN OF THE SUB-MARINERS?
NOT YET, MEDUSA--THE PRESSURE OF THE DEPTHS MIGHT BE AFFECTING THEIR COMMUNICATORS. JEAN, COULD YOU--
NO, WAIT--NAMORA?
SHE-HULK--KZZ--WE'VE FOUND--
IT'S BEAUTIFUL, BARONESS...
IT'S--IT'S...
WE CAN HEAR--WE CAN HEAR MUSIC, BARONESS.
WE CAN SEE--WHAT CAN'T WE SEE?

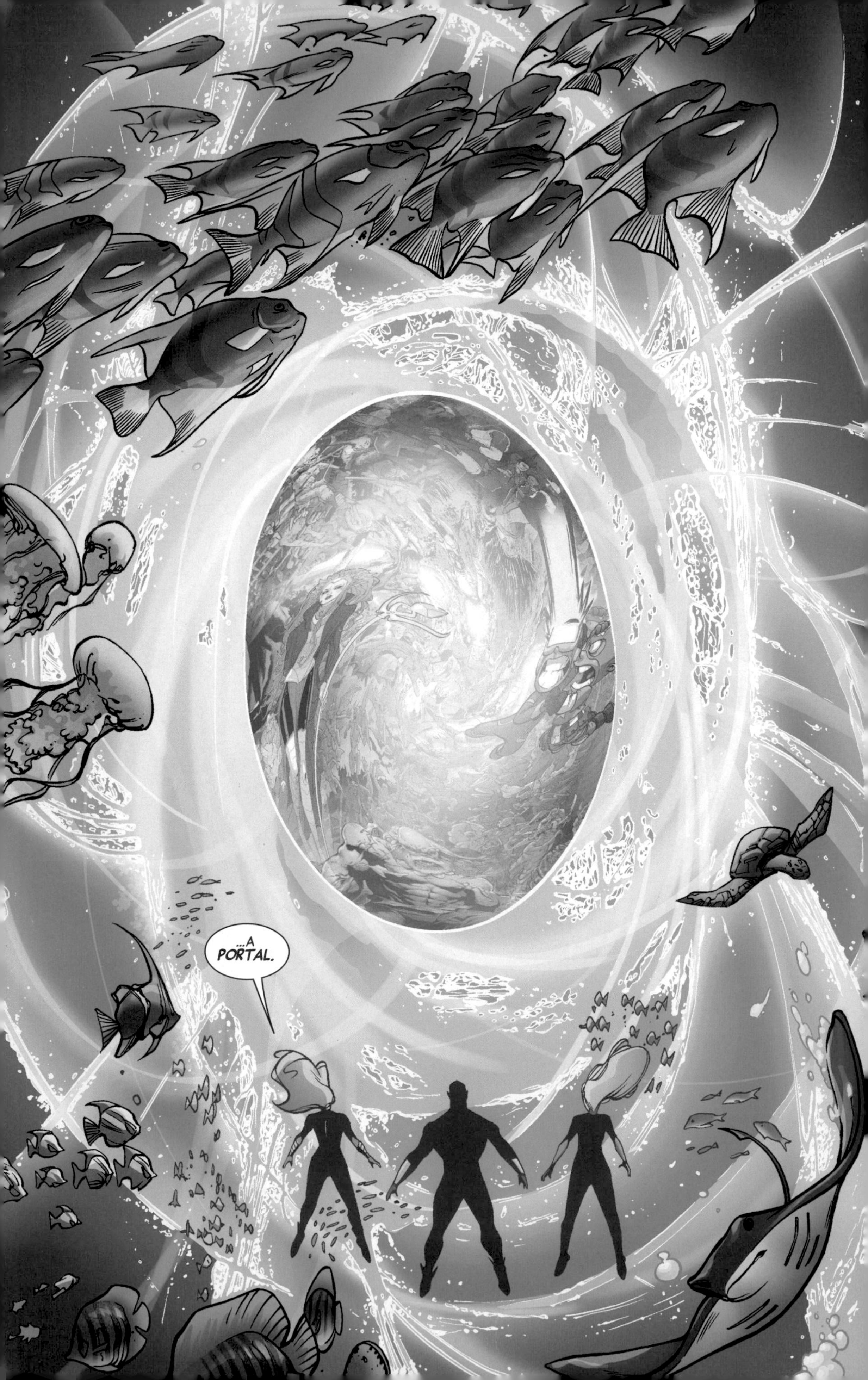
...A PORTAL.

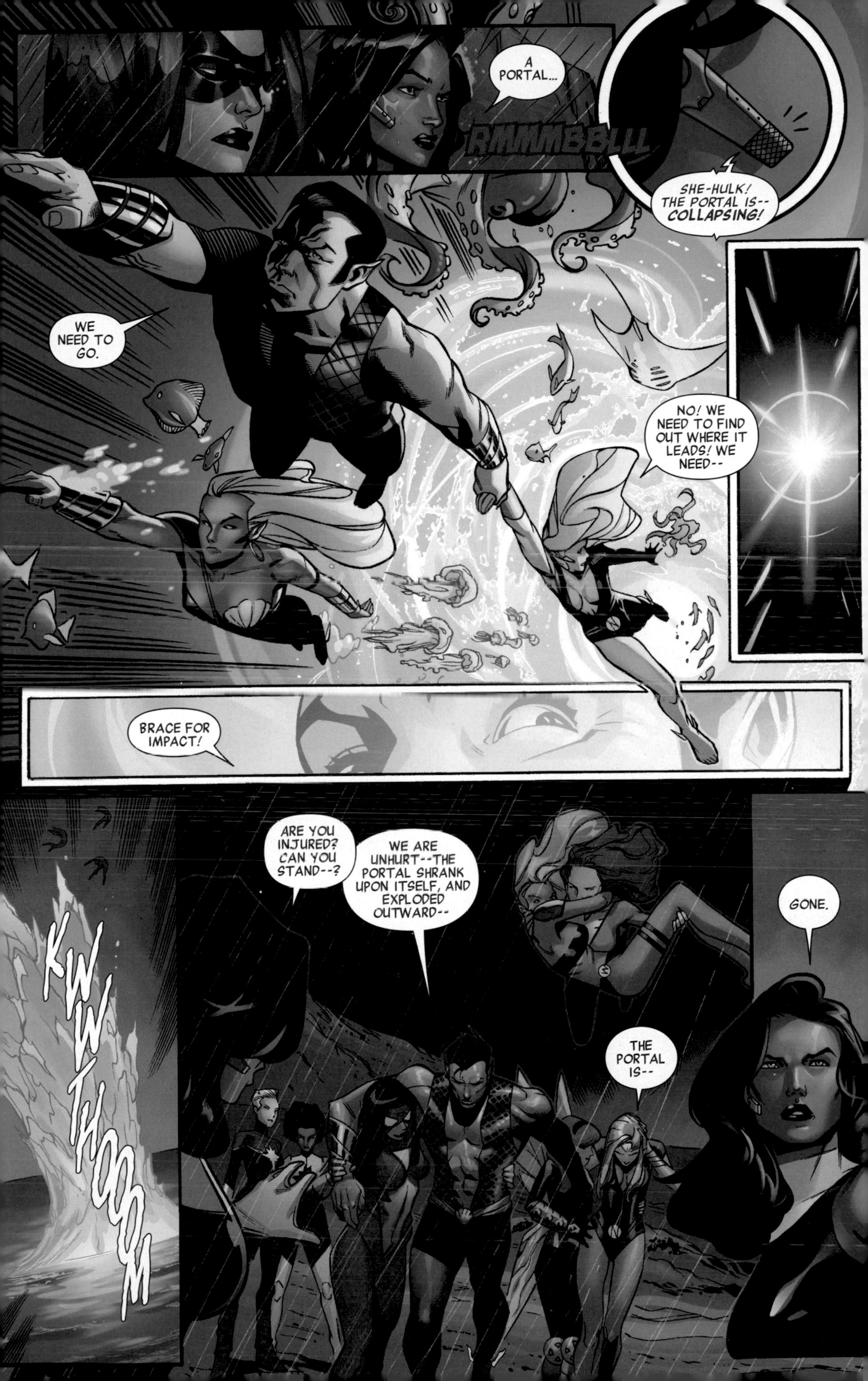
A PORTAL...
RMMMBBLLL
SHE-HULK! THE PORTAL IS-- COLLAPSING!
WE NEED TO GO.
NO! WE NEED TO FIND OUT WHERE IT LEADS! WE NEED--
BRACE FOR IMPACT!
KWWTHOOOM
ARE YOU INJURED? CAN YOU STAND--?
WE ARE UNHURT--THE PORTAL SHRANK UPON ITSELF, AND EXPLODED OUTWARD--
THE PORTAL IS--
GONE.

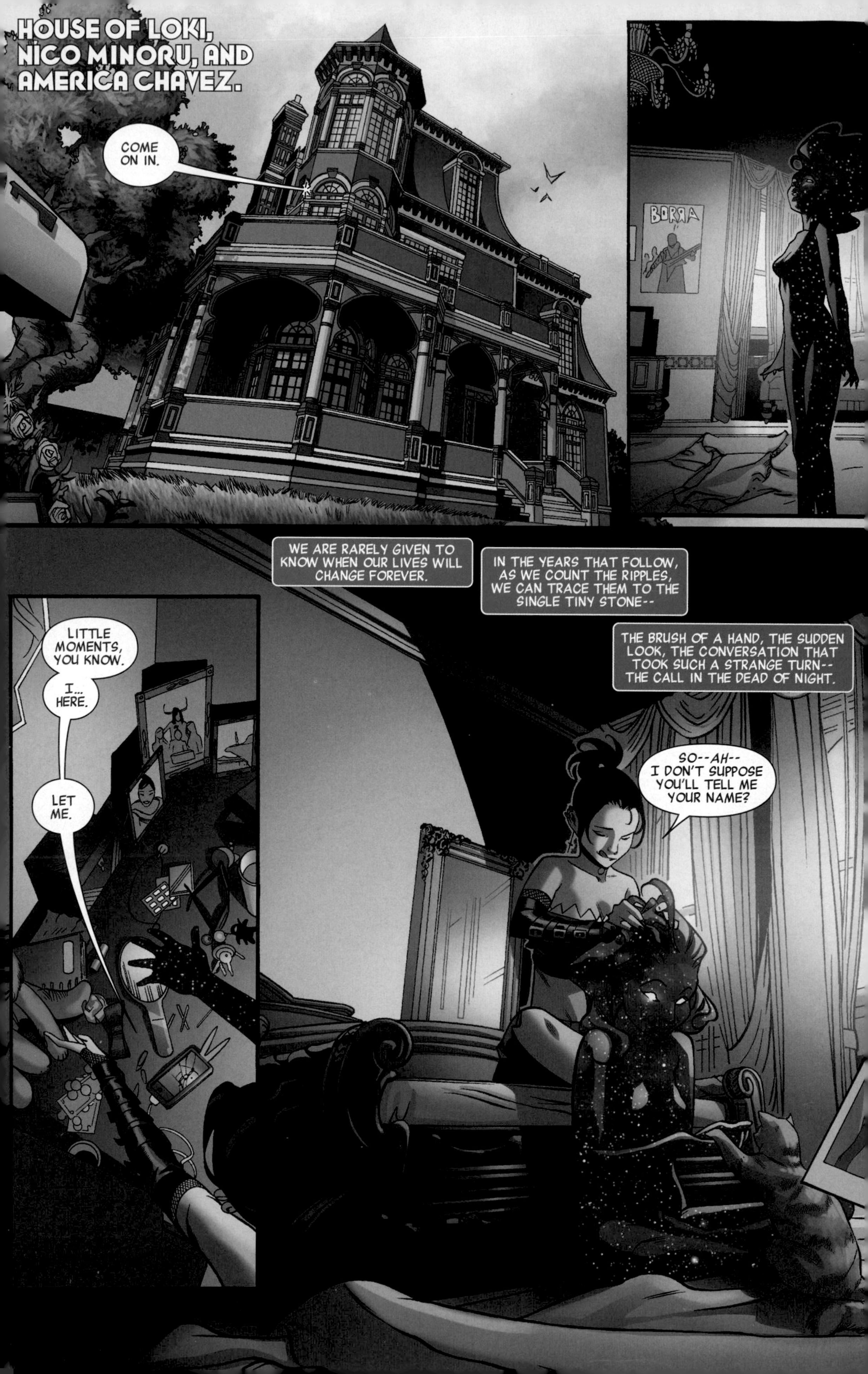
HOUSE OF LOKI, NICO MINORU, AND AMERICA CHAVEZ.
COME ON IN.
BORRA
WE ARE RARELY GIVEN TO KNOW WHEN OUR LIVES WILL CHANGE FOREVER.
IN THE YEARS THAT FOLLOW, AS WE COUNT THE RIPPLES, WE CAN TRACE THEM TO THE SINGLE TINY STONE--
THE BRUSH OF A HAND, THE SUDDEN LOOK, THE CONVERSATION THAT TOOK SUCH A STRANGE TURN-- THE CALL IN THE DEAD OF NIGHT.
LITTLE MOMENTS, YOU KNOW.
I... HERE.
LET ME.
SO--AH-- I DON'T SUPPOSE YOU'LL TELL ME YOUR NAME?

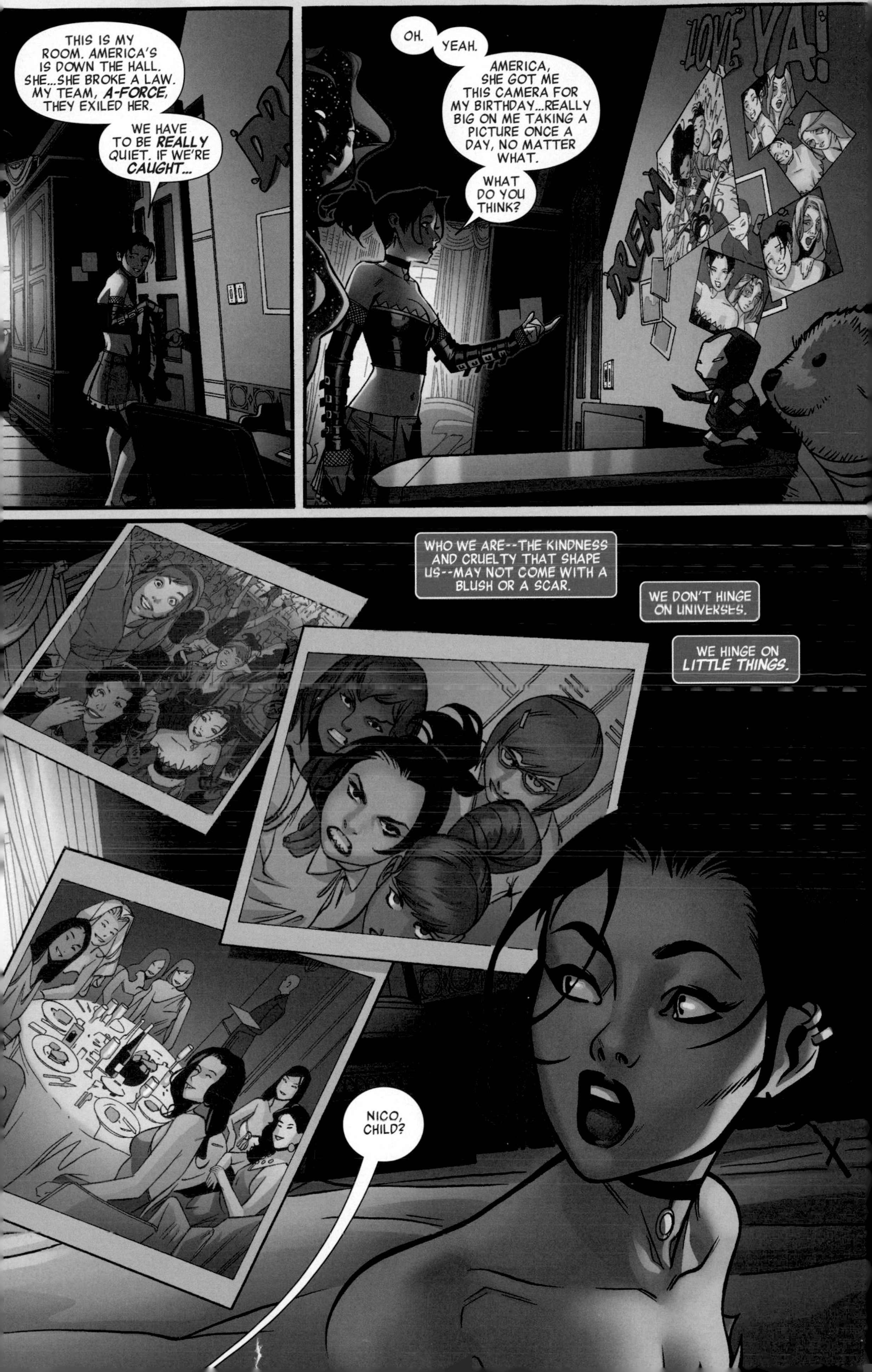

THIS IS MY ROOM. AMERICA'S IS DOWN THE HALL. SHE...SHE BROKE A LAW. MY TEAM, A-FORCE, THEY EXILED HER.
WE HAVE TO BE REALLY QUIET. IF WE'RE CAUGHT...
OH.
YEAH.
AMERICA, SHE GOT ME THIS CAMERA FOR MY BIRTHDAY...REALLY BIG ON ME TAKING A PICTURE ONCE A DAY, NO MATTER WHAT.
WHAT DO YOU THINK?
LOVE YA!
DREAM
WHO WE ARE--THE KINDNESS AND CRUELTY THAT SHAPE US--MAY NOT COME WITH A BLUSH OR A SCAR.
WE DON'T HINGE ON UNIVERSES.
WE HINGE ON LITTLE THINGS.
NICO, CHILD?

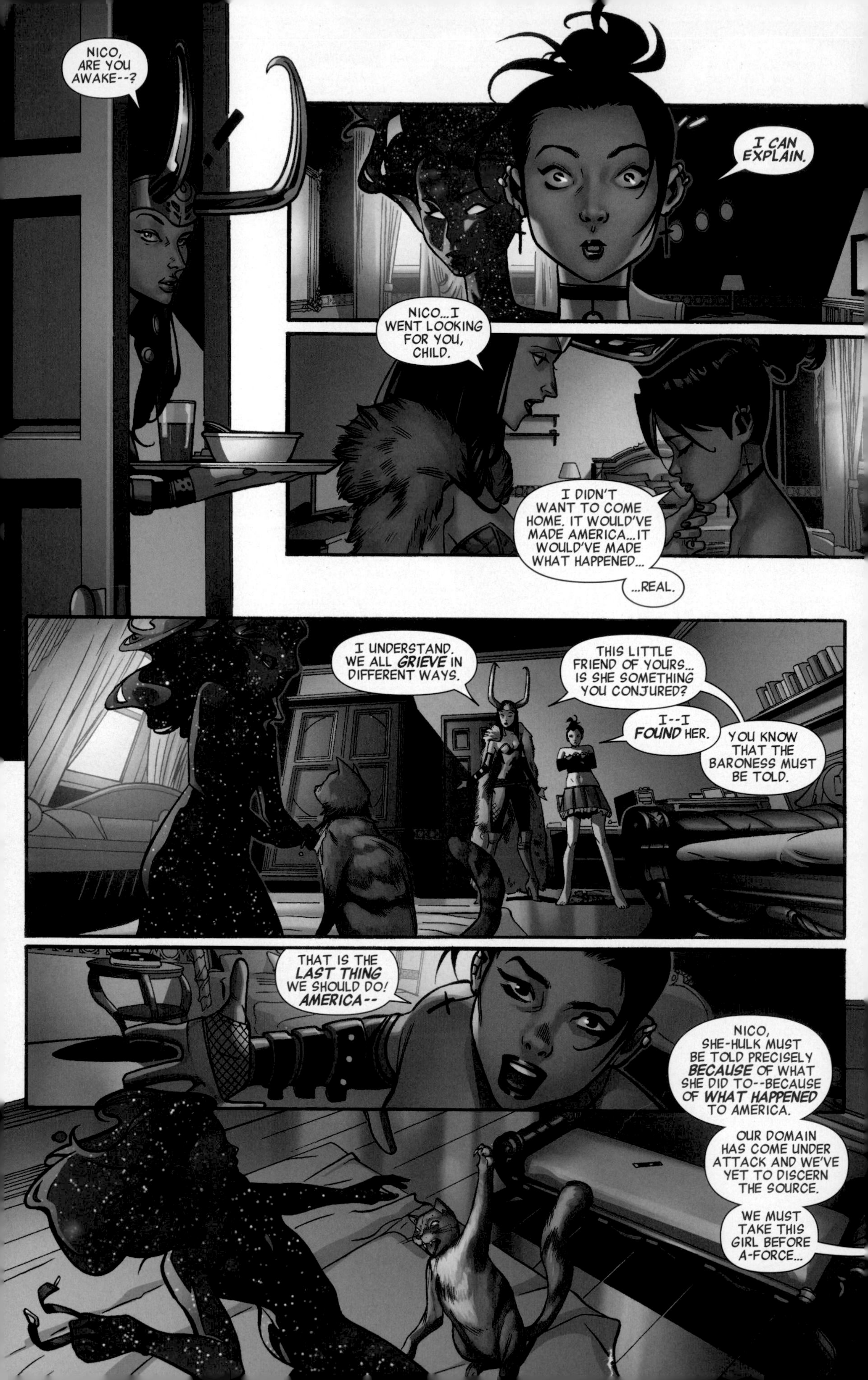
NICO, ARE YOU AWAKE--?
I CAN EXPLAIN.
NICO...I WENT LOOKING FOR YOU, CHILD.
I DIDN'T WANT TO COME HOME. IT WOULD'VE MADE AMERICA...IT WOULD'VE MADE WHAT HAPPENED...
...REAL.
I UNDERSTAND. WE ALL GRIEVE IN DIFFERENT WAYS.
THIS LITTLE FRIEND OF YOURS... IS SHE SOMETHING YOU CONJURED?
I--I FOUND HER.
YOU KNOW THAT THE BARONESS MUST BE TOLD.
THAT IS THE LAST THING WE SHOULD DO! AMERICA--
NICO, SHE-HULK MUST BE TOLD PRECISELY BECAUSE OF WHAT SHE DID TO--BECAUSE OF WHAT HAPPENED TO AMERICA.
OUR DOMAIN HAS COME UNDER ATTACK AND WE'VE YET TO DISCERN THE SOURCE.
WE MUST TAKE THIS GIRL BEFORE A-FORCE...

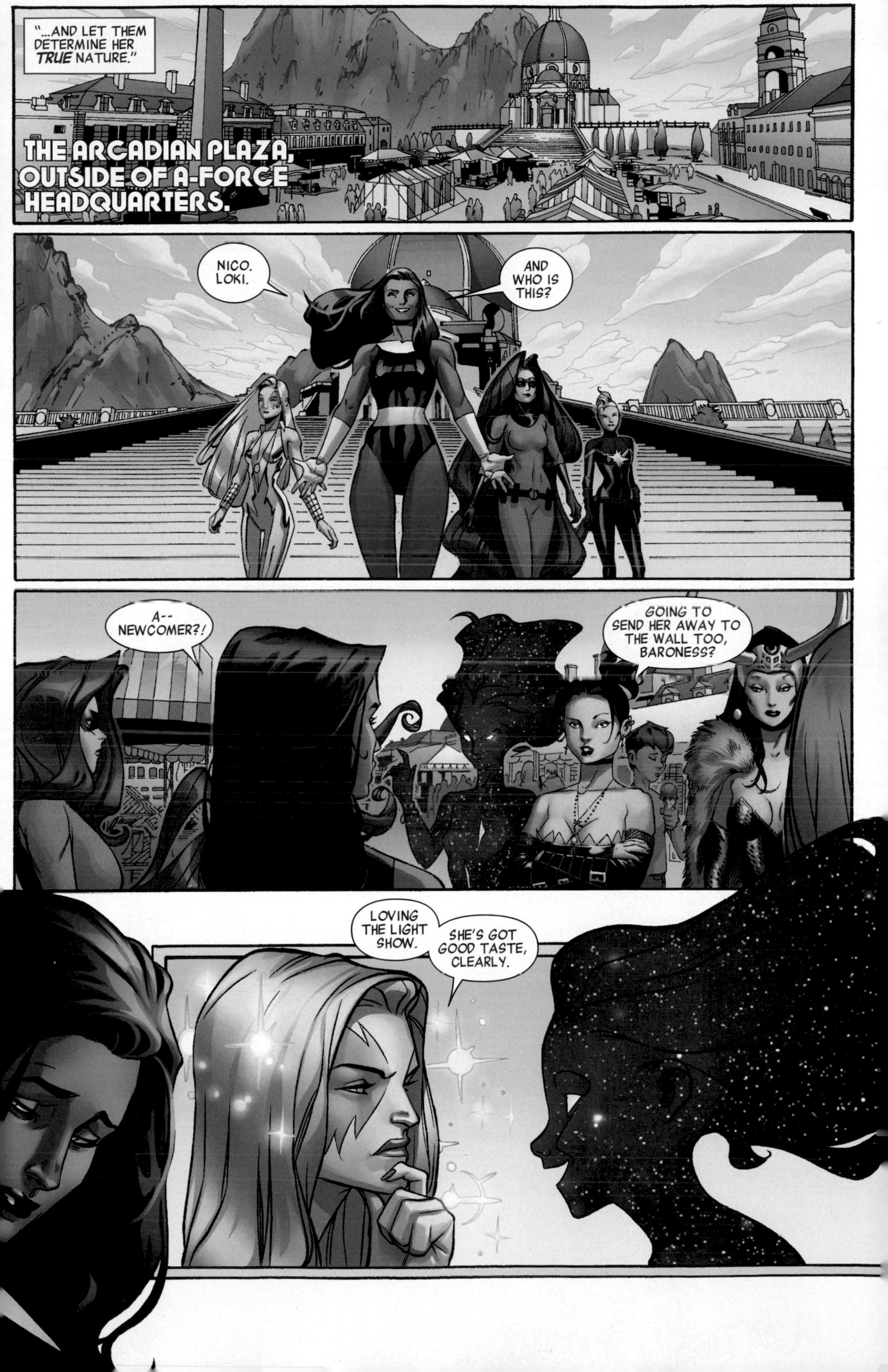
"...AND LET THEM DETERMINE HER *TRUE* NATURE."
THE ARCADIAN PLAZA, OUTSIDE OF A-FORCE HEADQUARTERS.
NICO. LOKI.
AND WHO IS THIS?
A-- NEWCOMER?!
GOING TO SEND HER AWAY TO THE WALL TOO, BARONESS?
LOVING THE LIGHT SHOW.
SHE'S GOT GOOD TASTE, CLEARLY.

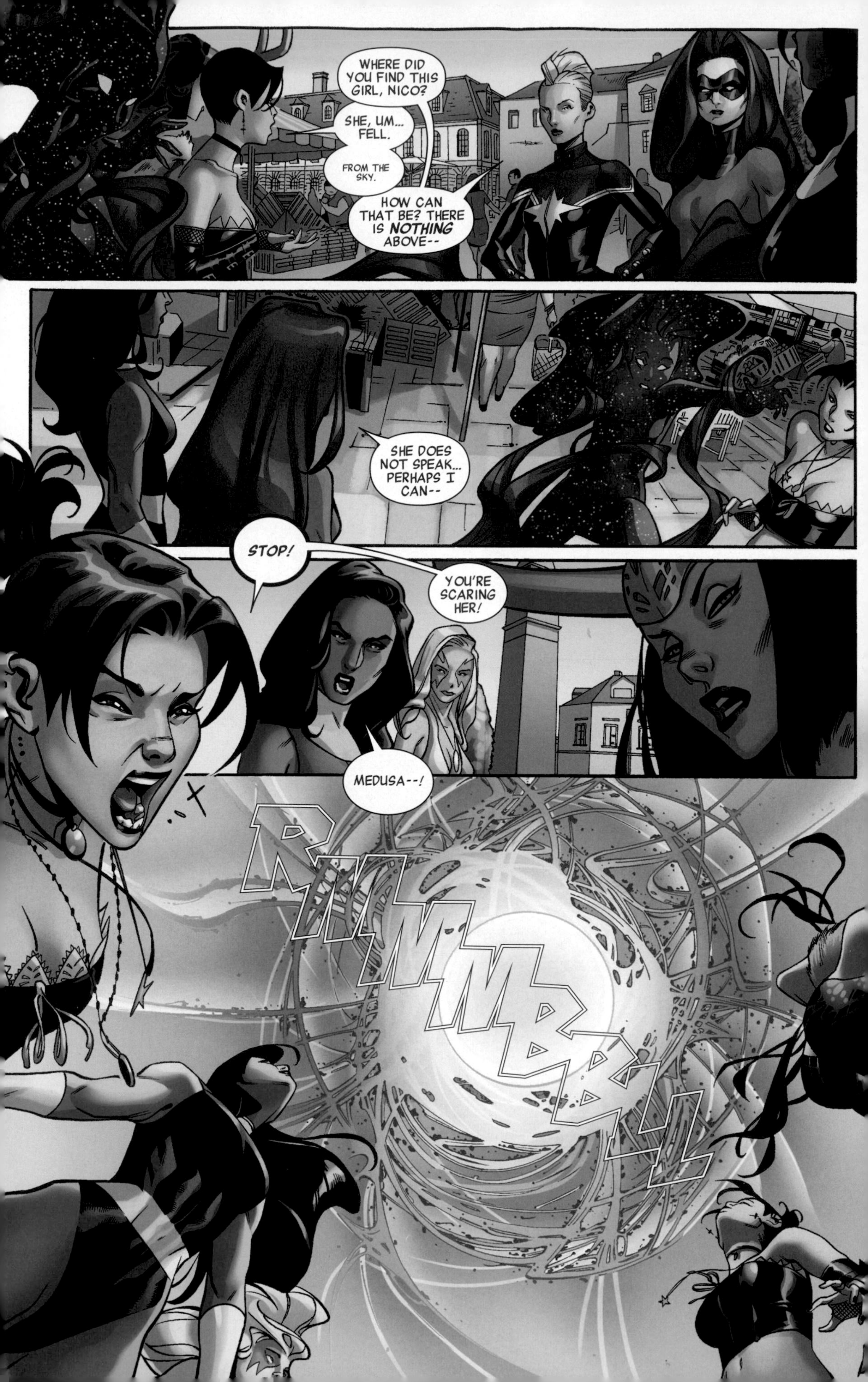
WHERE DID YOU FIND THIS GIRL, NICO?
SHE, UM... FELL.
FROM THE SKY.
HOW CAN THAT BE? THERE IS NOTHING ABOVE--
SHE DOES NOT SPEAK... PERHAPS I CAN--
STOP!
YOU'RE SCARING HER!
MEDUSA--!
RMMBBL

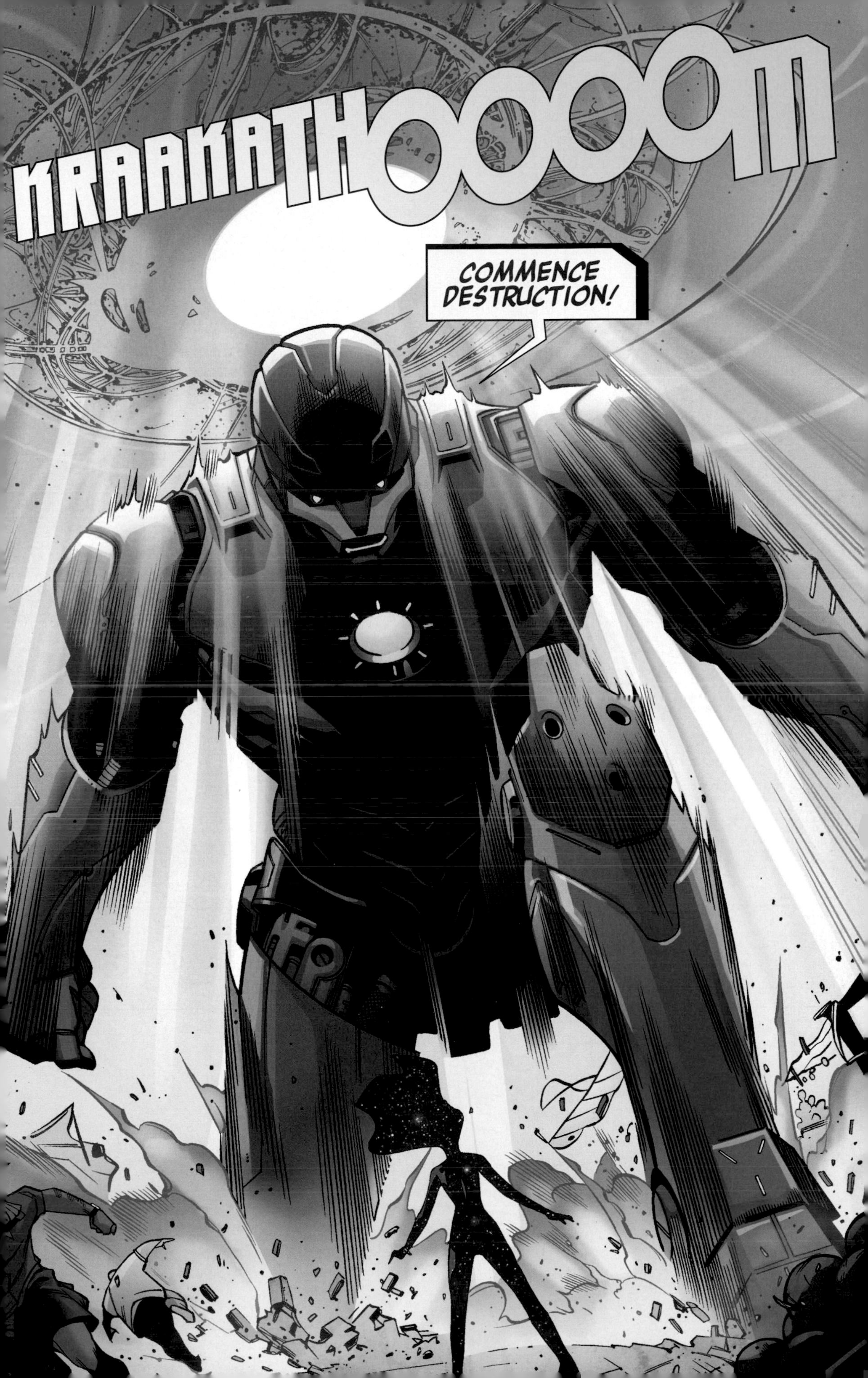
KRAAKATHOOOOM
COMMENCE DESTRUCTION!

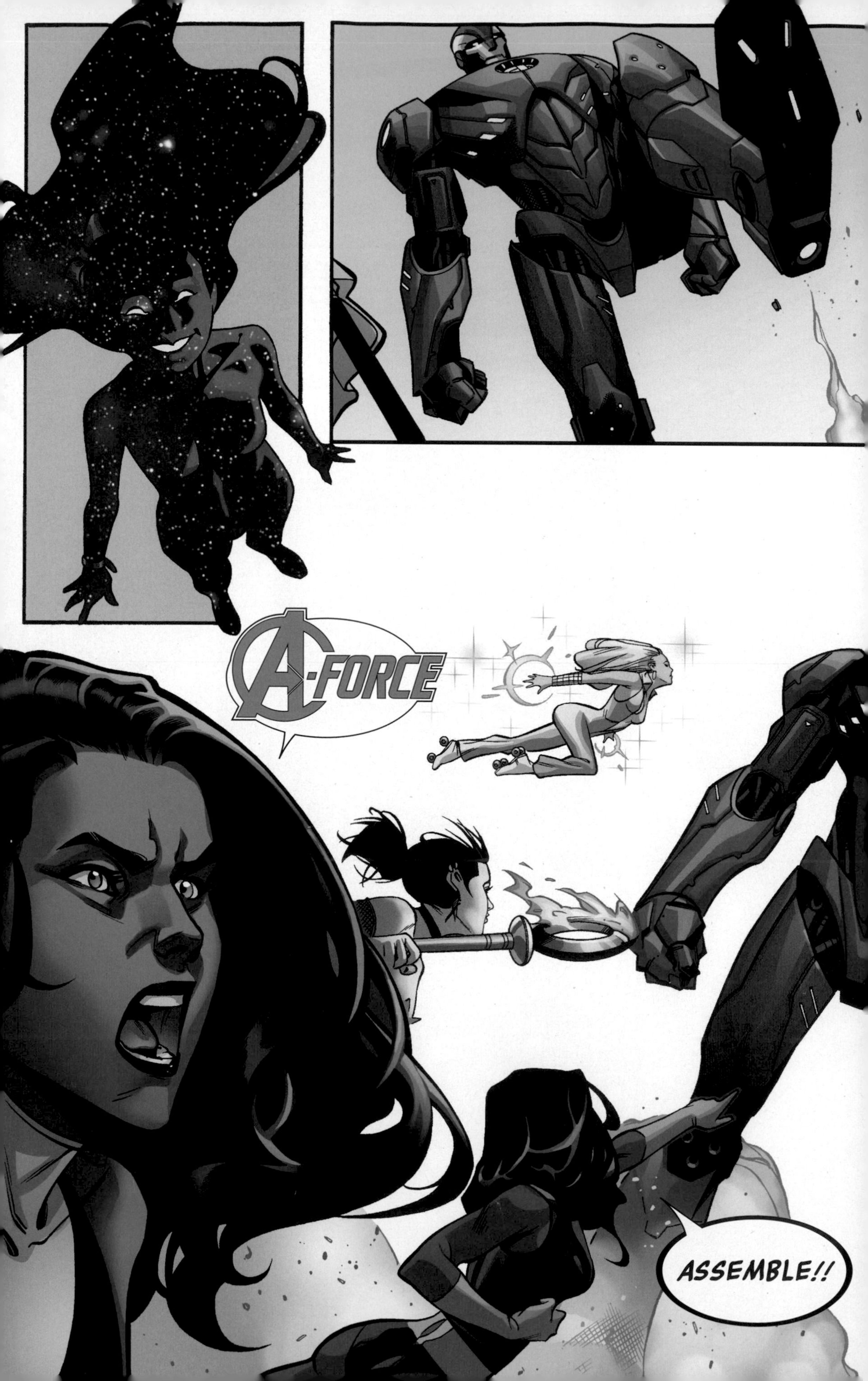
A-FORCE
ASSEMBLE!!

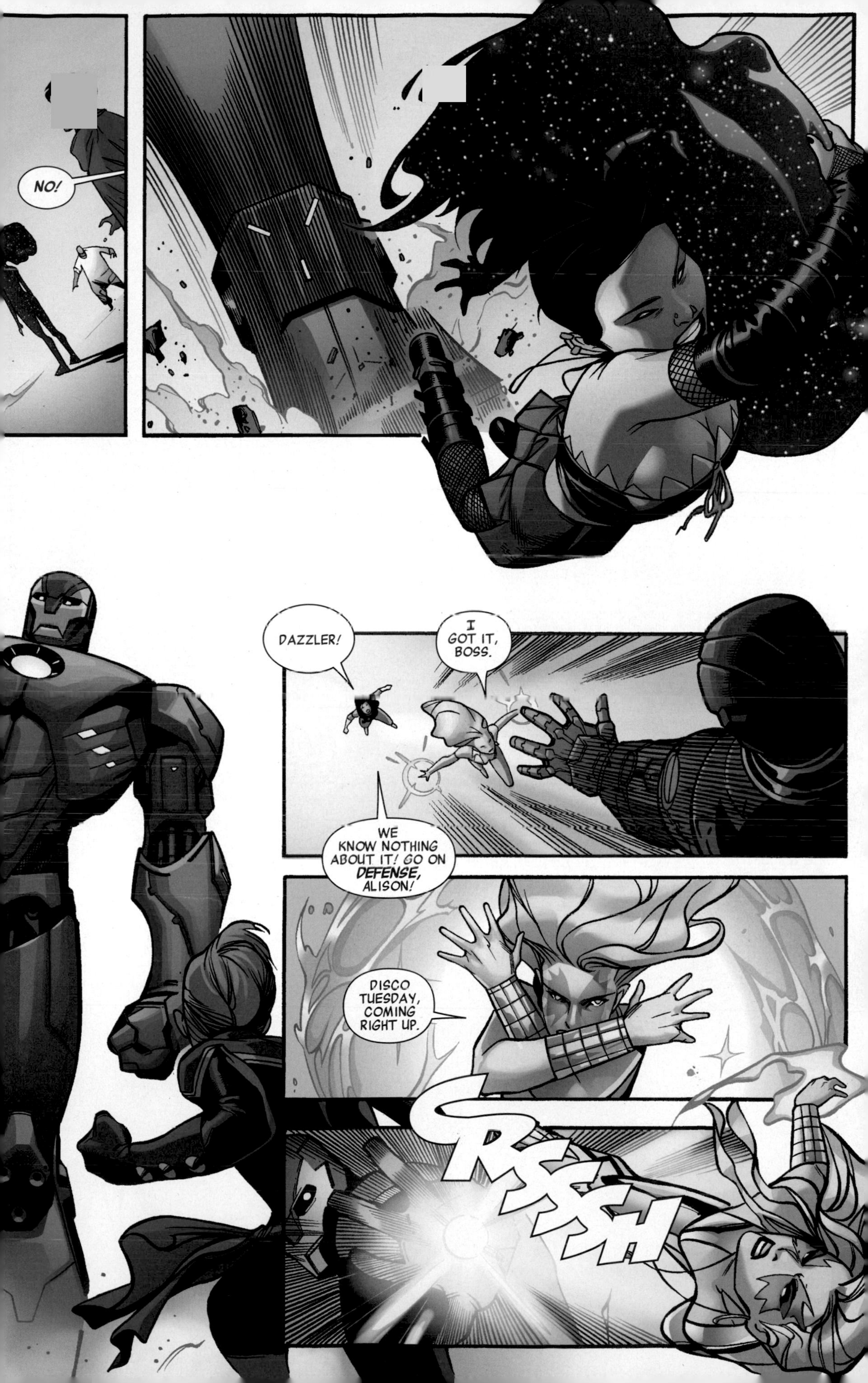
NO!
DAZZLER!
I GOT IT, BOSS.
WE KNOW NOTHING ABOUT IT! GO ON DEFENSE, ALISON!
DISCO TUESDAY, COMING RIGHT UP.
CRSSH

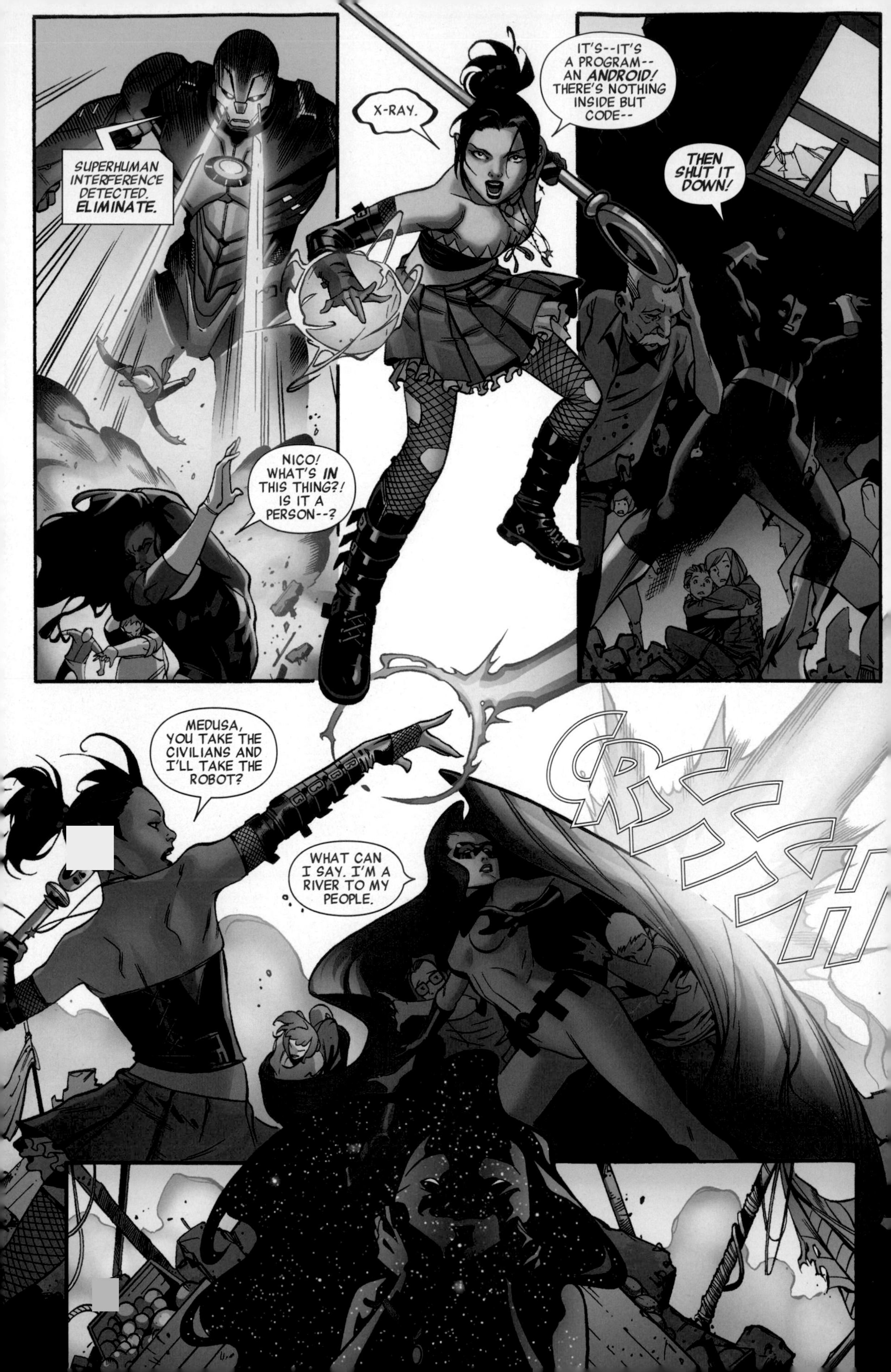
SUPERHUMAN INTERFERENCE DETECTED. ELIMINATE.
X-RAY.
IT'S--IT'S A PROGRAM-- AN ANDROID! THERE'S NOTHING INSIDE BUT CODE--
THEN SHUT IT DOWN!
NICO! WHAT'S IN THIS THING?! IS IT A PERSON--?
MEDUSA, YOU TAKE THE CIVILIANS AND I'LL TAKE THE ROBOT?
WHAT CAN I SAY. I'M A RIVER TO MY PEOPLE.
CRRAAAASH

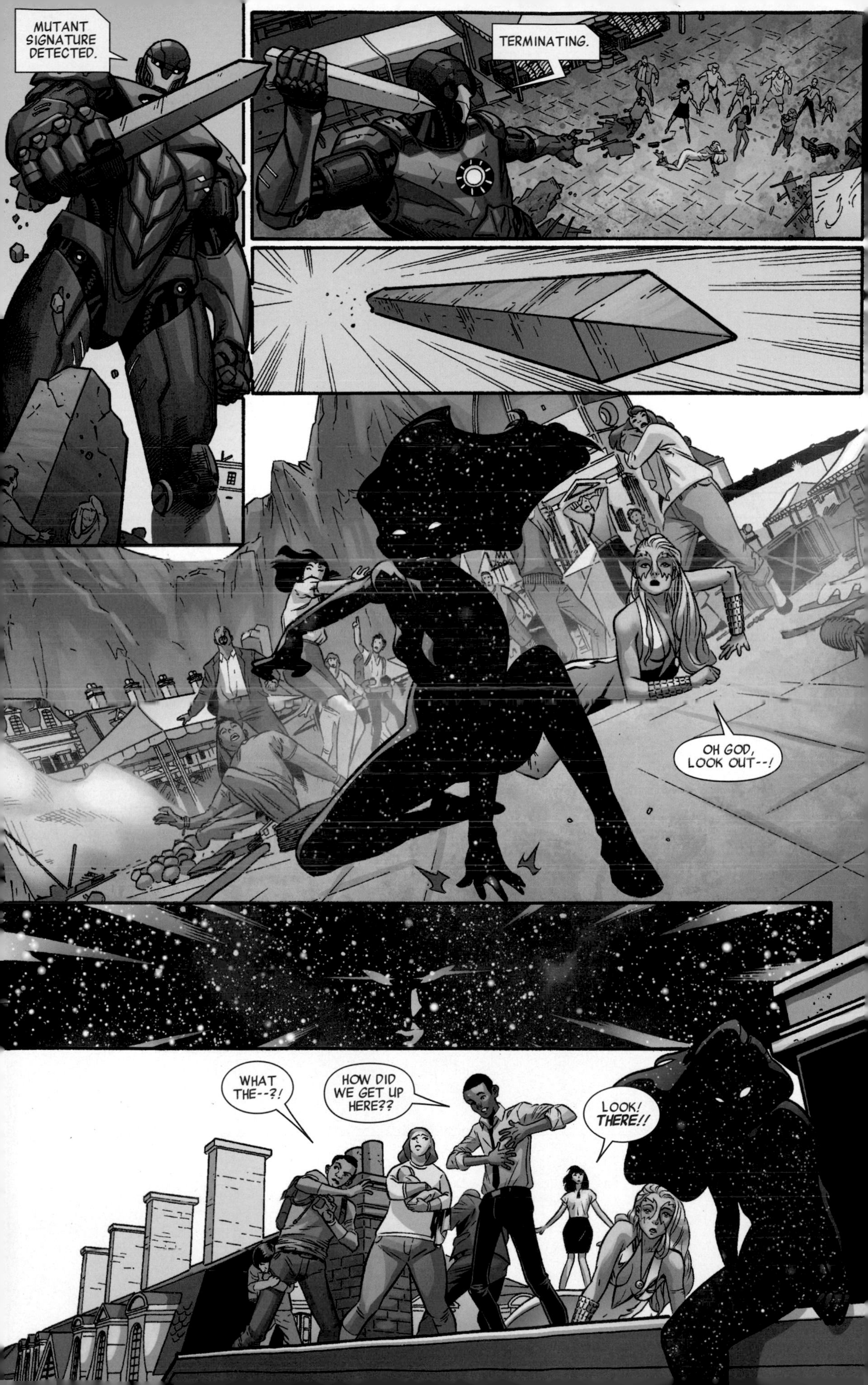
MUTANT SIGNATURE DETECTED.
TERMINATING.
OH GOD, LOOK OUT--!
WHAT THE--?!
HOW DID WE GET UP HERE??
LOOK! THERE!!

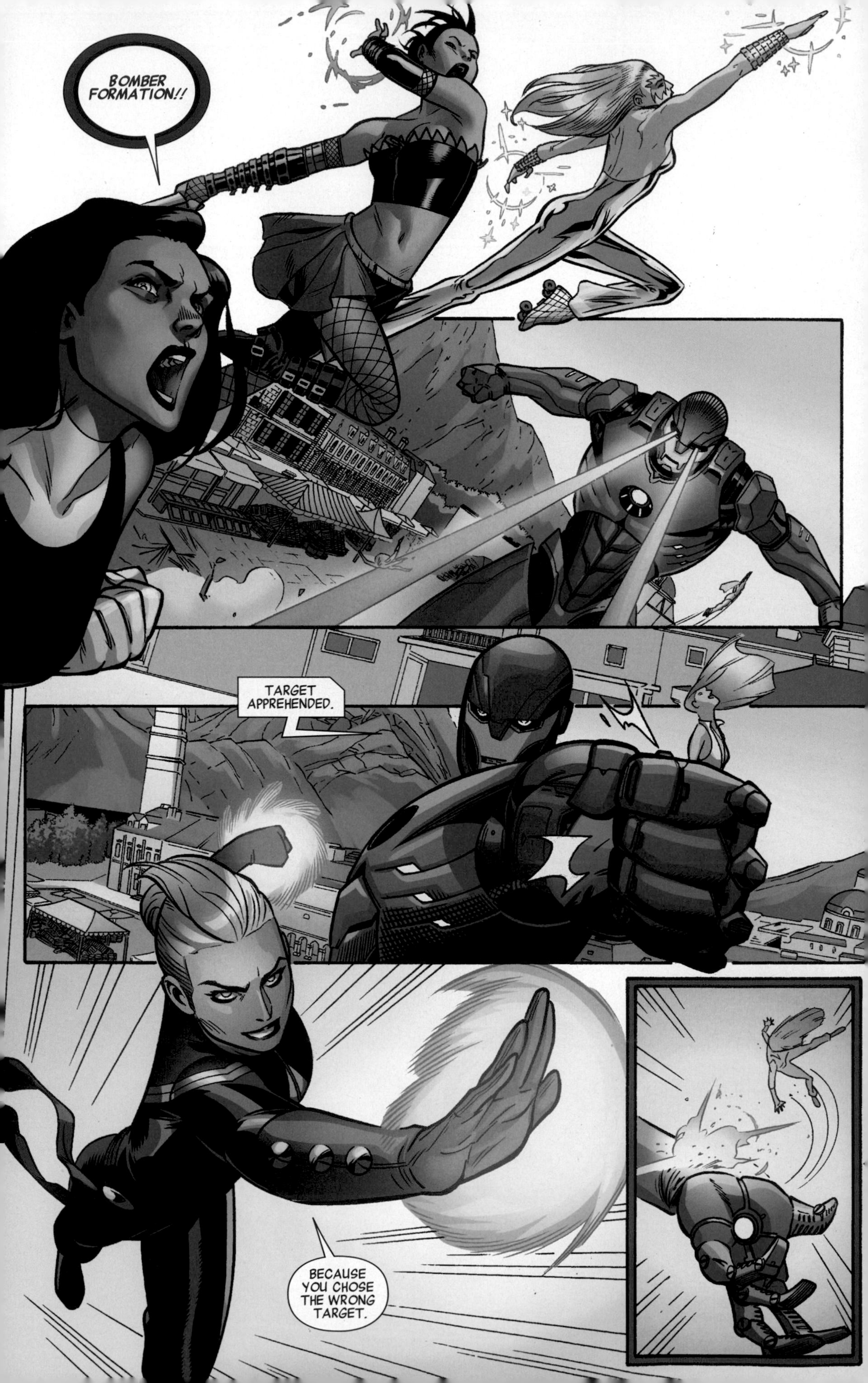
BOMBER FORMATION!!
TARGET APPREHENDED.
BECAUSE YOU CHOSE THE WRONG TARGET.

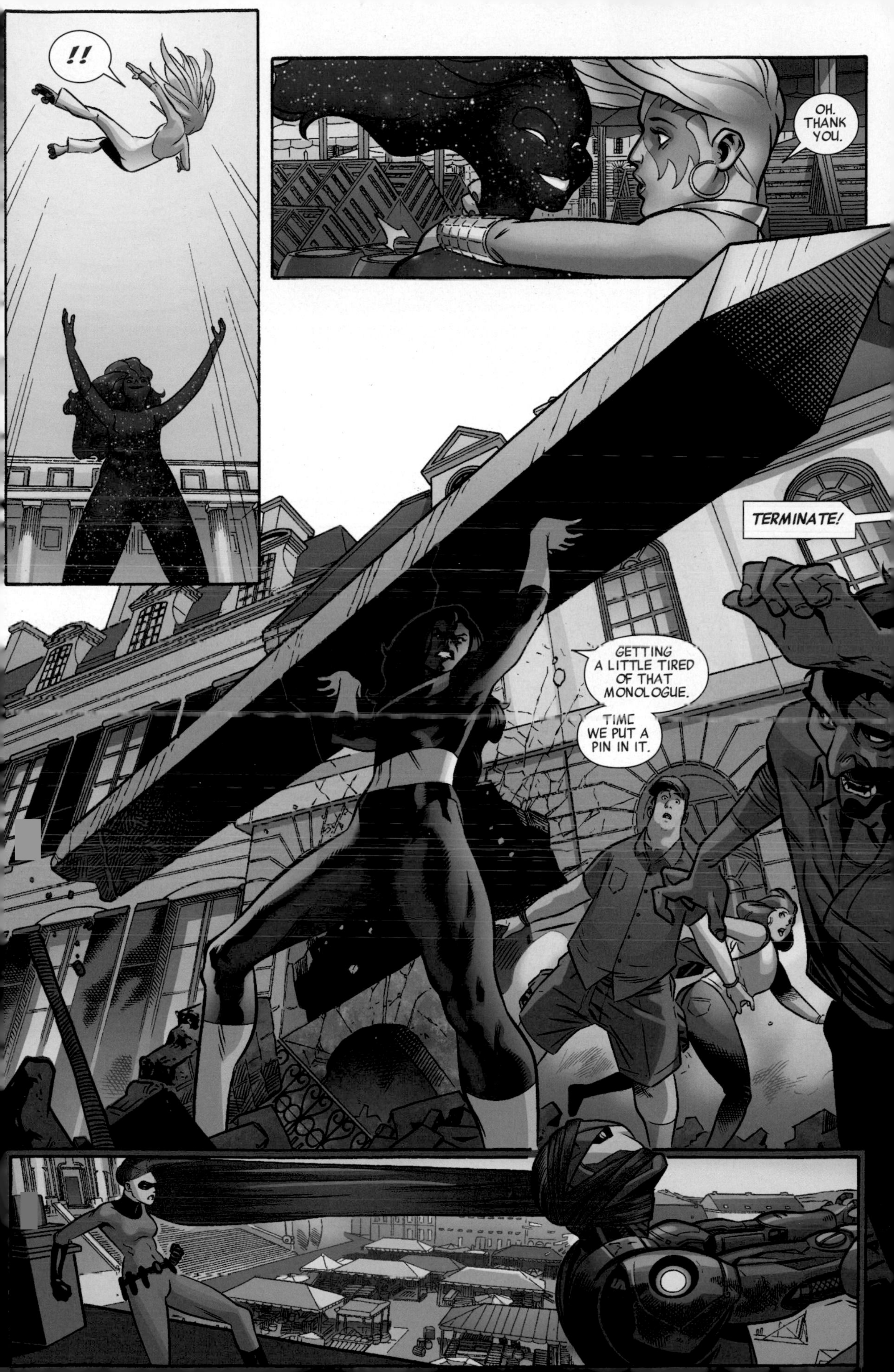
!!
OH. THANK YOU.
TERMINATE!
GETTING A LITTLE TIRED OF THAT MONOLOGUE.
TIME WE PUT A PIN IN IT.

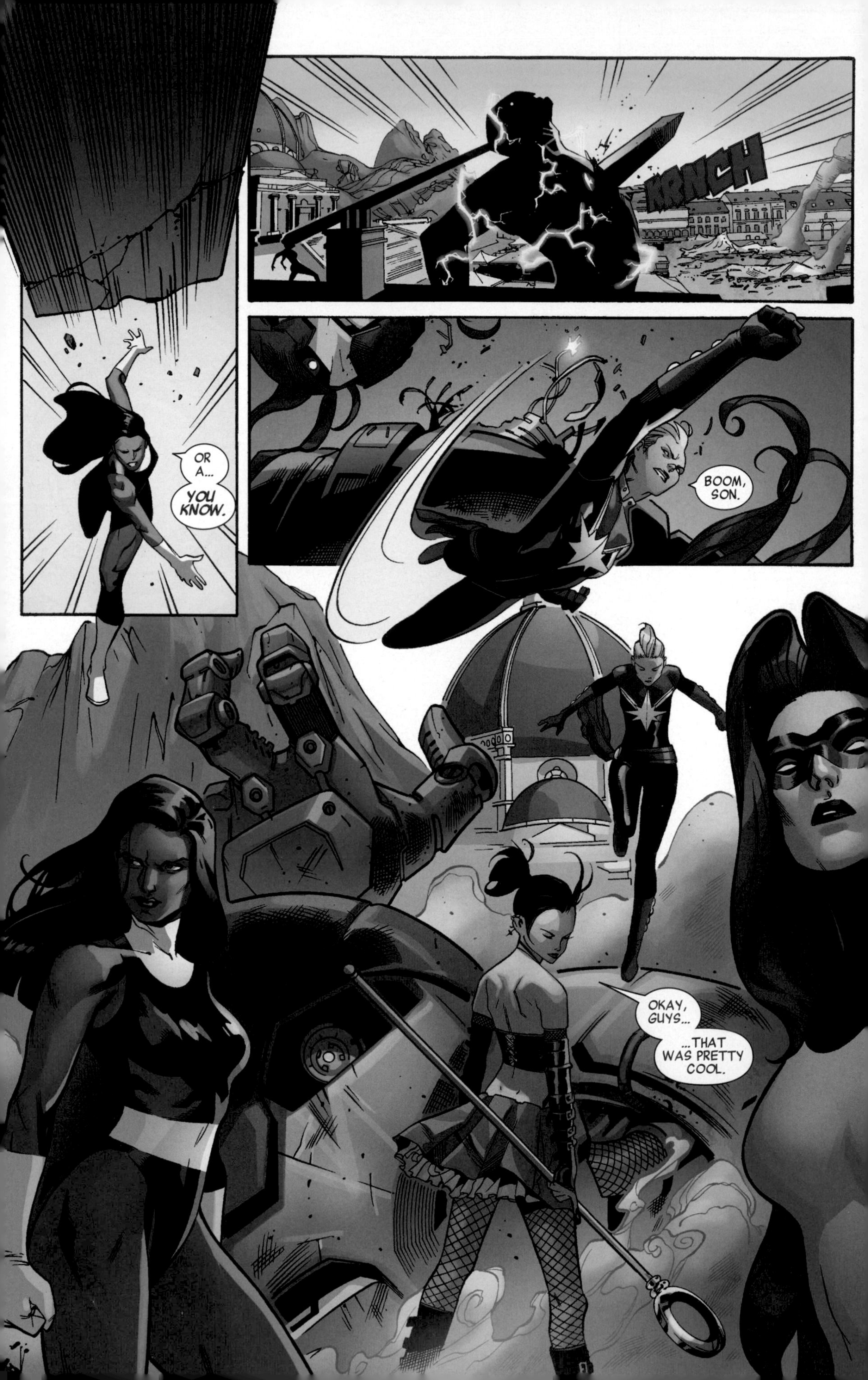
KRNCH
OR A... YOU KNOW.
BOOM, SON.
OKAY, GUYS...
...THAT WAS PRETTY COOL.

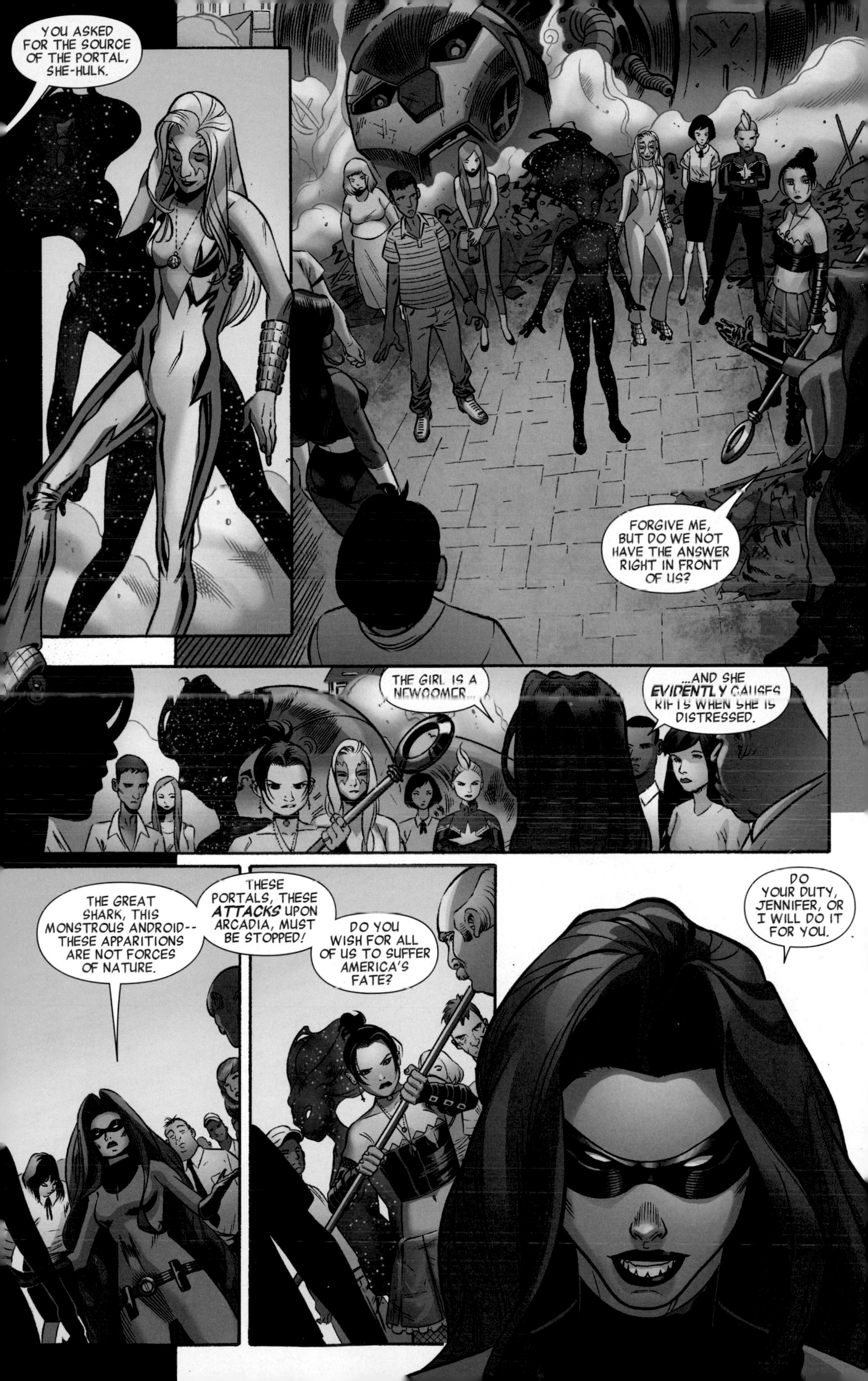
YOU ASKED FOR THE SOURCE OF THE PORTAL, SHE-HULK.
FORGIVE ME, BUT DO WE NOT HAVE THE ANSWER RIGHT IN FRONT OF US?
THE GIRL IS A NEWCOMER...
...AND SHE EVIDENTLY CAUSES RIFTS WHEN SHE IS DISTRESSED.
THE GREAT SHARK, THIS MONSTROUS ANDROID-- THESE APPARITIONS ARE NOT FORCES OF NATURE.
THESE PORTALS, THESE ATTACKS UPON ARCADIA, MUST BE STOPPED!
DO YOU WISH FOR ALL OF US TO SUFFER AMERICA'S FATE?
DO YOUR DUTY, JENNIFER, OR I WILL DO IT FOR YOU.

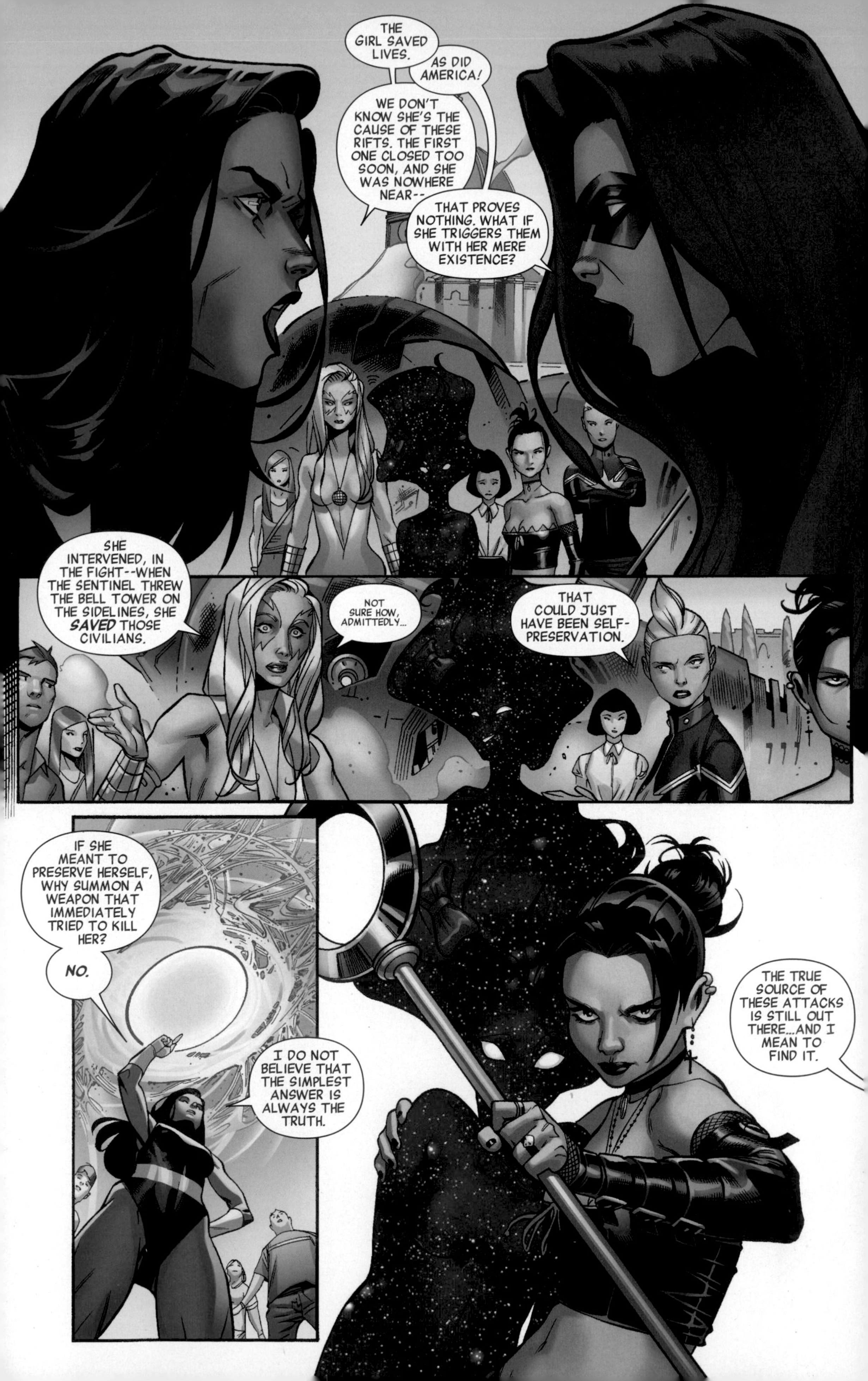

THE GIRL SAVED LIVES.
AS DID AMERICA!
WE DON'T KNOW SHE'S THE CAUSE OF THESE RIFTS. THE FIRST ONE CLOSED TOO SOON, AND SHE WAS NOWHERE NEAR--
THAT PROVES NOTHING. WHAT IF SHE TRIGGERS THEM WITH HER MERE EXISTENCE?
SHE INTERVENED, IN THE FIGHT--WHEN THE SENTINEL THREW THE BELL TOWER ON THE SIDELINES, SHE SAVED THOSE CIVILIANS.
NOT SURE HOW, ADMITTEDLY...
THAT COULD JUST HAVE BEEN SELF-PRESERVATION.
IF SHE MEANT TO PRESERVE HERSELF, WHY SUMMON A WEAPON THAT IMMEDIATELY TRIED TO KILL HER?
NO.
I DO NOT BELIEVE THAT THE SIMPLEST ANSWER IS ALWAYS THE TRUTH.
THE TRUE SOURCE OF THESE ATTACKS IS STILL OUT THERE...AND I MEAN TO FIND IT.

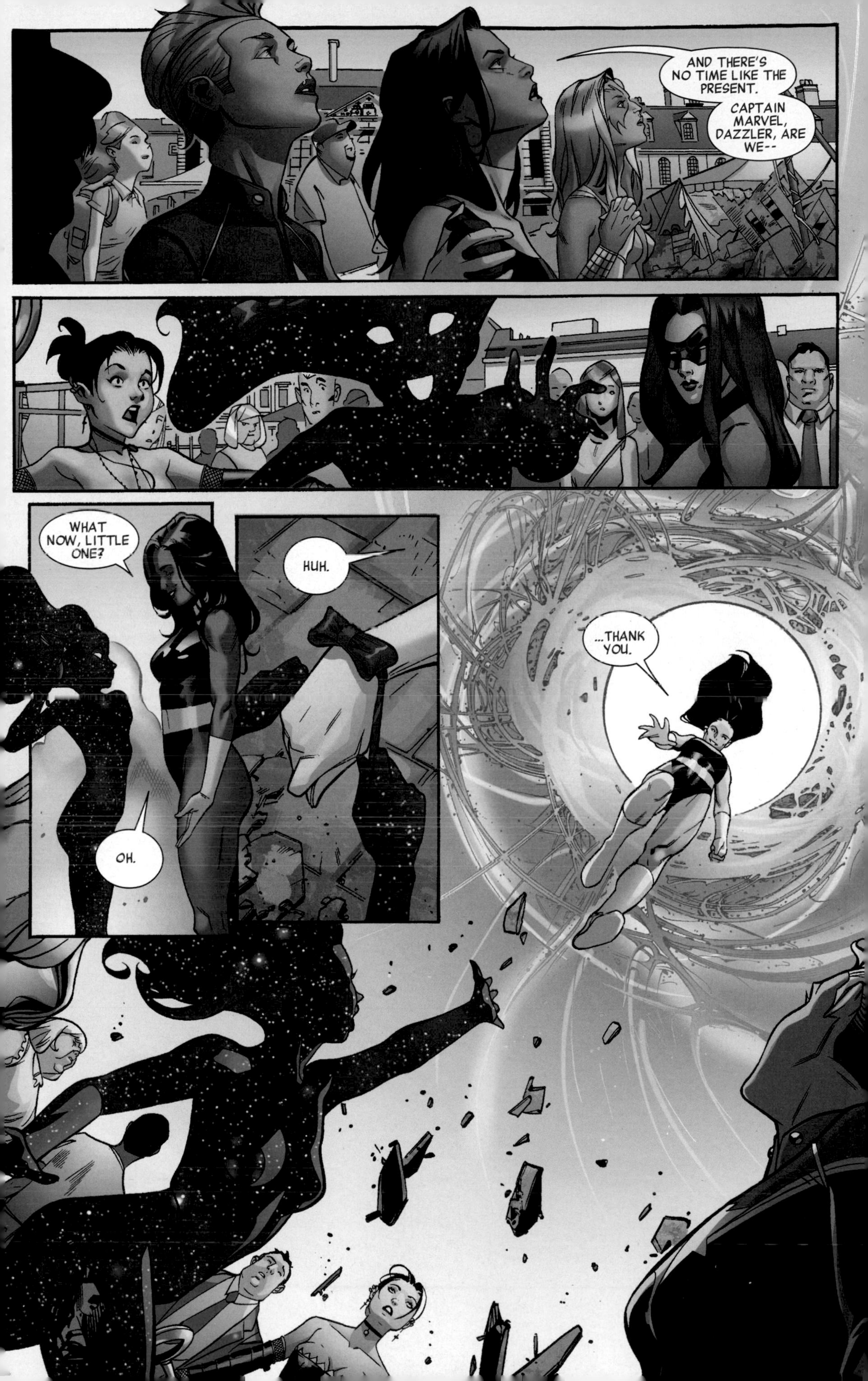
AND THERE'S NO TIME LIKE THE PRESENT.
CAPTAIN MARVEL, DAZZLER, ARE WE--
WHAT NOW, LITTLE ONE?
OH.
HUH.
...THANK YOU.

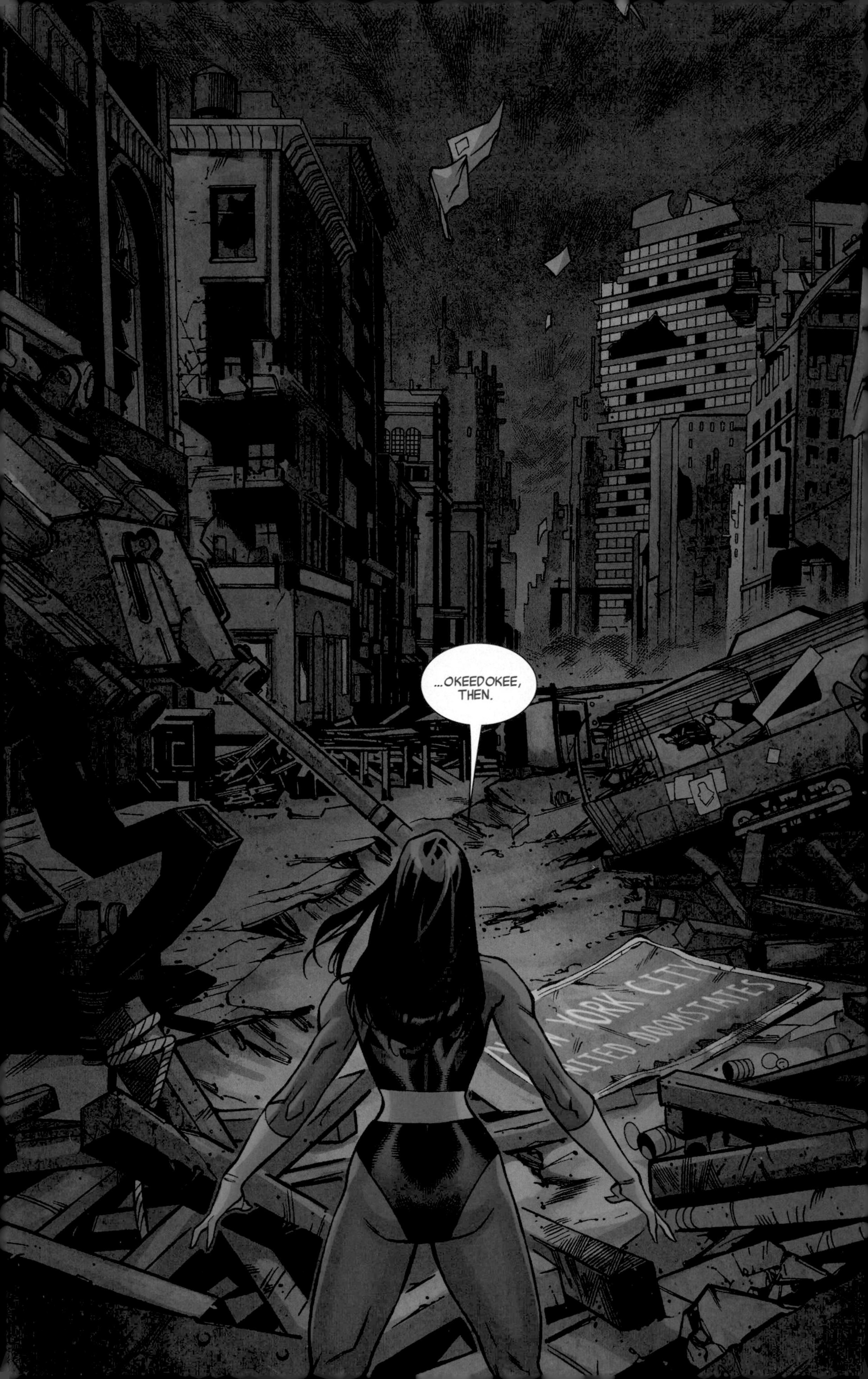
...OKEEDOKEE, THEN.
YORK CITY
DOOMSTATES

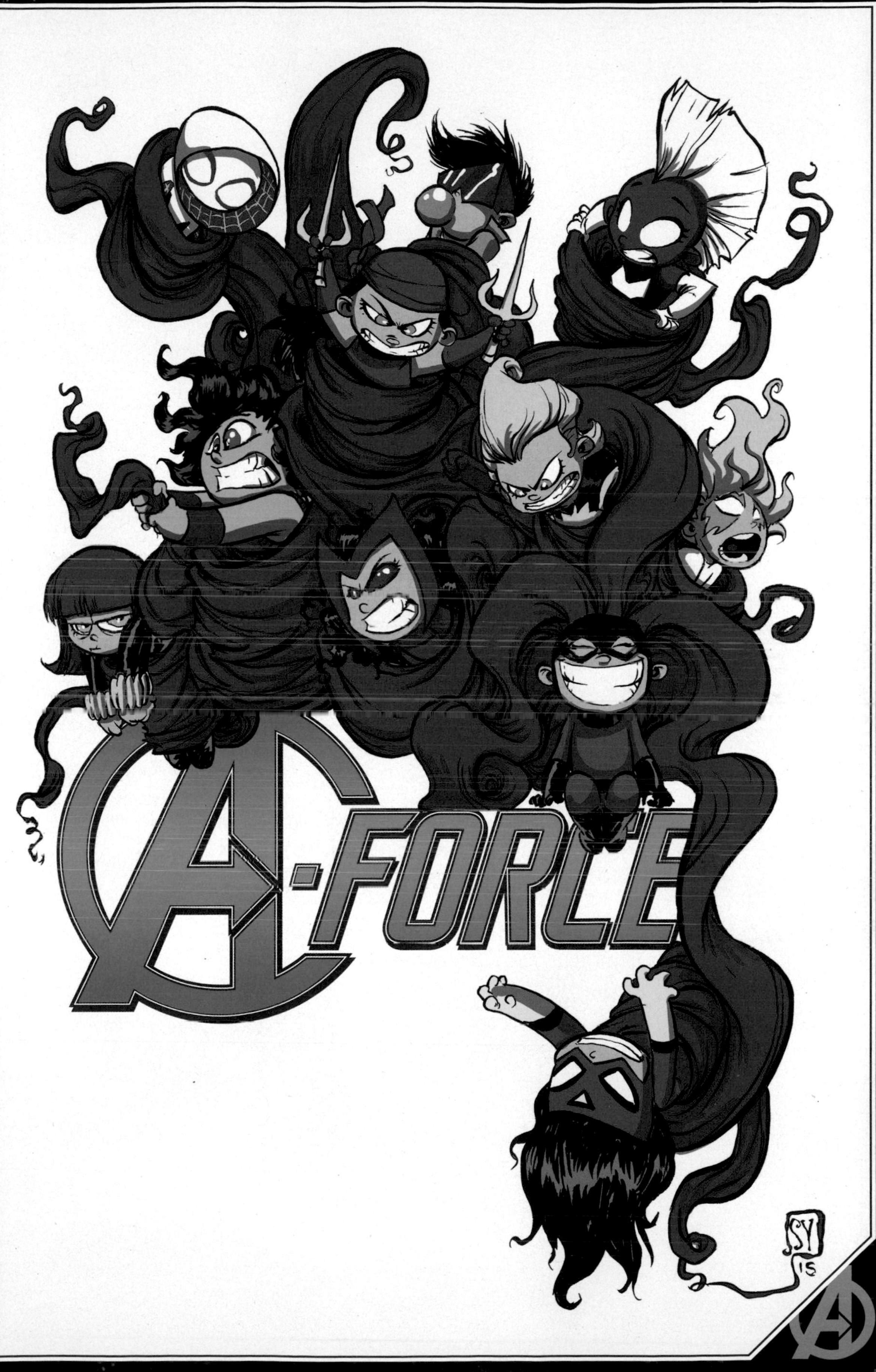
A-FORCE

#1 VARIANT BY **SKOTTIE YOUNG**

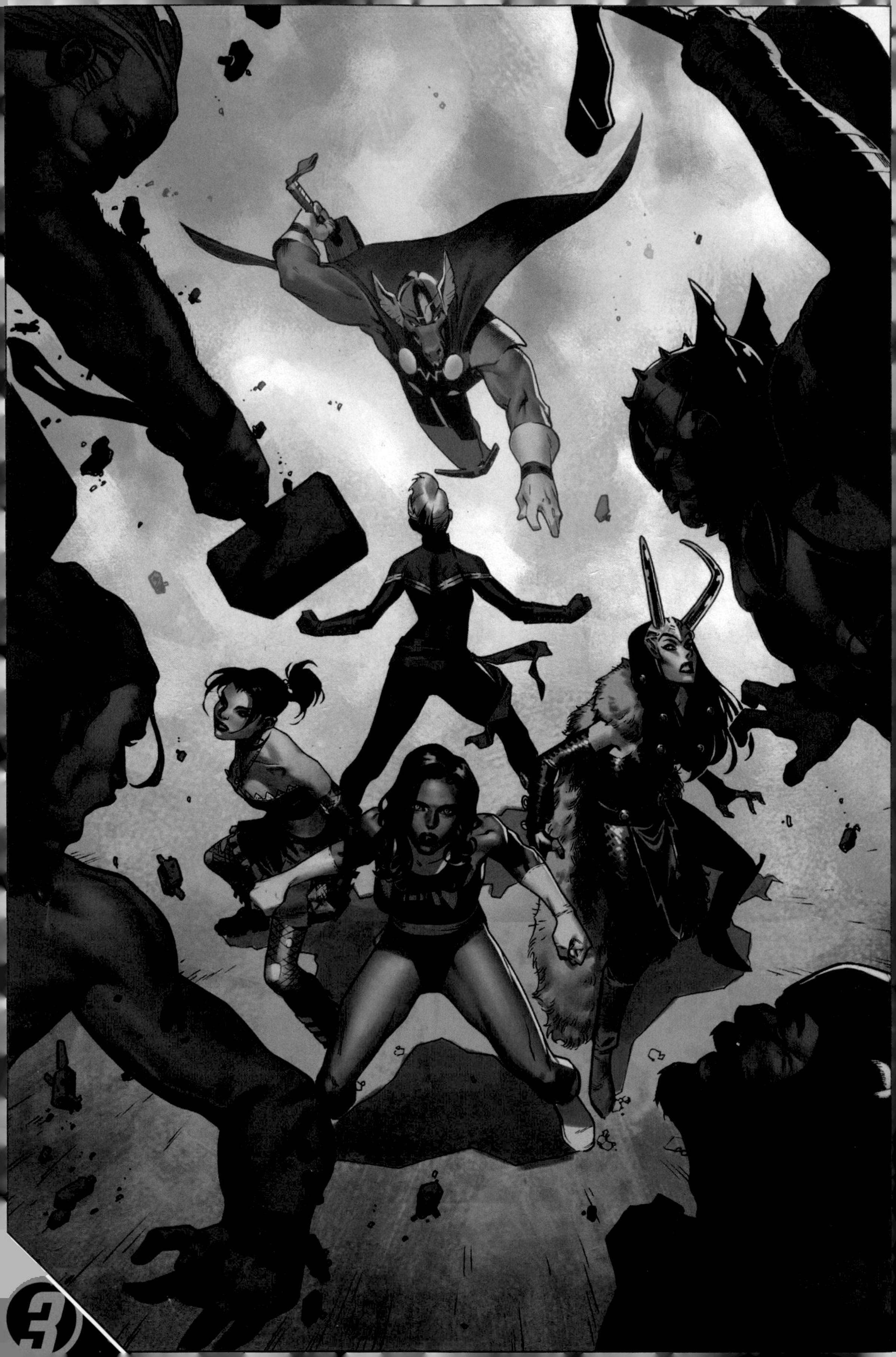

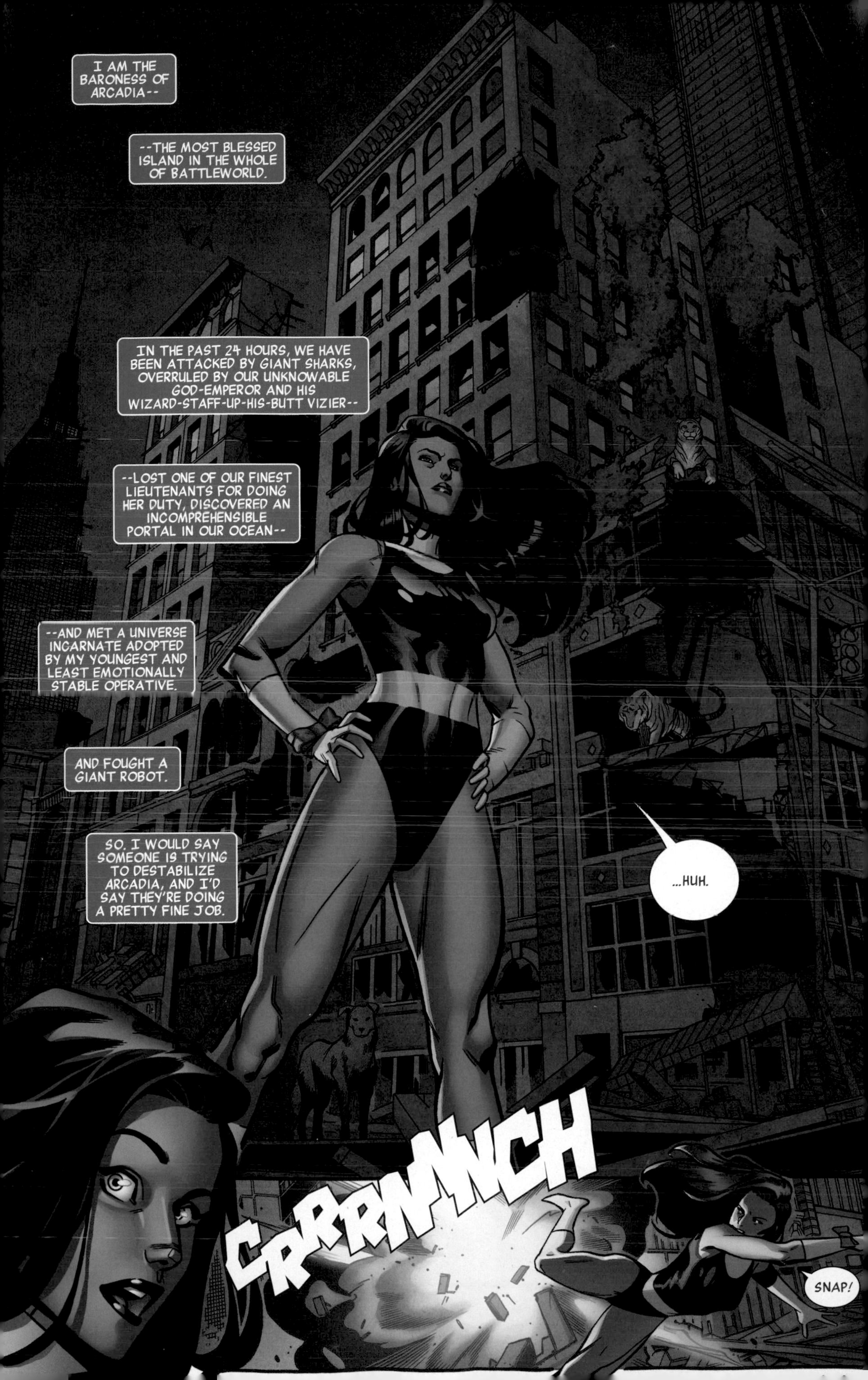
I AM THE BARONESS OF ARCADIA--
--THE MOST BLESSED ISLAND IN THE WHOLE OF BATTLEWORLD.
IN THE PAST 24 HOURS, WE HAVE BEEN ATTACKED BY GIANT SHARKS, OVERRULED BY OUR UNKNOWABLE GOD-EMPEROR AND HIS WIZARD-STAFF-UP-HIS-BUTT VIZIER--
--LOST ONE OF OUR FINEST LIEUTENANTS FOR DOING HER DUTY, DISCOVERED AN INCOMPREHENSIBLE PORTAL IN OUR OCEAN--
--AND MET A UNIVERSE INCARNATE ADOPTED BY MY YOUNGEST AND LEAST EMOTIONALLY STABLE OPERATIVE.
AND FOUGHT A GIANT ROBOT.
SO, I WOULD SAY SOMEONE IS TRYING TO DESTABILIZE ARCADIA, AND I'D SAY THEY'RE DOING A PRETTY FINE JOB.
...HUH.
CRRRNNNCH
SNAP!

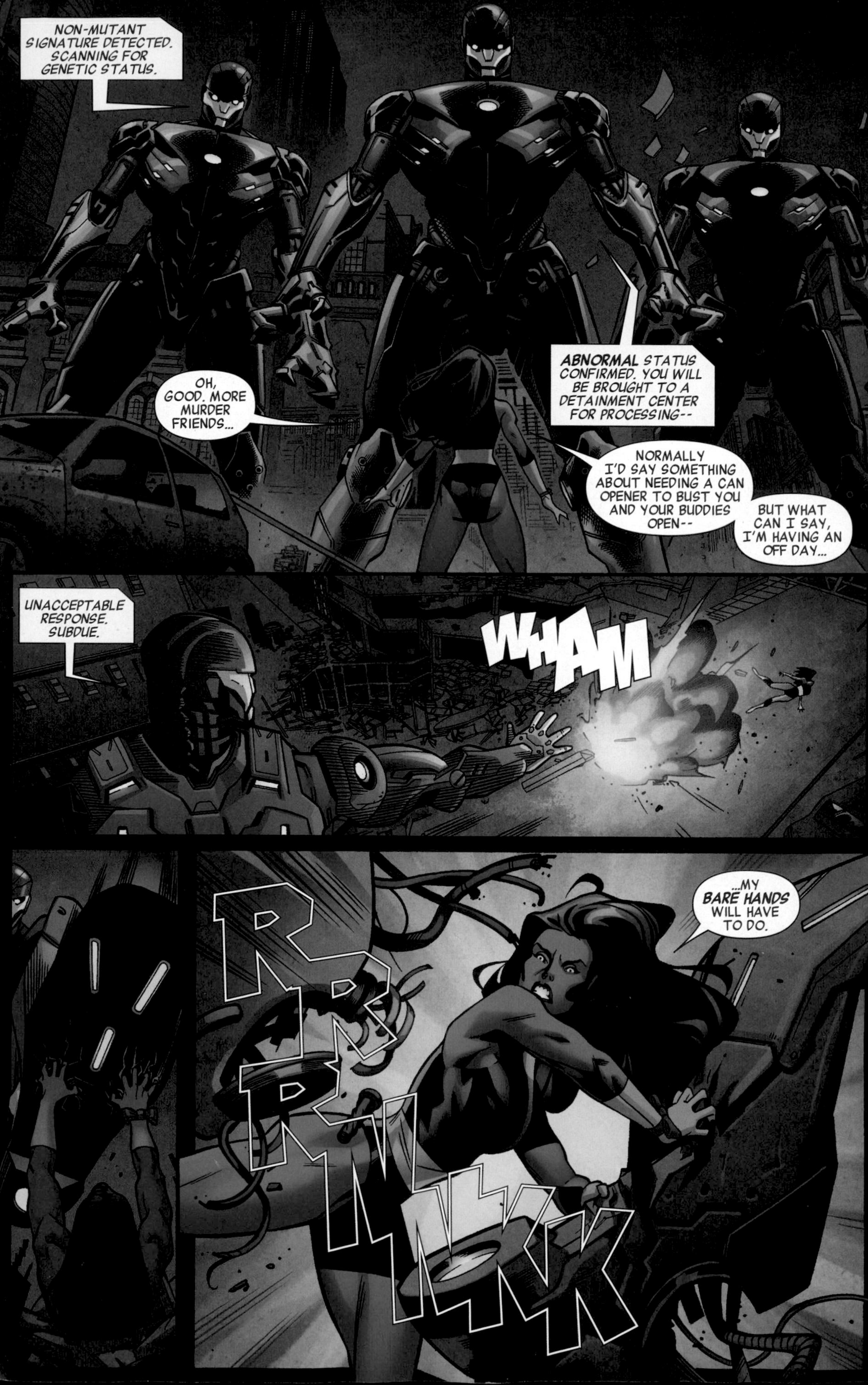
NON-MUTANT SIGNATURE DETECTED. SCANNING FOR GENETIC STATUS.
OH, GOOD. MORE MURDER FRIENDS...
ABNORMAL STATUS CONFIRMED. YOU WILL BE BROUGHT TO A DETAINMENT CENTER FOR PROCESSING--
NORMALLY I'D SAY SOMETHING ABOUT NEEDING A CAN OPENER TO BUST YOU AND YOUR BUDDIES OPEN--
BUT WHAT CAN I SAY, I'M HAVING AN OFF DAY...
UNACCEPTABLE RESPONSE. SUBDUE.
WHAM
...MY BARE HANDS WILL HAVE TO DO.
RRNNK

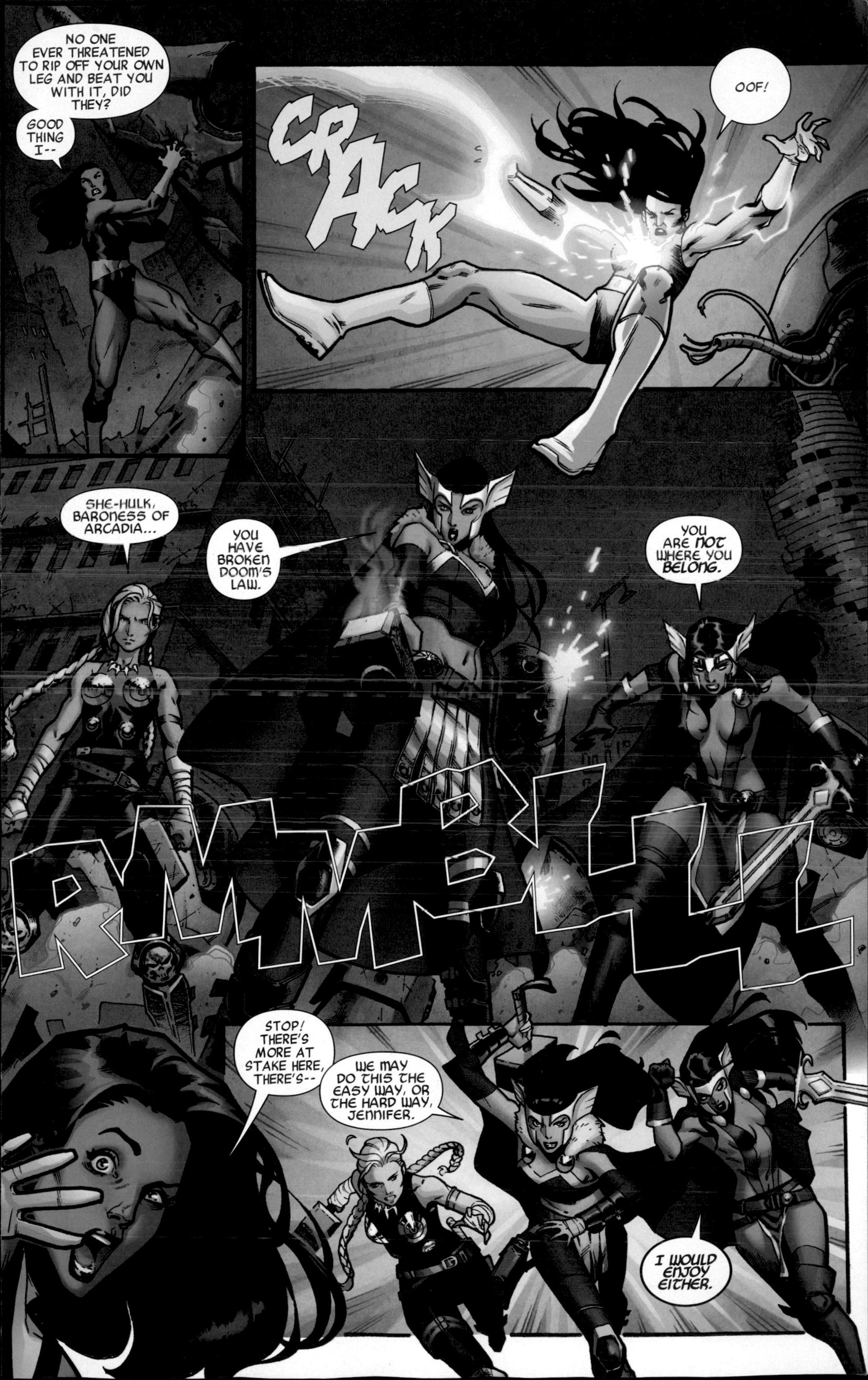
NO ONE EVER THREATENED TO RIP OFF YOUR OWN LEG AND BEAT YOU WITH IT, DID THEY?
GOOD THING I--
CRACK
OOF!
SHE-HULK, BARONESS OF ARCADIA...
YOU HAVE BROKEN DOOM'S LAW.
YOU ARE NOT WHERE YOU BELONG.
STOP! THERE'S MORE AT STAKE HERE, THERE'S--
WE MAY DO THIS THE EASY WAY, OR THE HARD WAY, JENNIFER.
I WOULD ENJOY EITHER.

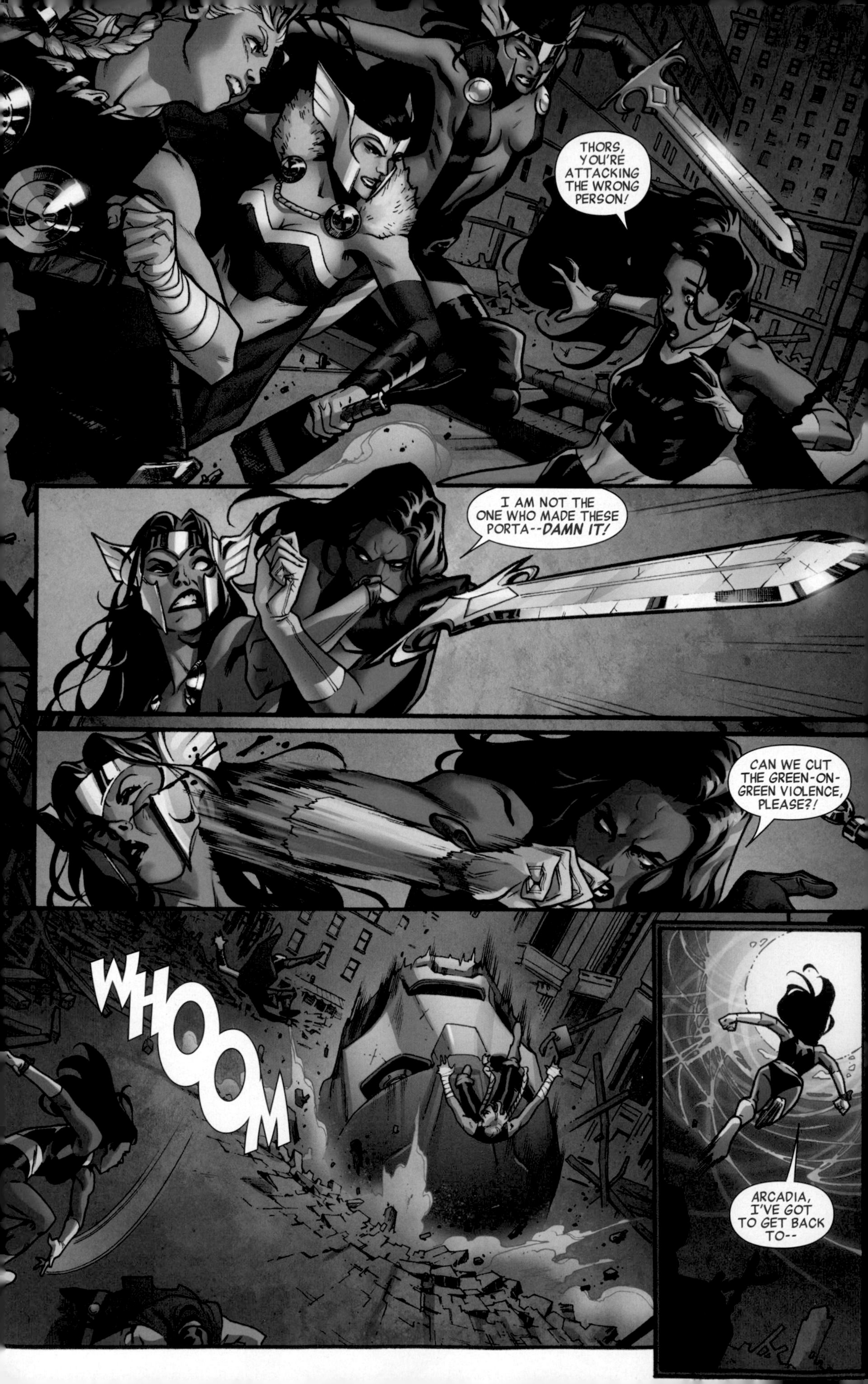

THORS, YOU'RE ATTACKING THE WRONG PERSON!
I AM NOT THE ONE WHO MADE THESE PORTA--DAMN IT!
CAN WE CUT THE GREEN-ON-GREEN VIOLENCE, PLEASE?!
WHOOM
ARCADIA, I'VE GOT TO GET BACK TO--

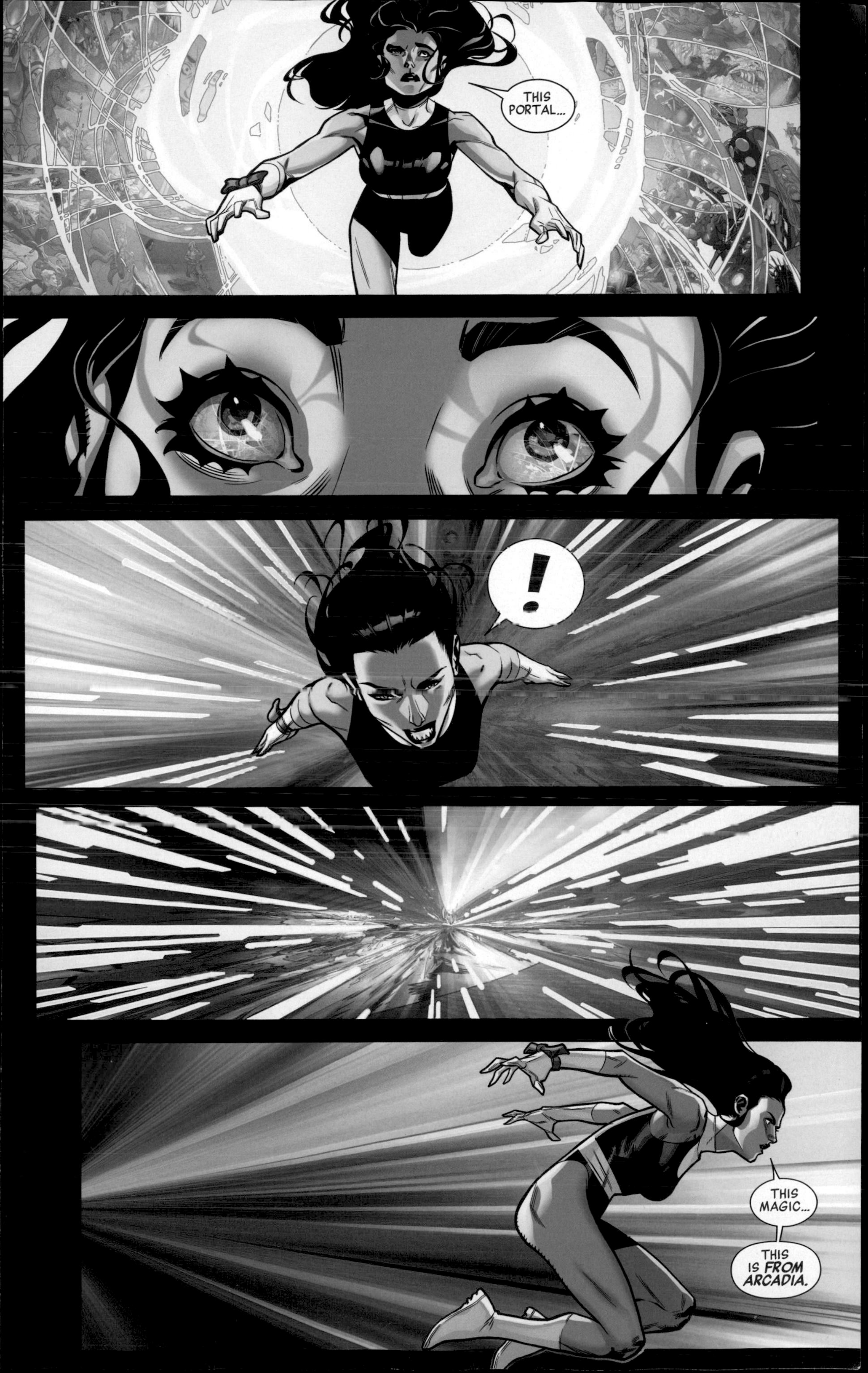
THIS PORTAL...
!
THIS MAGIC...
THIS IS FROM ARCADIA.

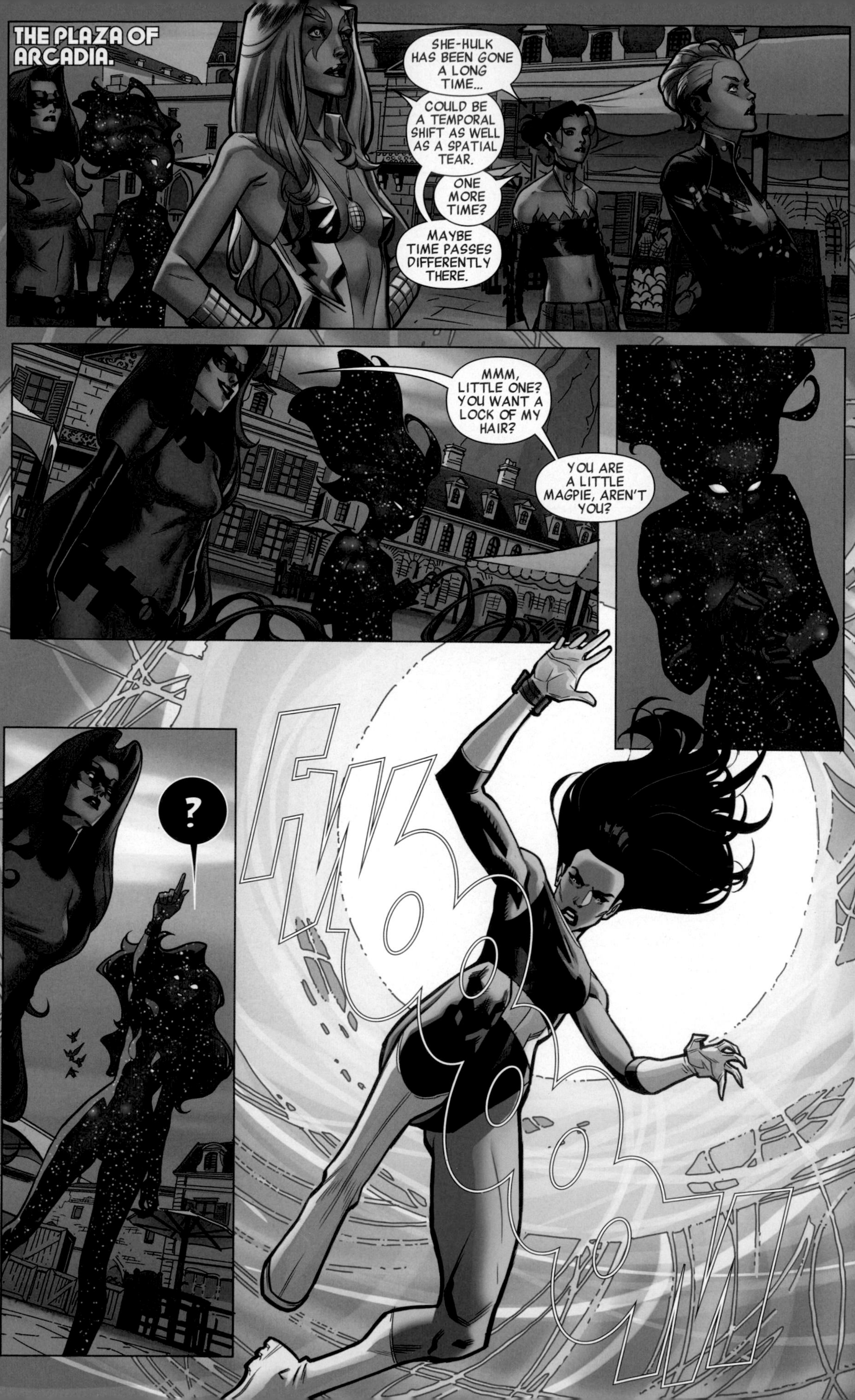
THE PLAZA OF ARCADIA.
SHE-HULK HAS BEEN GONE A LONG TIME...
COULD BE A TEMPORAL SHIFT AS WELL AS A SPATIAL TEAR.
ONE MORE TIME?
MAYBE TIME PASSES DIFFERENTLY THERE.
MMM, LITTLE ONE? YOU WANT A LOCK OF MY HAIR?
YOU ARE A LITTLE MAGPIE, AREN'T YOU?
?
FWOOOOOOM

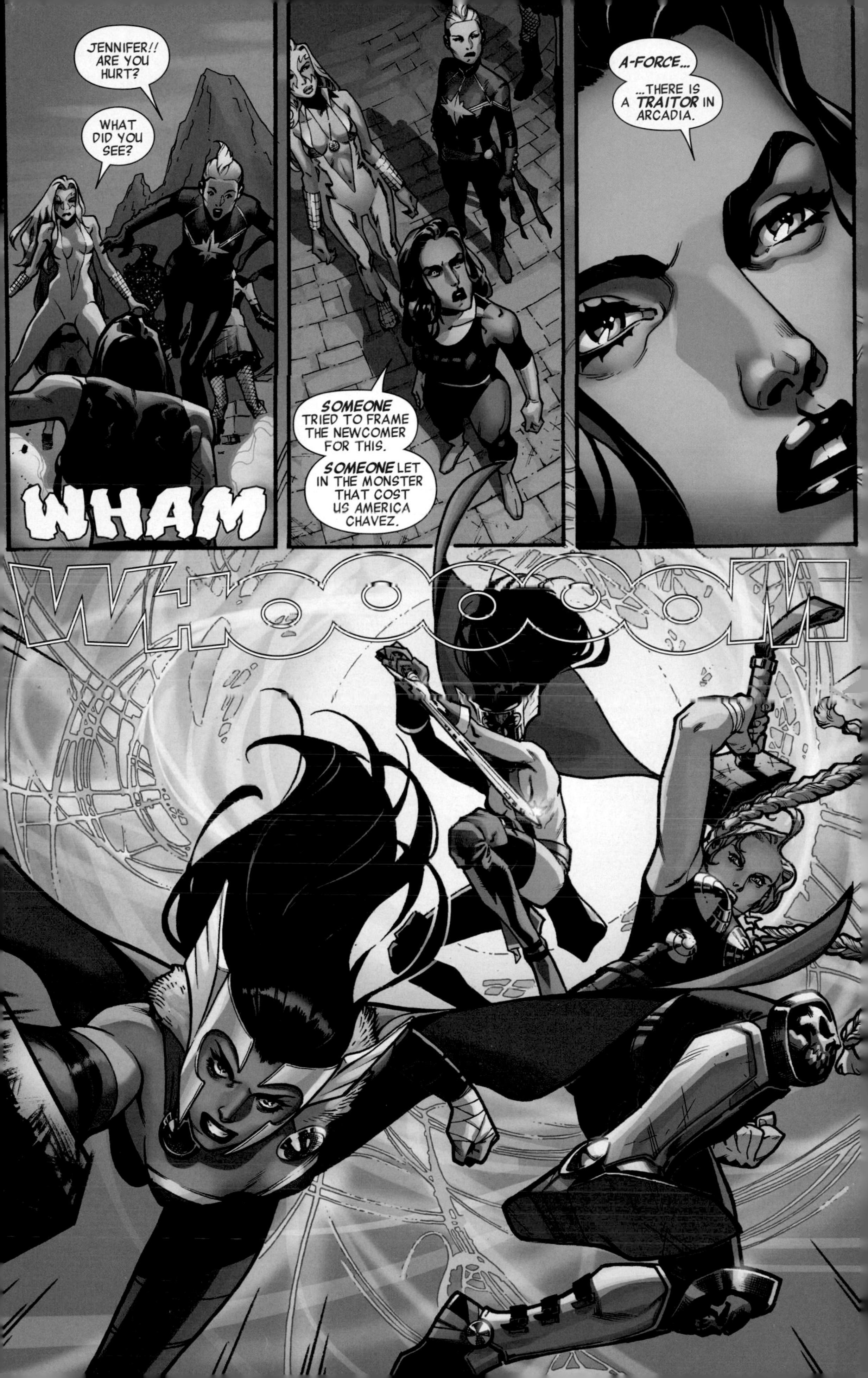
JENNIFER!! ARE YOU HURT?
WHAT DID YOU SEE?
WHAM
SOMEONE TRIED TO FRAME THE NEWCOMER FOR THIS.
SOMEONE LET IN THE MONSTER THAT COST US AMERICA CHAVEZ.
A-FORCE...
...THERE IS A TRAITOR IN ARCADIA.
WHOOOOOOM

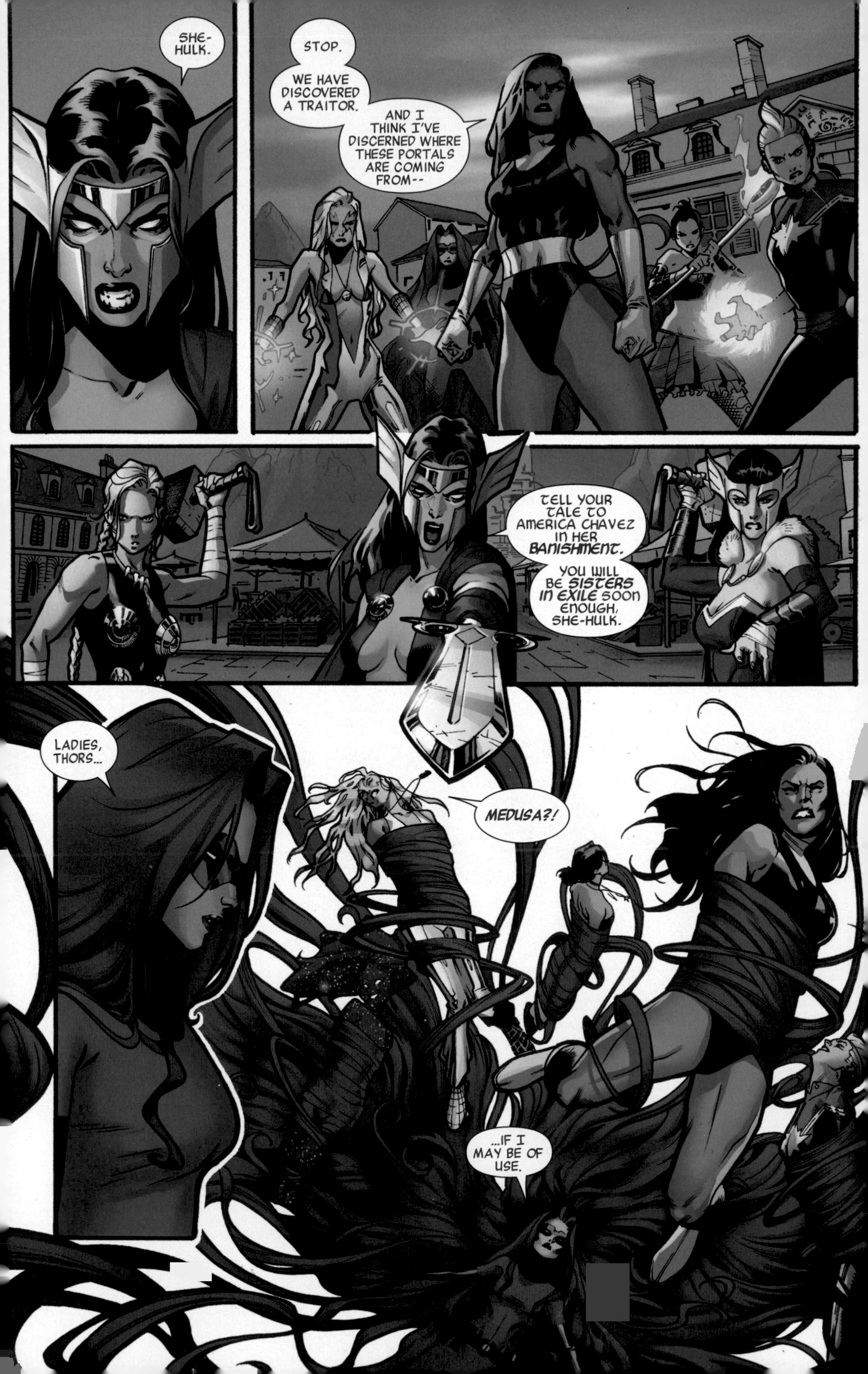
SHE-HULK.
STOP.
WE HAVE DISCOVERED A TRAITOR.
AND I THINK I'VE DISCERNED WHERE THESE PORTALS ARE COMING FROM--
TELL YOUR TALE TO AMERICA CHAVEZ IN HER BANISHMENT.
YOU WILL BE SISTERS IN EXILE SOON ENOUGH, SHE-HULK.
LADIES, THORS...
MEDUSA?!
...IF I MAY BE OF USE.

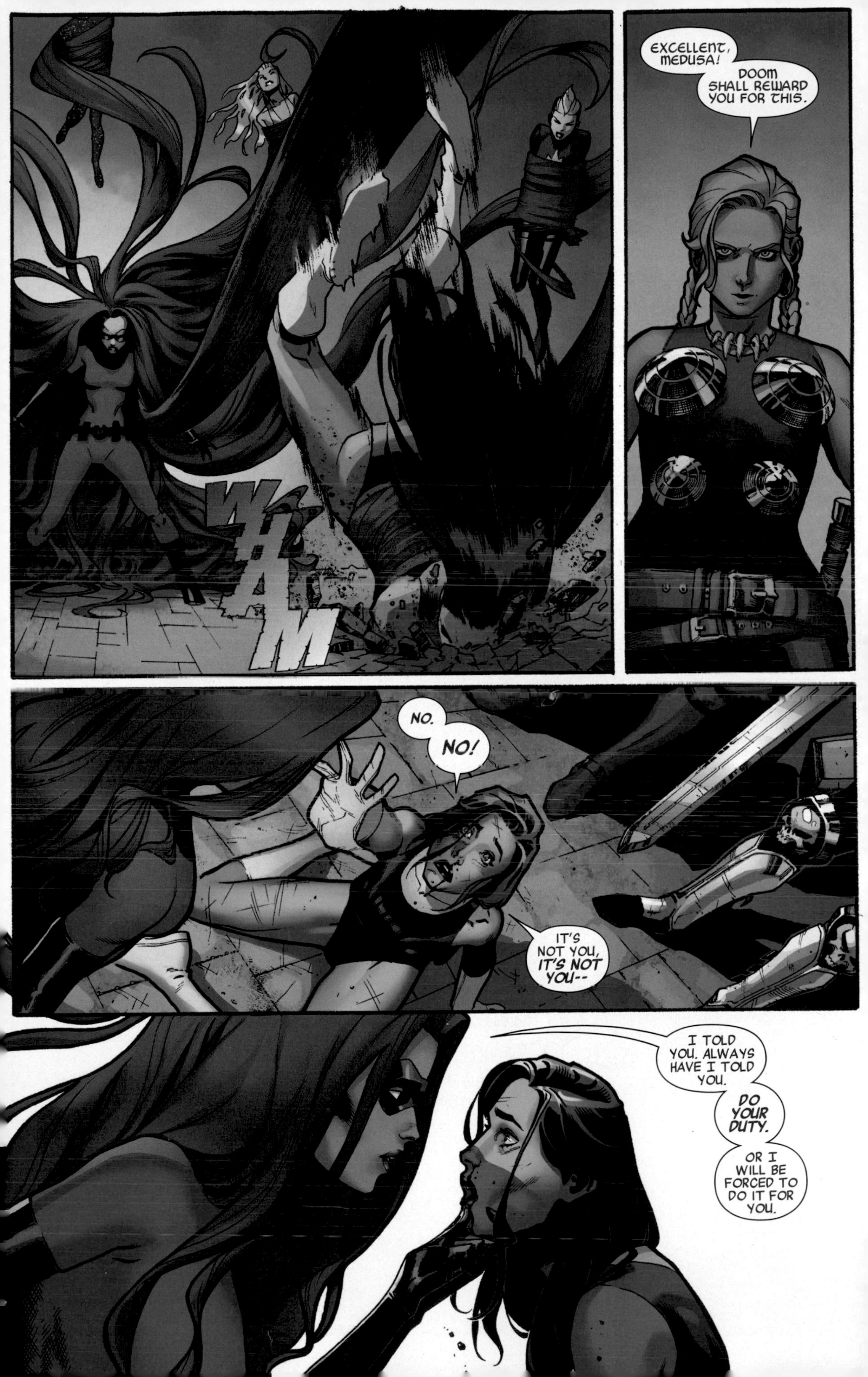
WHAM
EXCELLENT, MEDUSA!
DOOM SHALL REWARD YOU FOR THIS.
NO.
NO!
IT'S NOT YOU, IT'S NOT YOU--
I TOLD YOU. ALWAYS HAVE I TOLD YOU.
DO YOUR DUTY.
OR I WILL BE FORCED TO DO IT FOR YOU.

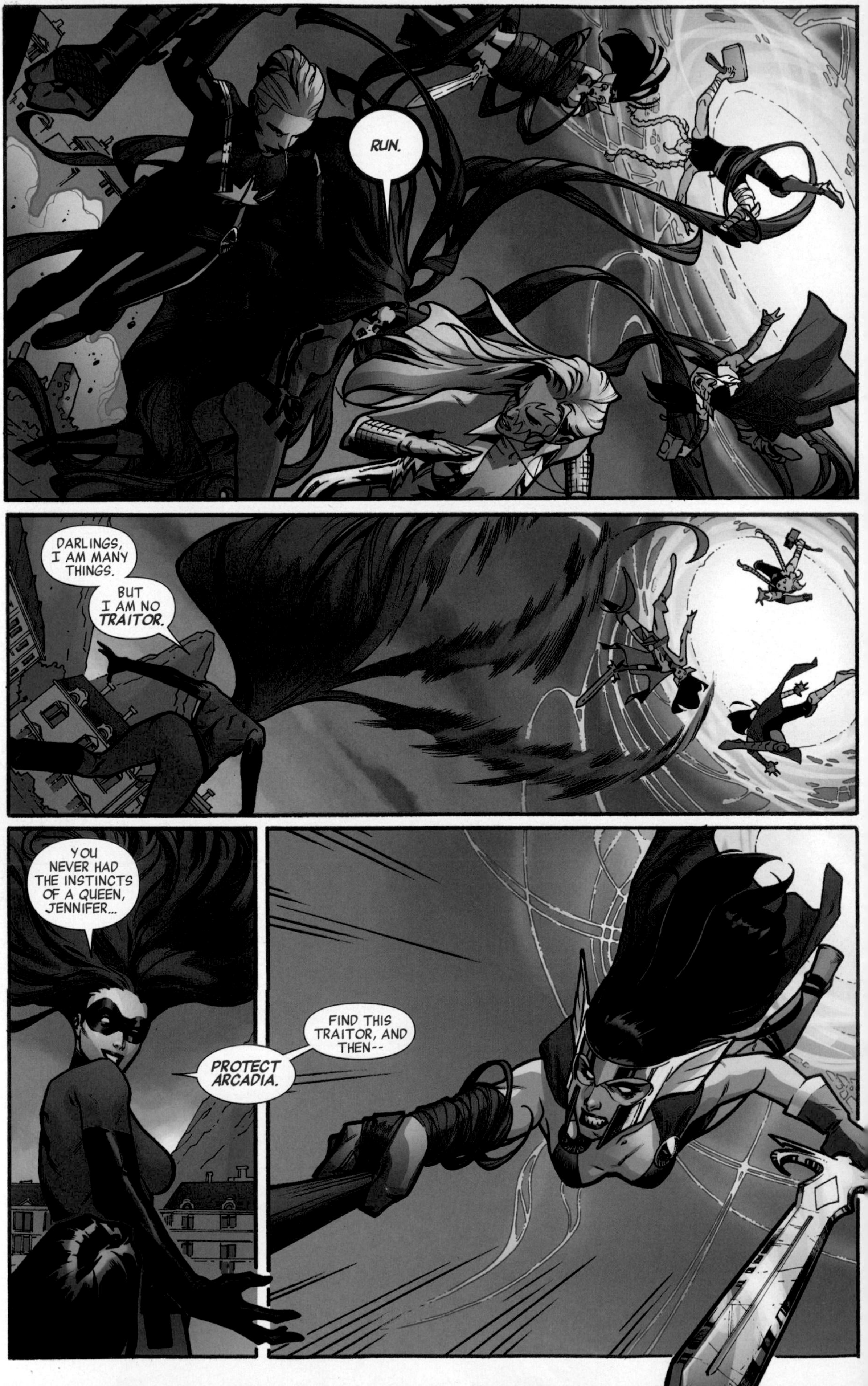
RUN.
DARLINGS, I AM MANY THINGS.
BUT I AM NO TRAITOR.
YOU NEVER HAD THE INSTINCTS OF A QUEEN, JENNIFER...
FIND THIS TRAITOR, AND THEN--
PROTECT ARCADIA.

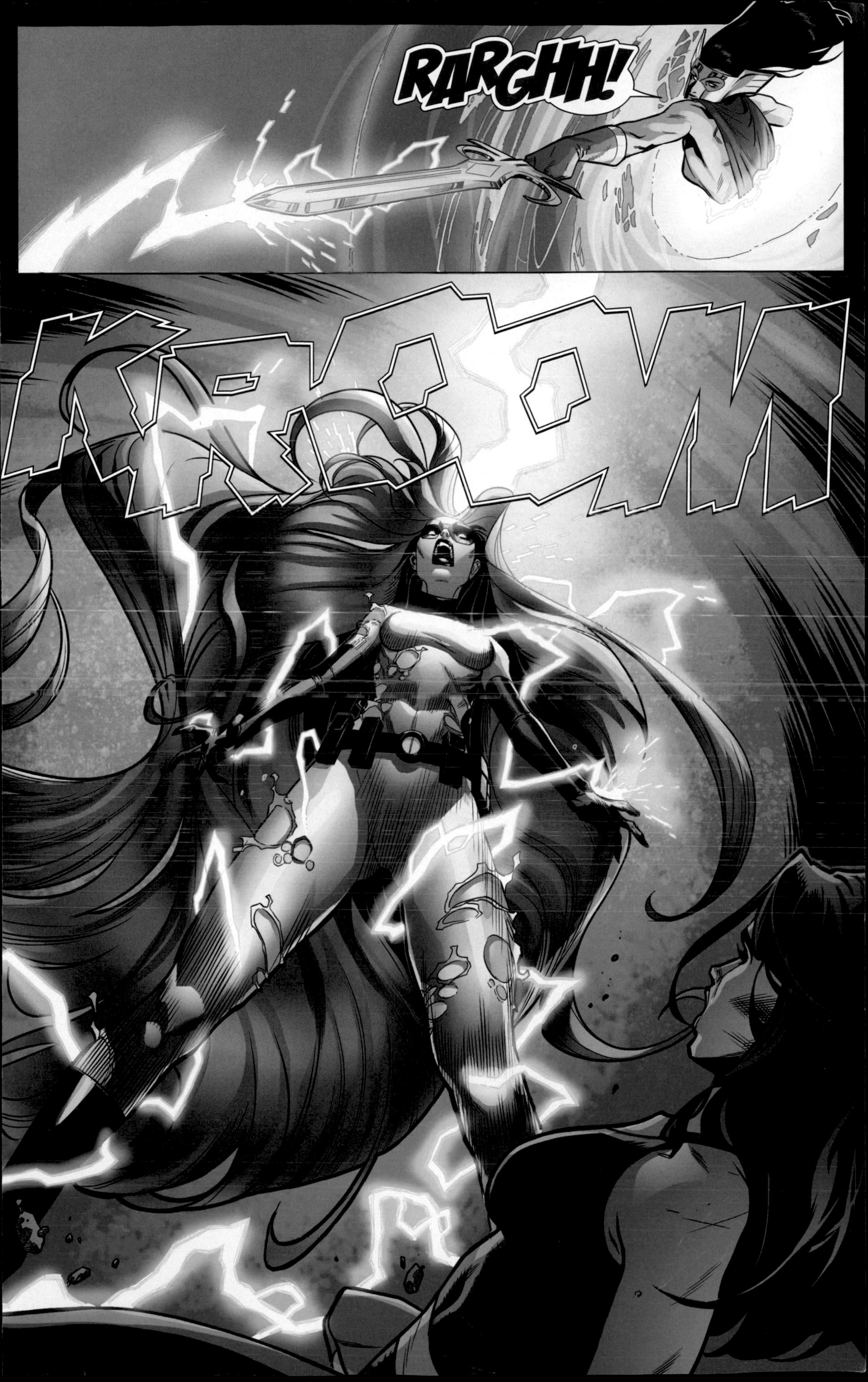
RARGHH!
KRAKOOM

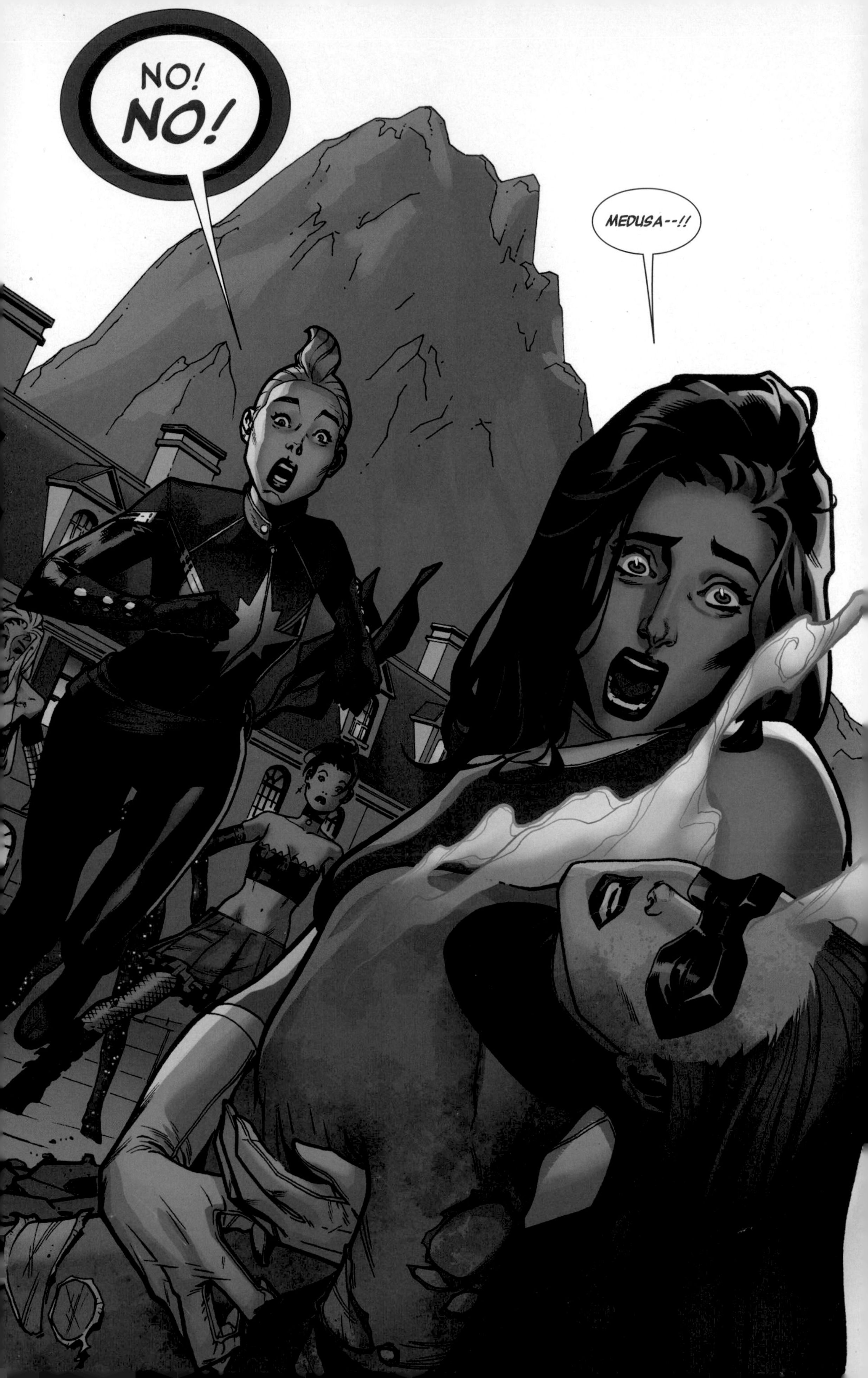
NO! NO!
MEDUSA--!!

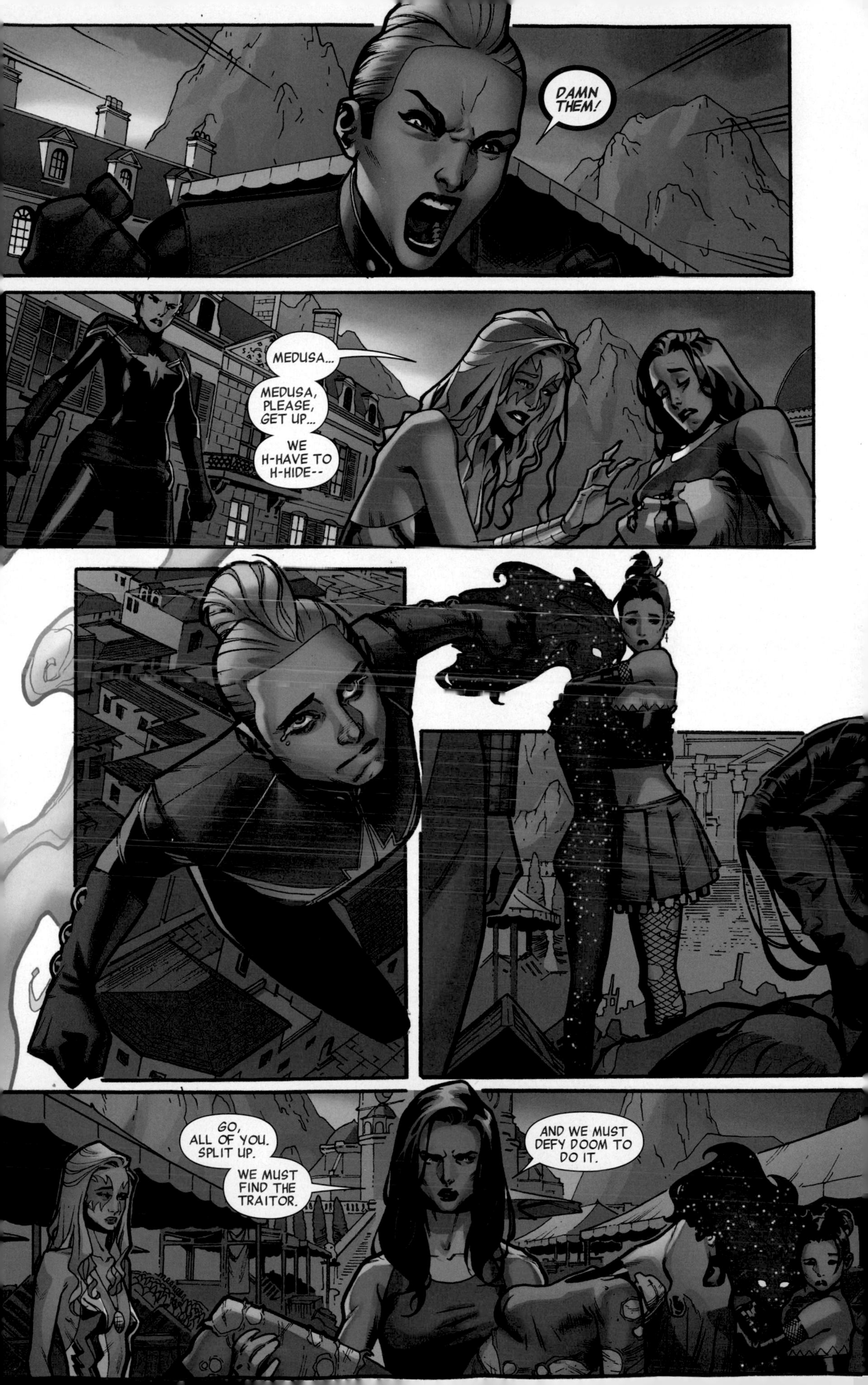
DAMN THEM!
MEDUSA...
MEDUSA, PLEASE, GET UP...
WE H-HAVE TO H-HIDE--
GO, ALL OF YOU. SPLIT UP.
WE MUST FIND THE TRAITOR.
AND WE MUST DEFY DOOM TO DO IT.

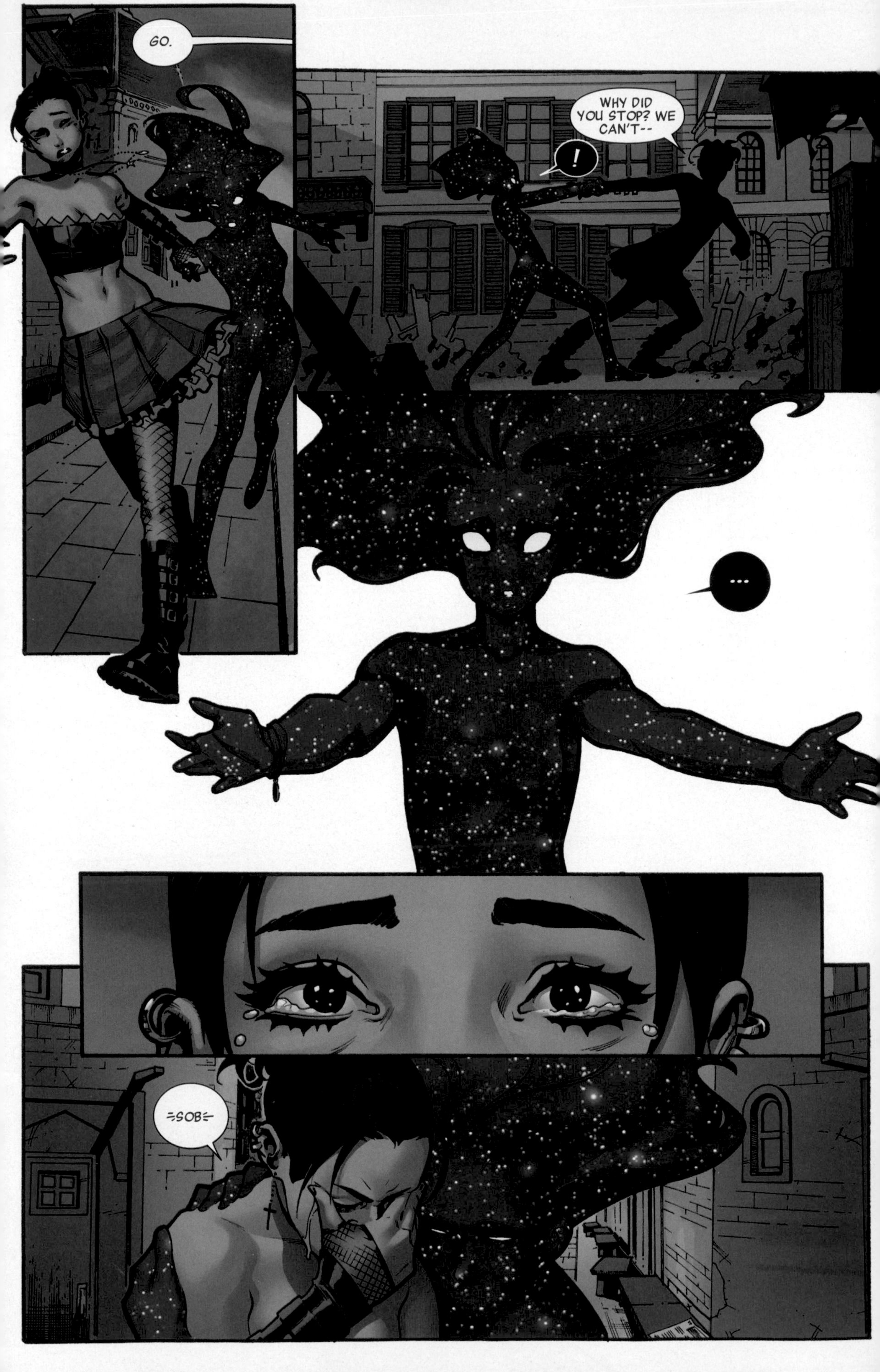
GO.
WHY DID YOU STOP? WE CAN'T--
!
...
=SOB=

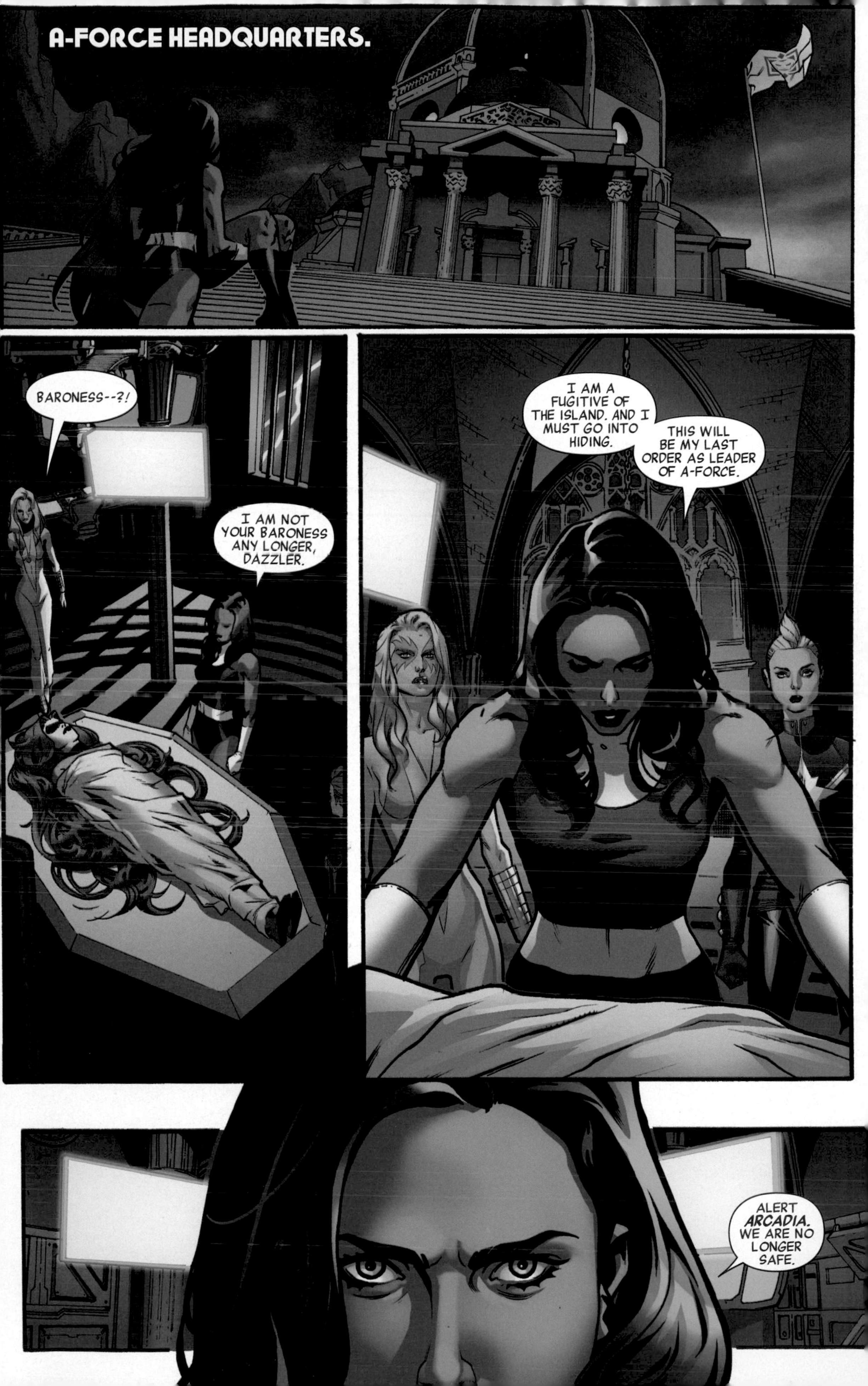
A-FORCE HEADQUARTERS.
BARONESS--?!
I AM NOT YOUR BARONESS ANY LONGER, DAZZLER.
I AM A FUGITIVE OF THE ISLAND. AND I MUST GO INTO HIDING.
THIS WILL BE MY LAST ORDER AS LEADER OF A-FORCE.
ALERT ARCADIA. WE ARE NO LONGER SAFE.

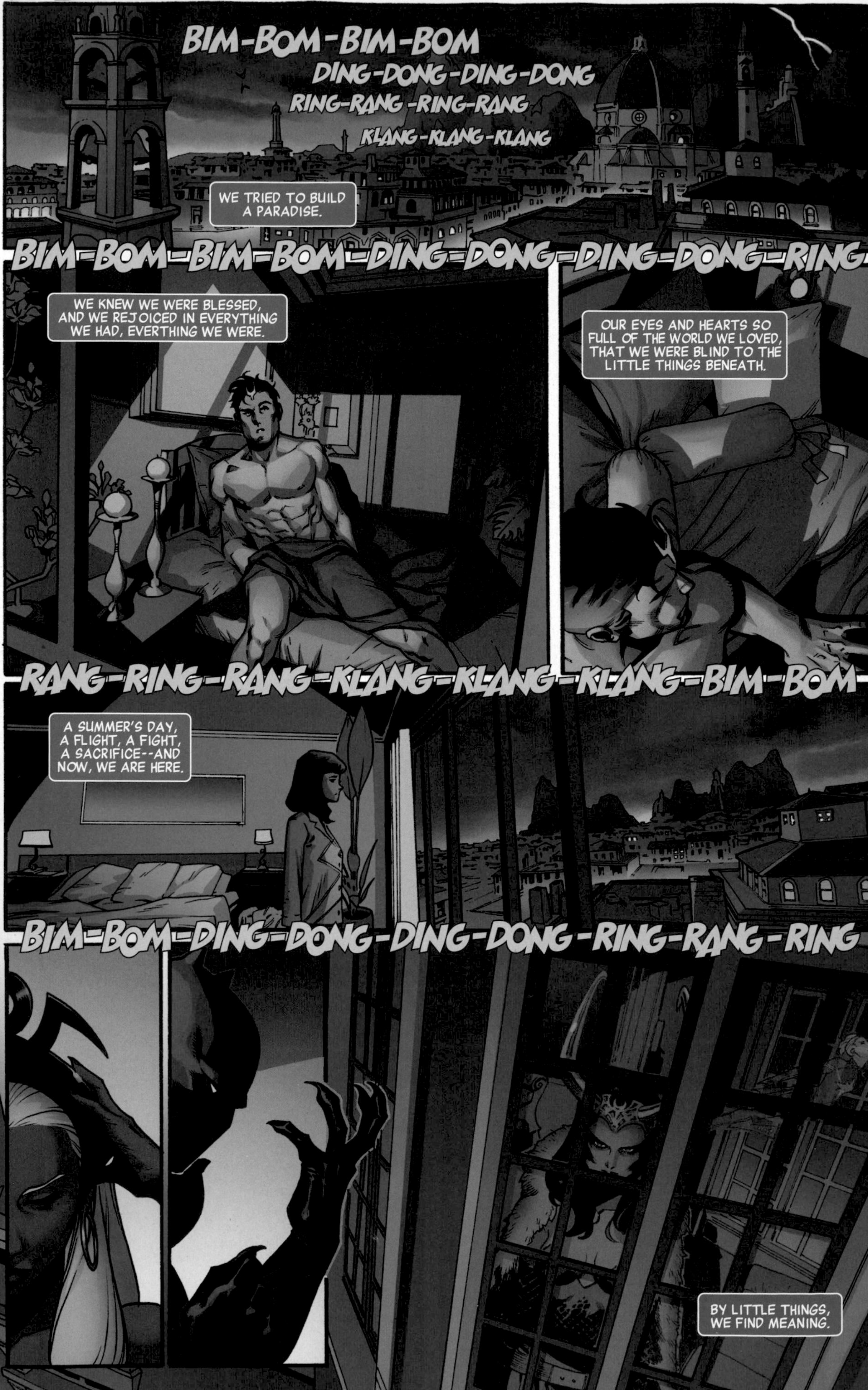

BIM-BOM-BIM-BOM
DING-DONG-DING-DONG
RING-RANG-RING-RANG
KLANG-KLANG-KLANG
WE TRIED TO BUILD A PARADISE.
BIM-BOM-BIM-BOM-DING-DONG-DING-DONG-RING
WE KNEW WE WERE BLESSED, AND WE REJOICED IN EVERYTHING WE HAD, EVERTHING WE WERE.
OUR EYES AND HEARTS SO FULL OF THE WORLD WE LOVED, THAT WE WERE BLIND TO THE LITTLE THINGS BENEATH.
RANG-RING-RANG-KLANG-KLANG-KLANG-BIM-BOM
A SUMMER'S DAY, A FLIGHT, A FIGHT, A SACRIFICE--AND NOW, WE ARE HERE.
BIM-BOM-DING-DONG-DING-DONG-RING-RANG-RING
BY LITTLE THINGS, WE FIND MEANING.

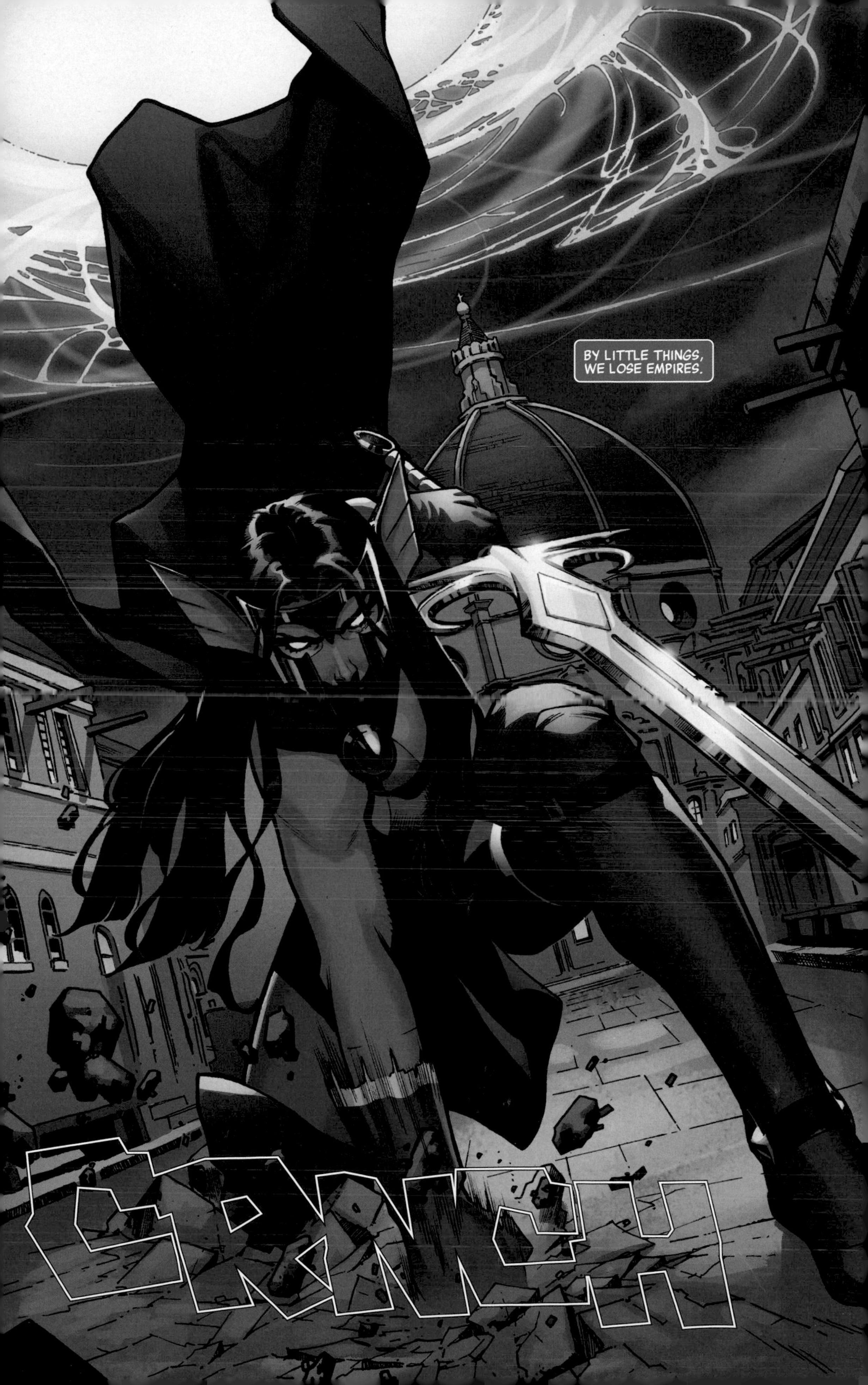
BY LITTLE THINGS, WE LOSE EMPIRES.
CRNCH

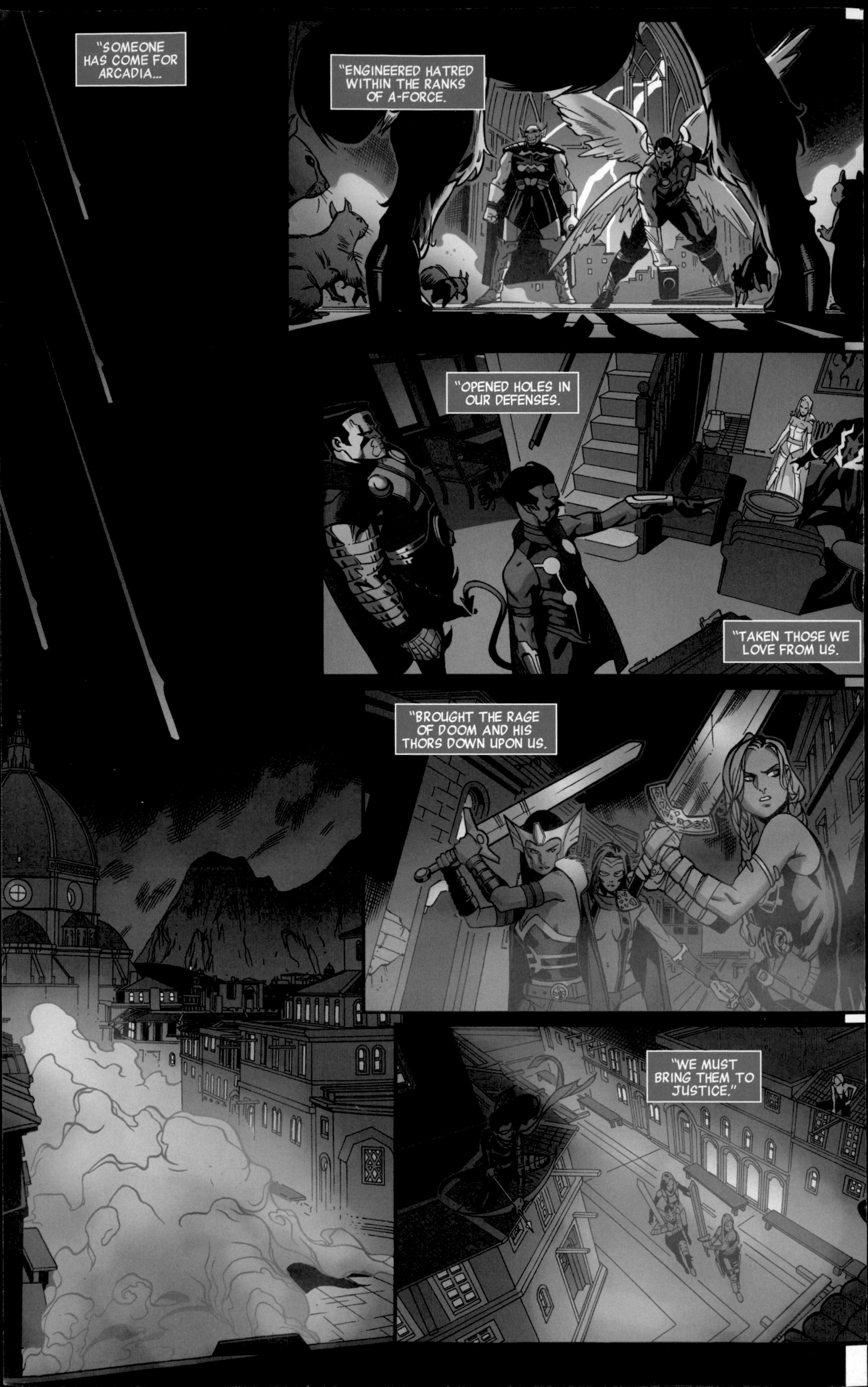
"SOMEONE HAS COME FOR ARCADIA...
"ENGINEERED HATRED WITHIN THE RANKS OF A-FORCE.
"OPENED HOLES IN OUR DEFENSES.
"TAKEN THOSE WE LOVE FROM US.
"BROUGHT THE RAGE OF DOOM AND HIS THORS DOWN UPON US.
"WE MUST BRING THEM TO JUSTICE."

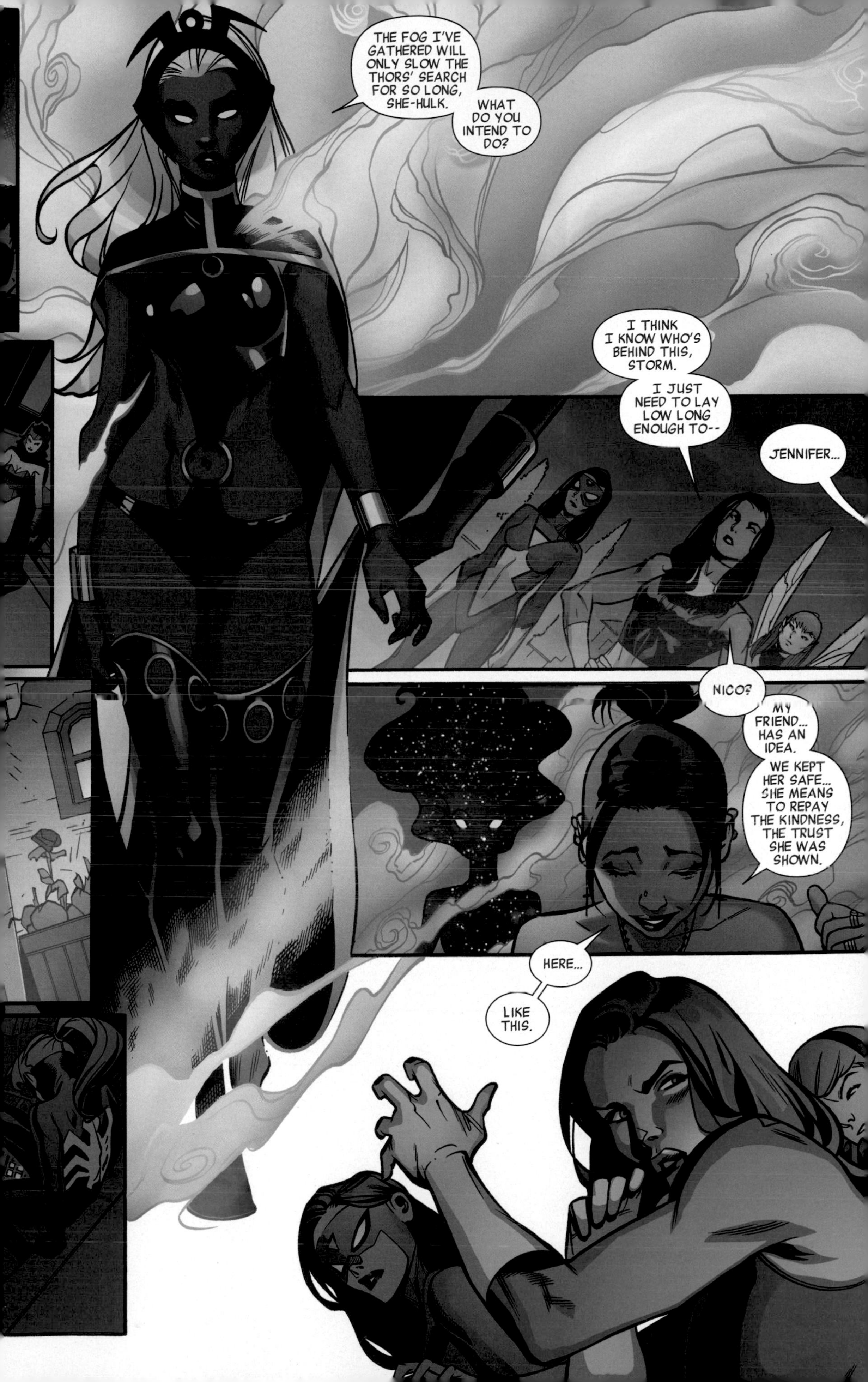
THE FOG I'VE GATHERED WILL ONLY SLOW THE THORS' SEARCH FOR SO LONG, SHE-HULK.
WHAT DO YOU INTEND TO DO?
I THINK I KNOW WHO'S BEHIND THIS, STORM.
I JUST NEED TO LAY LOW LONG ENOUGH TO--
JENNIFER...
NICO?
MY FRIEND... HAS AN IDEA.
WE KEPT HER SAFE... SHE MEANS TO REPAY THE KINDNESS, THE TRUST SHE WAS SHOWN.
HERE...
LIKE THIS.

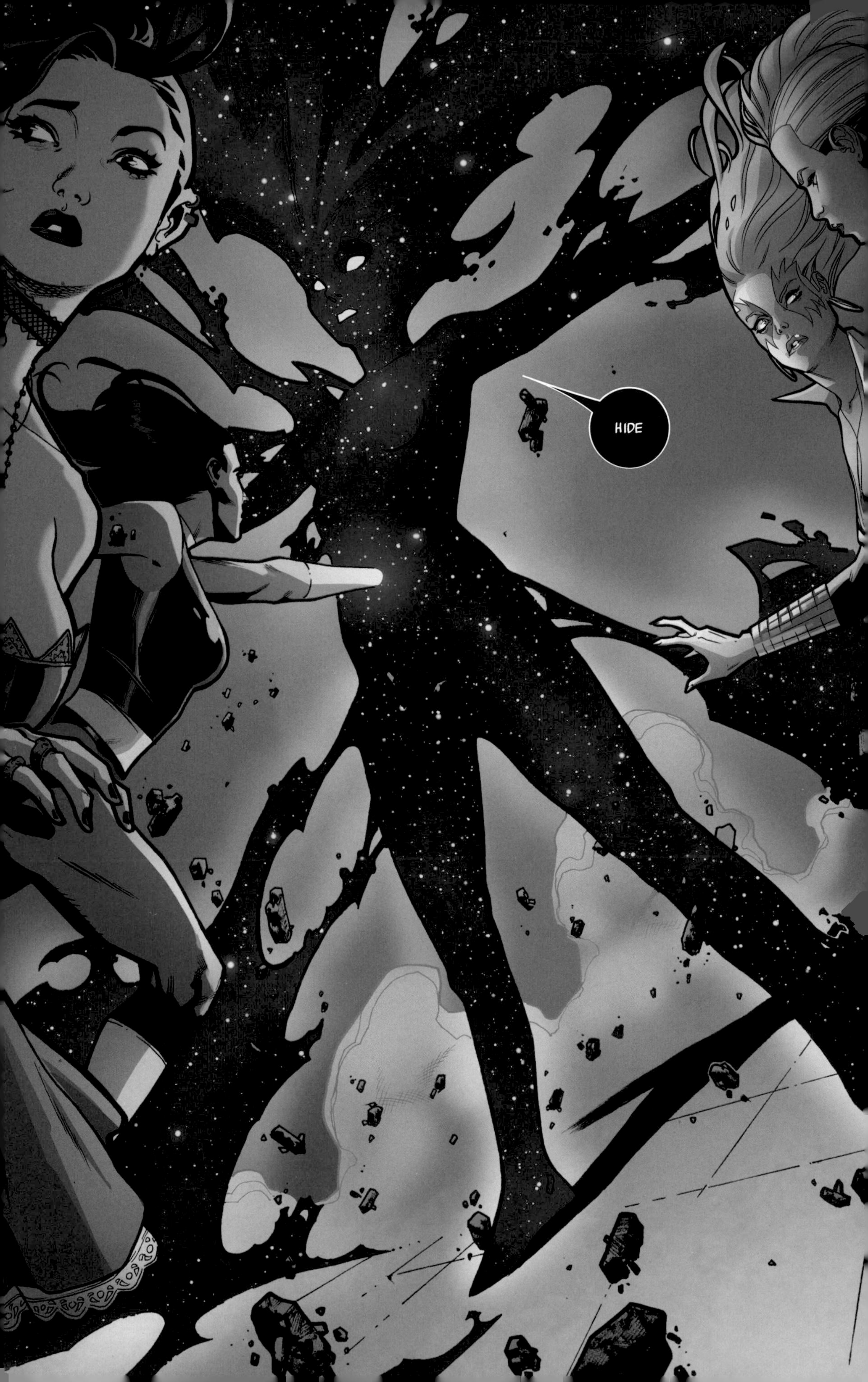
HIDE

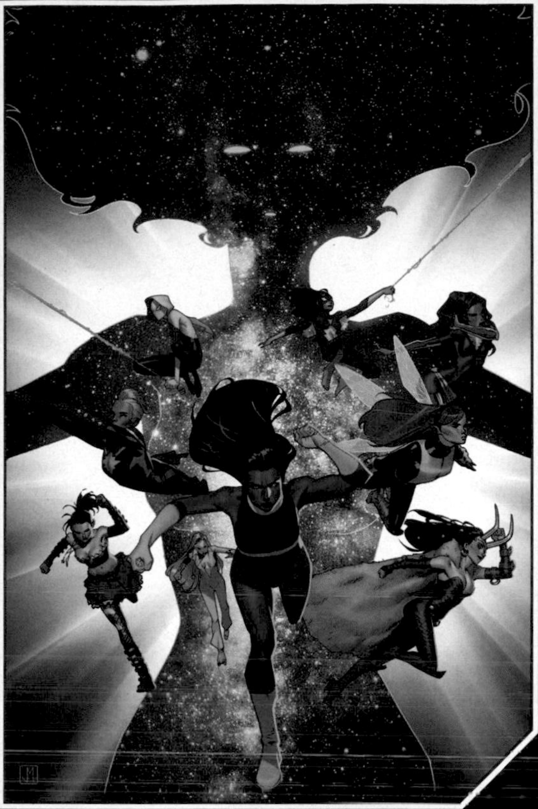

#1 VARIANT
BY **JORGE MOLINA**

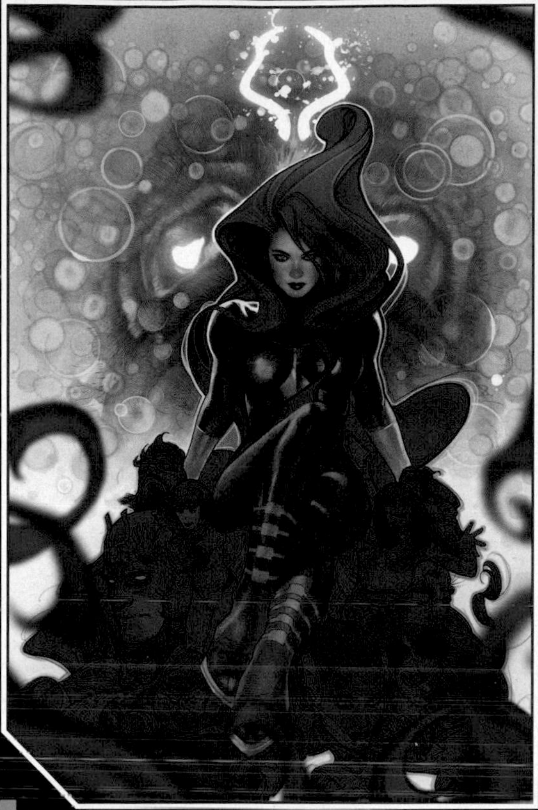

#1 INHUMANS 50TH ANNIVERSARY
VARIANT BY **ADAM HUGHES**

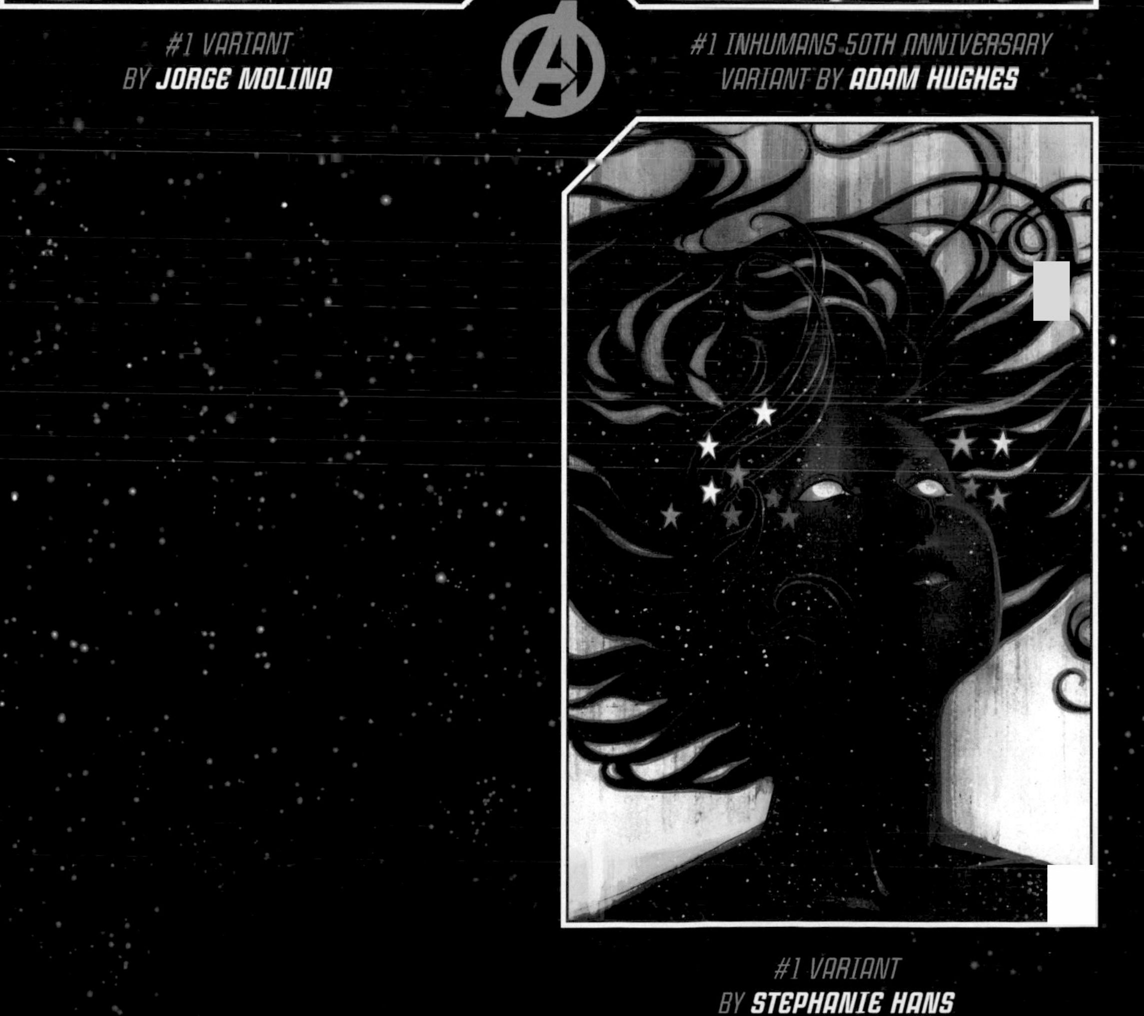

#1 VARIANT
BY **STEPHANIE HANS**

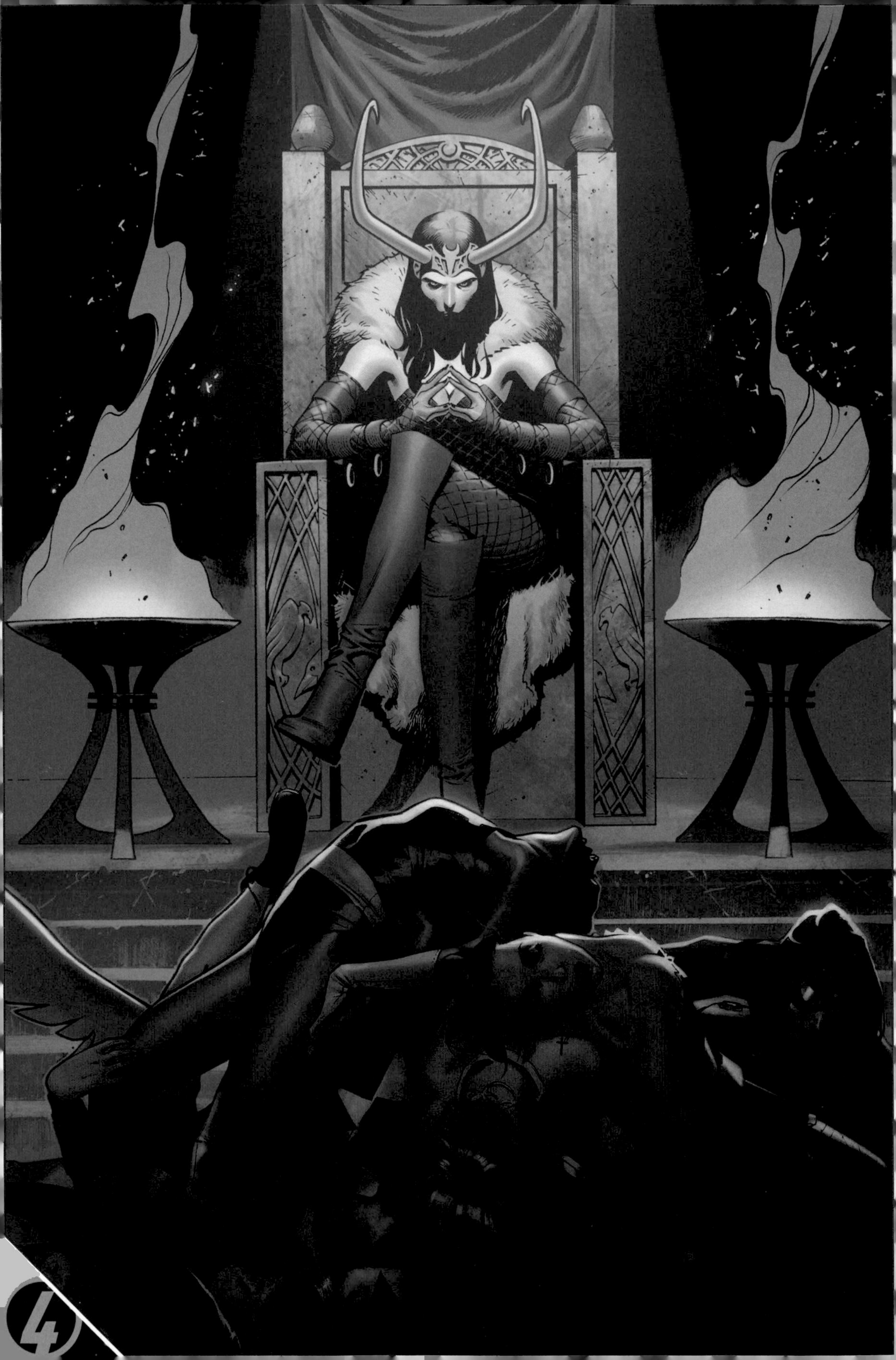

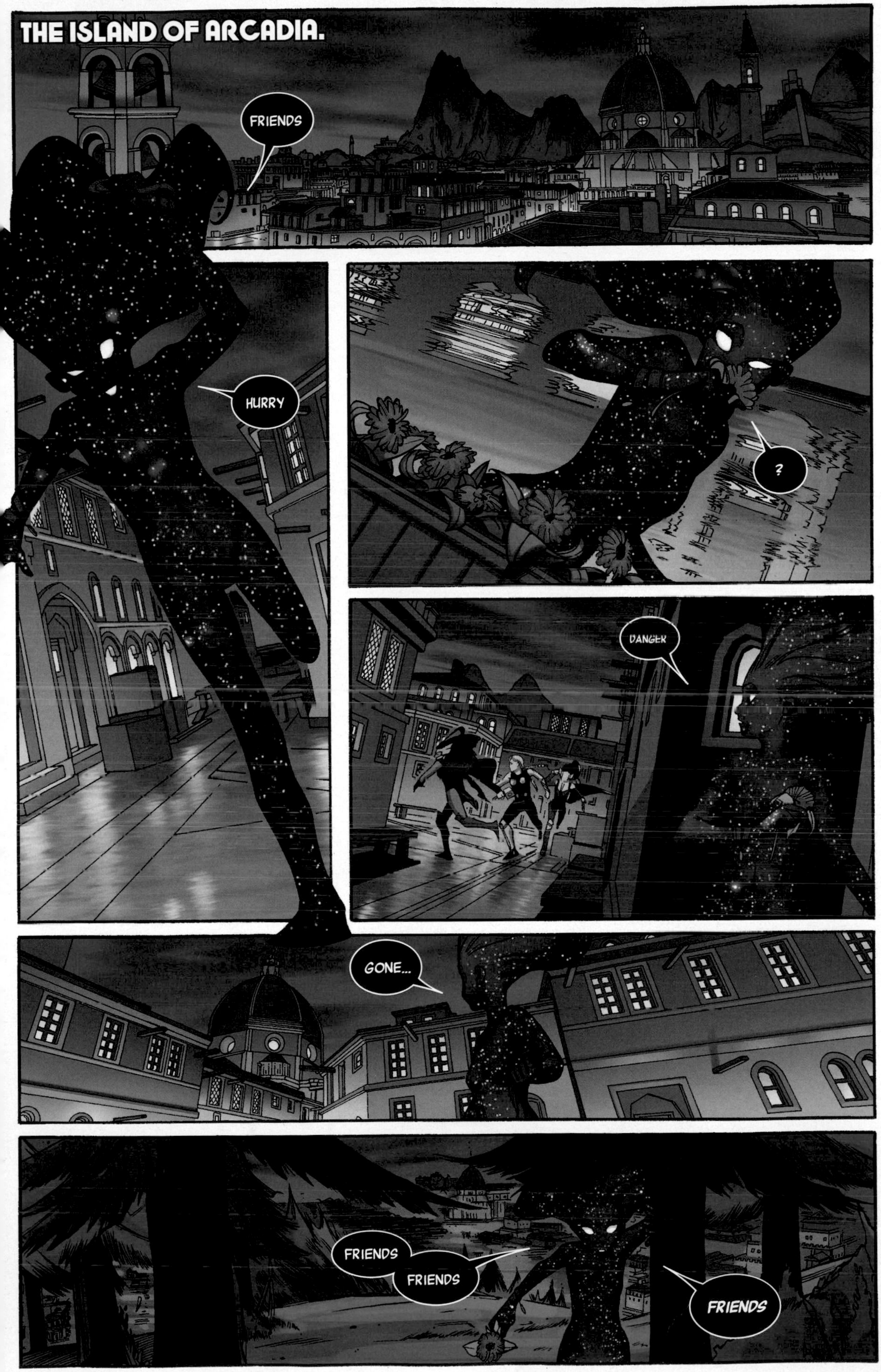
THE ISLAND OF ARCADIA.
FRIENDS
HURRY
?
DANGER
GONE...
FRIENDS
FRIENDS
FRIENDS

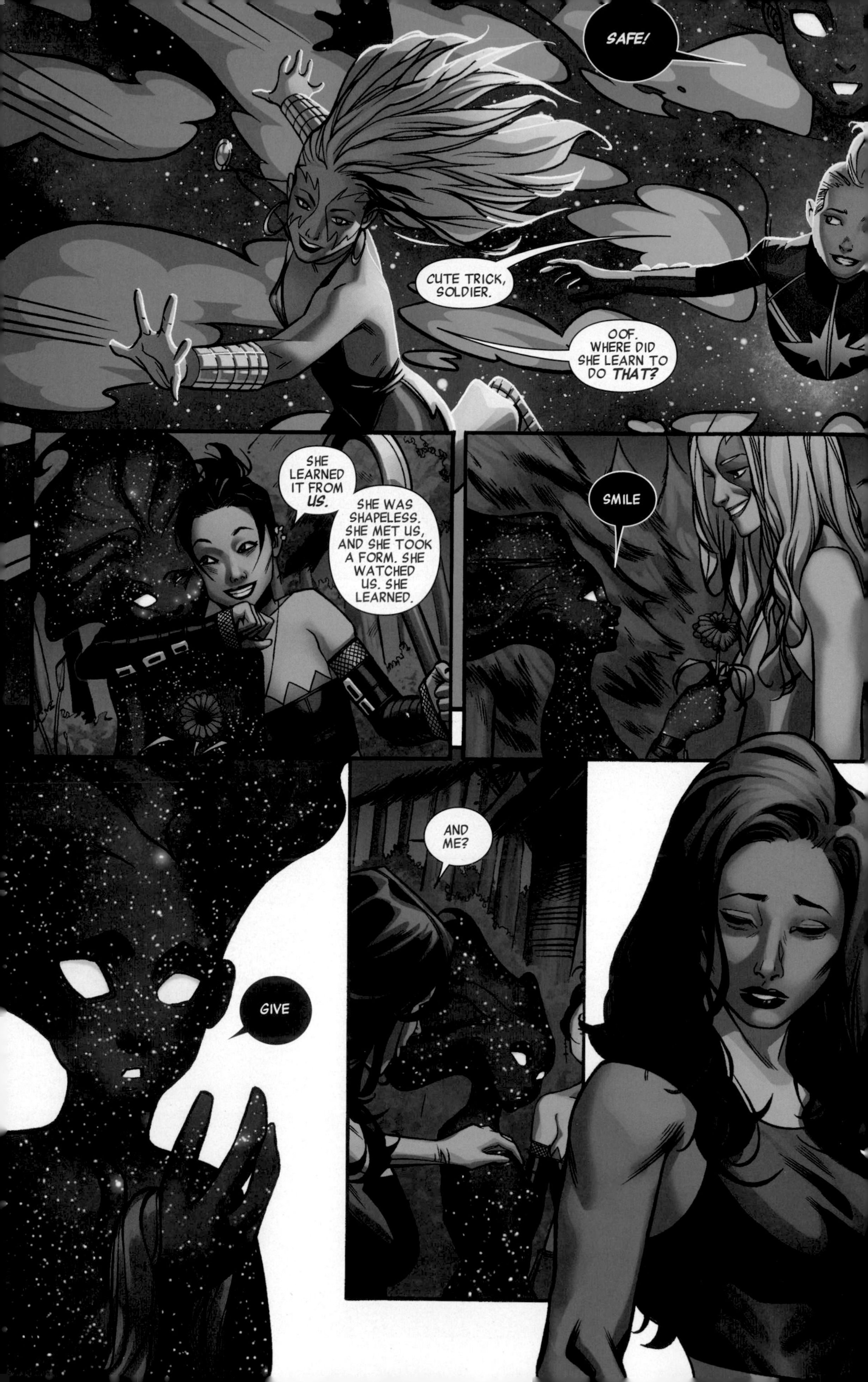
SAFE!
CUTE TRICK, SOLDIER.
OOF. WHERE DID SHE LEARN TO DO THAT?
SHE LEARNED IT FROM US.
SHE WAS SHAPELESS. SHE MET US, AND SHE TOOK A FORM. SHE WATCHED US. SHE LEARNED.
SMILE
GIVE
AND ME?

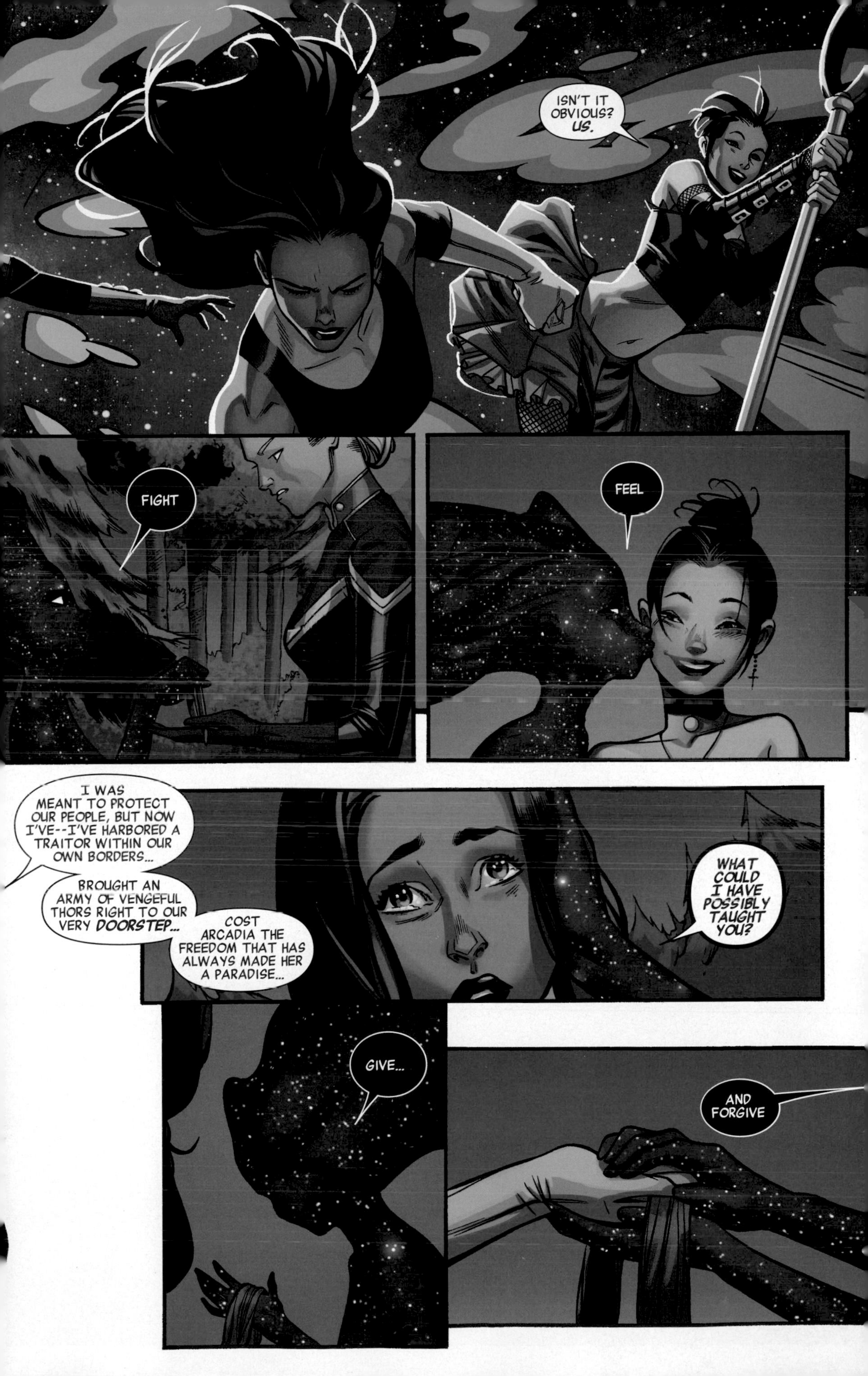
ISN'T IT OBVIOUS? US.
FIGHT
FEEL
I WAS MEANT TO PROTECT OUR PEOPLE, BUT NOW I'VE--I'VE HARBORED A TRAITOR WITHIN OUR OWN BORDERS...
BROUGHT AN ARMY OF VENGEFUL THORS RIGHT TO OUR VERY DOORSTEP...
COST ARCADIA THE FREEDOM THAT HAS ALWAYS MADE HER A PARADISE...
WHAT COULD I HAVE POSSIBLY TAUGHT YOU?
GIVE...
AND FORGIVE

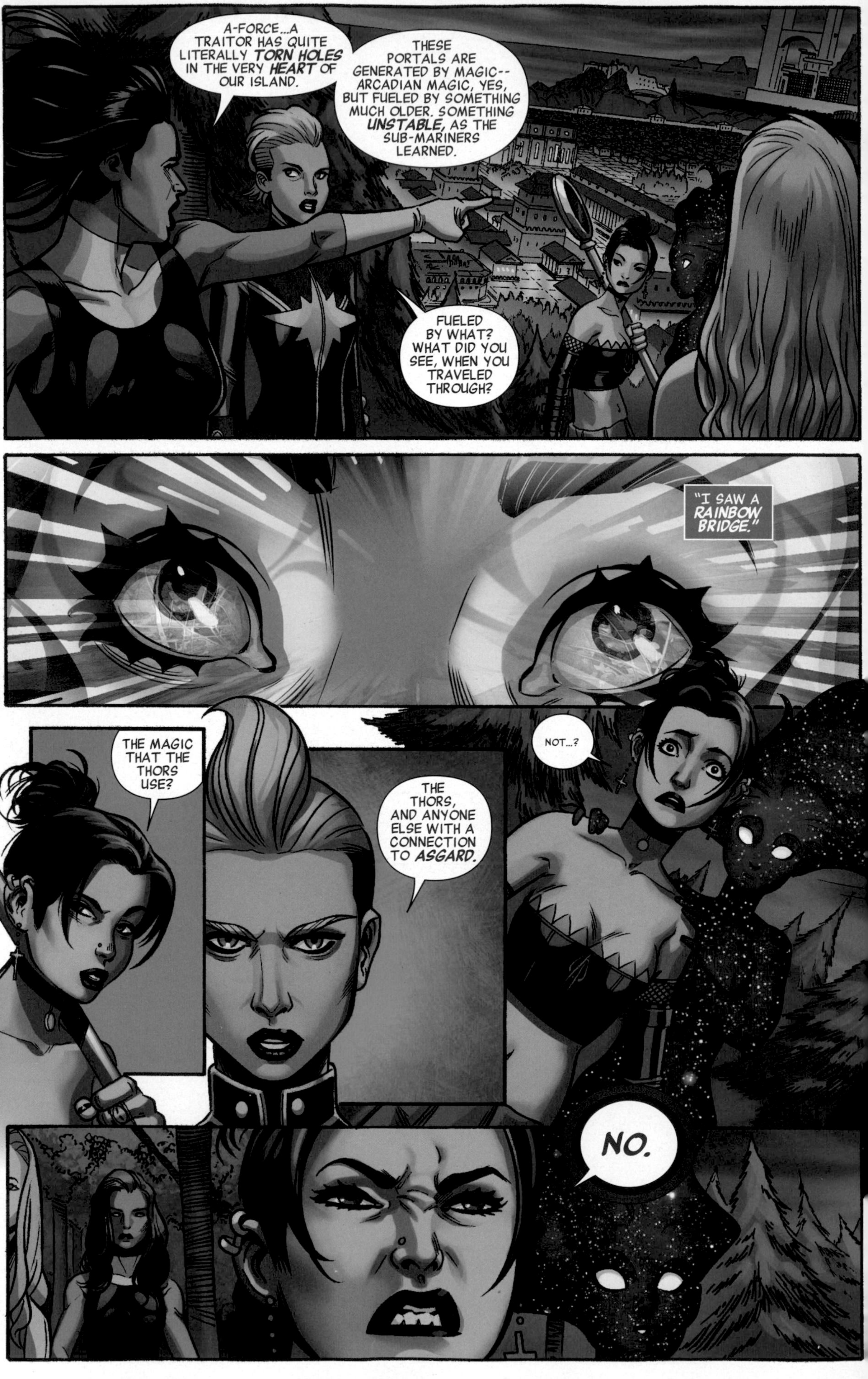
A-FORCE...A TRAITOR HAS QUITE LITERALLY TORN HOLES IN THE VERY HEART OF OUR ISLAND.
THESE PORTALS ARE GENERATED BY MAGIC-- ARCADIAN MAGIC, YES, BUT FUELED BY SOMETHING MUCH OLDER. SOMETHING UNSTABLE, AS THE SUB-MARINERS LEARNED.
FUELED BY WHAT? WHAT DID YOU SEE, WHEN YOU TRAVELED THROUGH?
"I SAW A RAINBOW BRIDGE."
THE MAGIC THAT THE THORS USE?
THE THORS, AND ANYONE ELSE WITH A CONNECTION TO ASGARD.
NOT...?
NO.

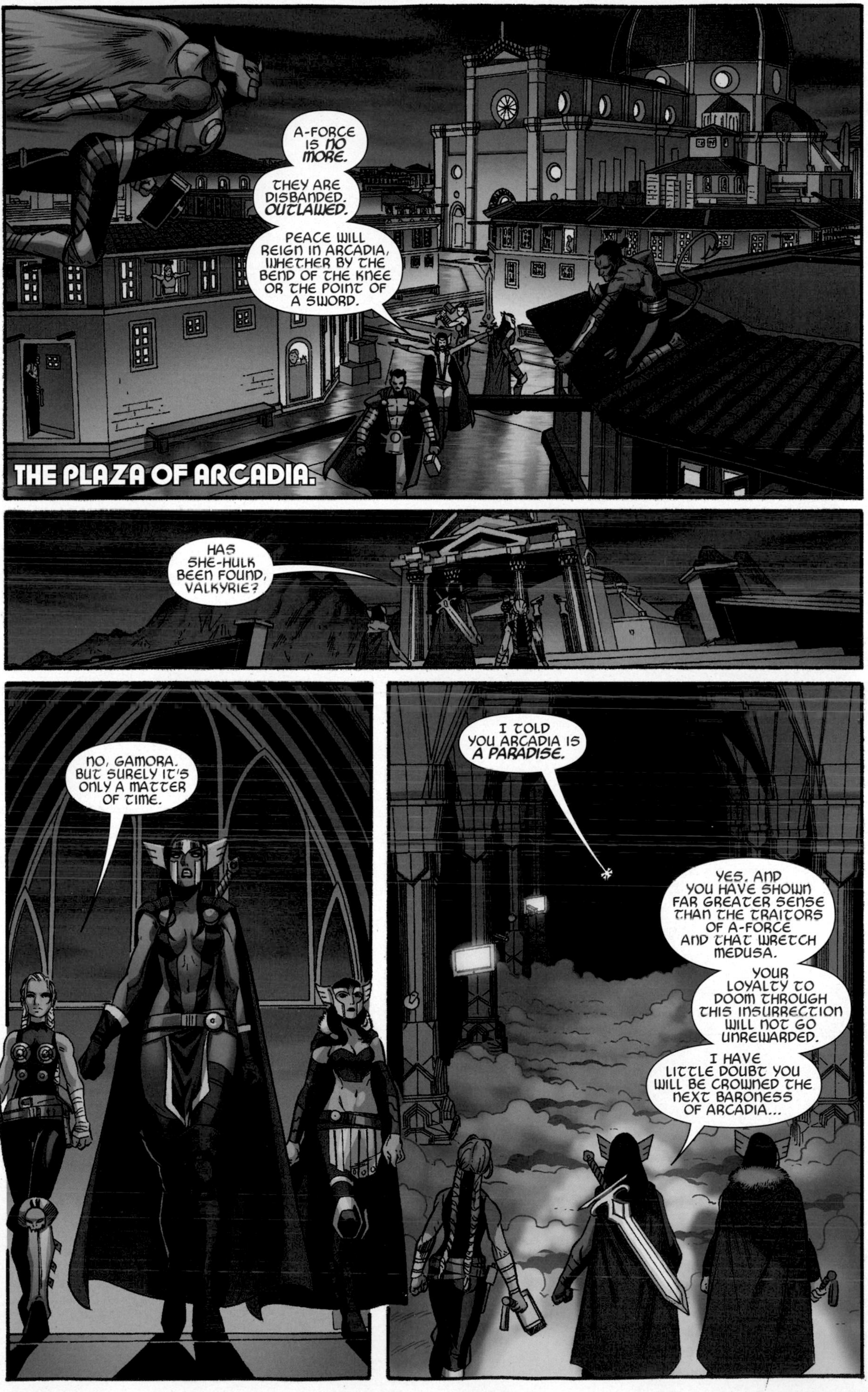
A-FORCE IS NO MORE.
THEY ARE DISBANDED. OUTLAWED.
PEACE WILL REIGN IN ARCADIA, WHETHER BY THE BEND OF THE KNEE OR THE POINT OF A SWORD.
THE PLAZA OF ARCADIA.
HAS SHE-HULK BEEN FOUND, VALKYRIE?
NO, GAMORA. BUT SURELY IT'S ONLY A MATTER OF TIME.
I TOLD YOU ARCADIA IS A PARADISE.
YES. AND YOU HAVE SHOWN FAR GREATER SENSE THAN THE TRAITORS OF A-FORCE AND THAT WRETCH MEDUSA.
YOUR LOYALTY TO DOOM THROUGH THIS INSURRECTION WILL NOT GO UNREWARDED.
I HAVE LITTLE DOUBT YOU WILL BE CROWNED THE NEXT BARONESS OF ARCADIA...

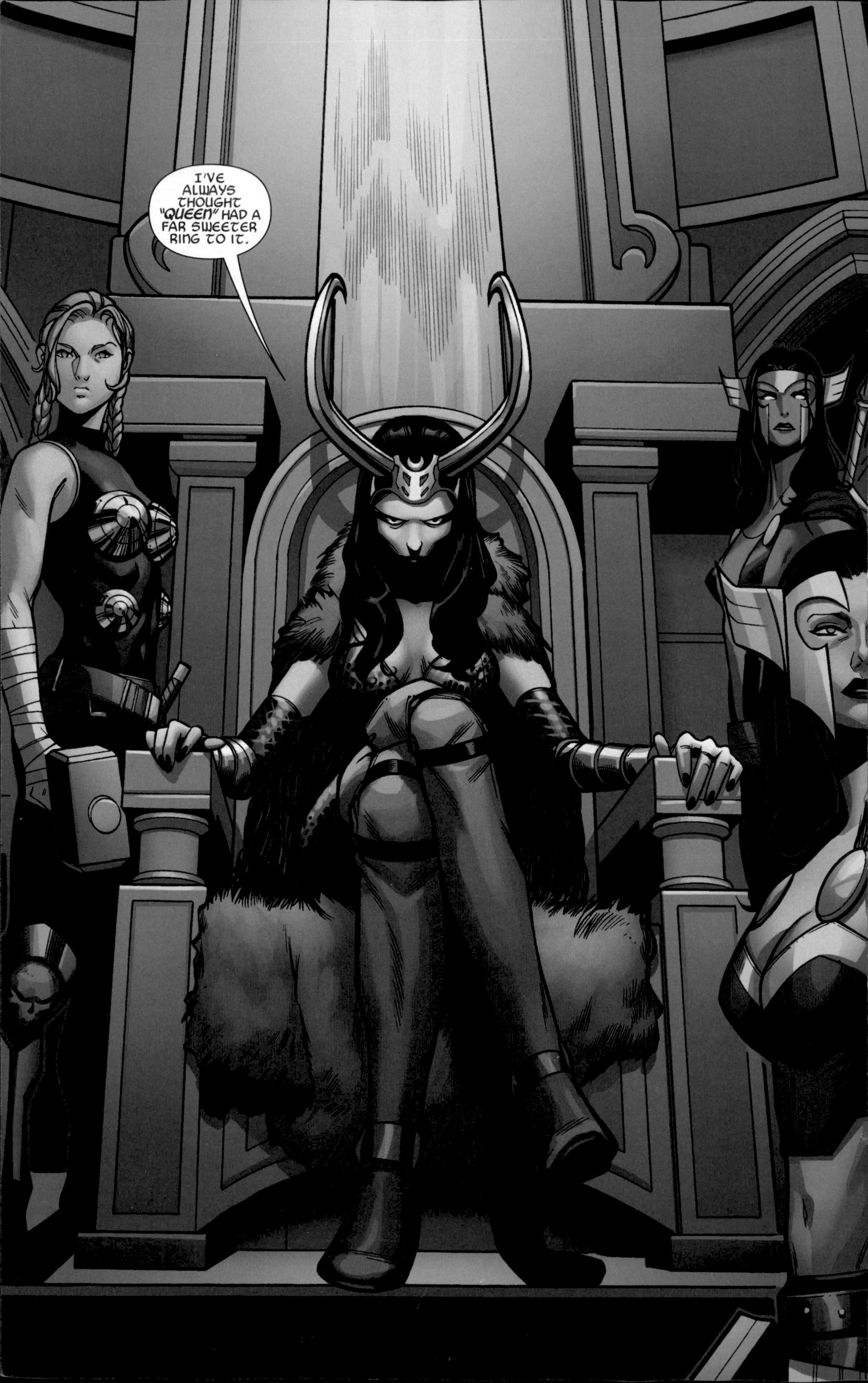
I'VE ALWAYS THOUGHT "QUEEN" HAD A FAR SWEETER RING TO IT.

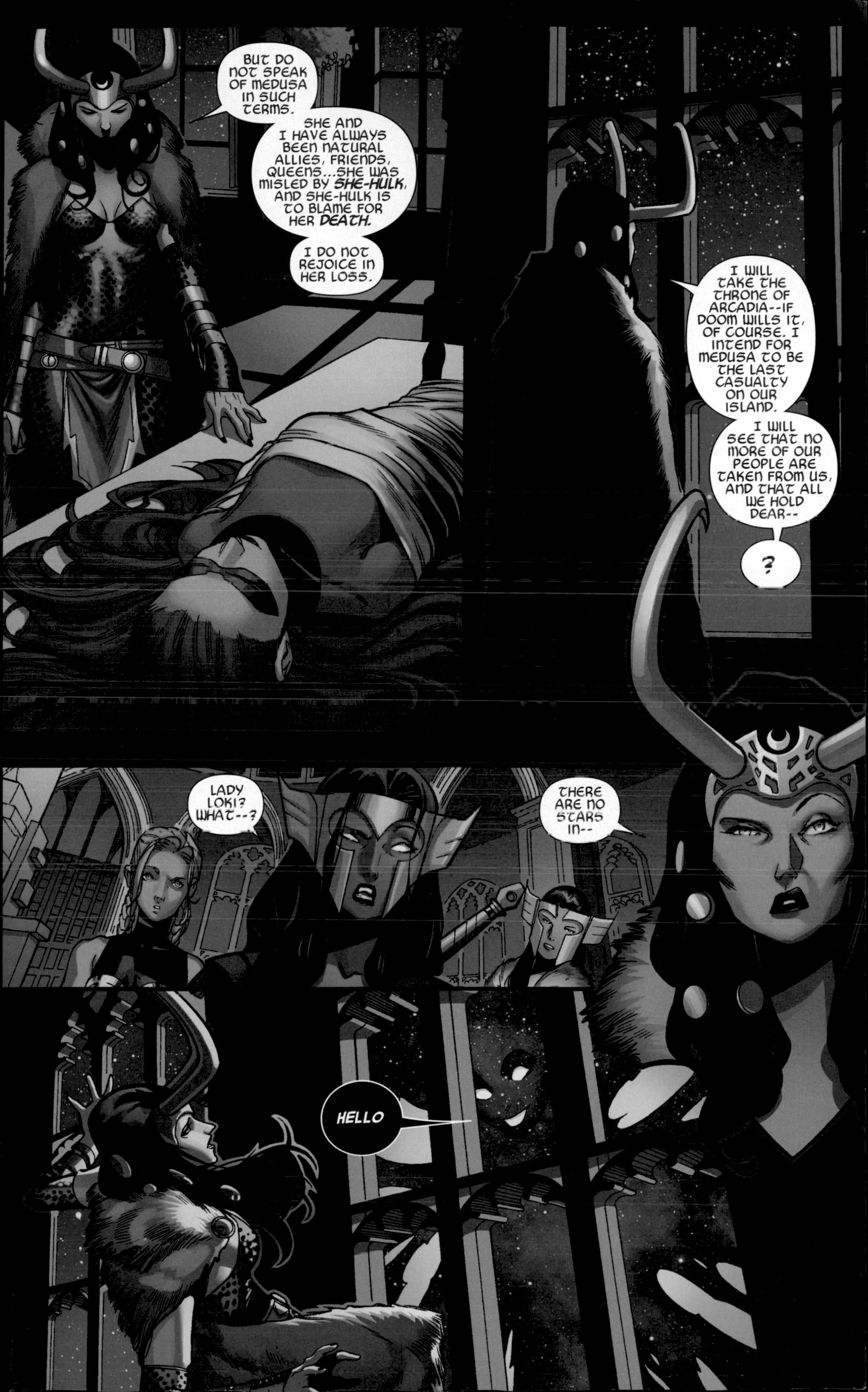
BUT DO NOT SPEAK OF MEDUSA IN SUCH TERMS.
SHE AND I HAVE ALWAYS BEEN NATURAL ALLIES, FRIENDS, QUEENS...SHE WAS MISLED BY SHE-HULK, AND SHE-HULK IS TO BLAME FOR HER DEATH.
I DO NOT REJOICE IN HER LOSS.
I WILL TAKE THE THRONE OF ARCADIA--IF DOOM WILLS IT, OF COURSE. I INTEND FOR MEDUSA TO BE THE LAST CASUALTY ON OUR ISLAND.
I WILL SEE THAT NO MORE OF OUR PEOPLE ARE TAKEN FROM US, AND THAT ALL WE HOLD DEAR--
?
LADY LOKI? WHAT--?
THERE ARE NO STARS IN--
HELLO

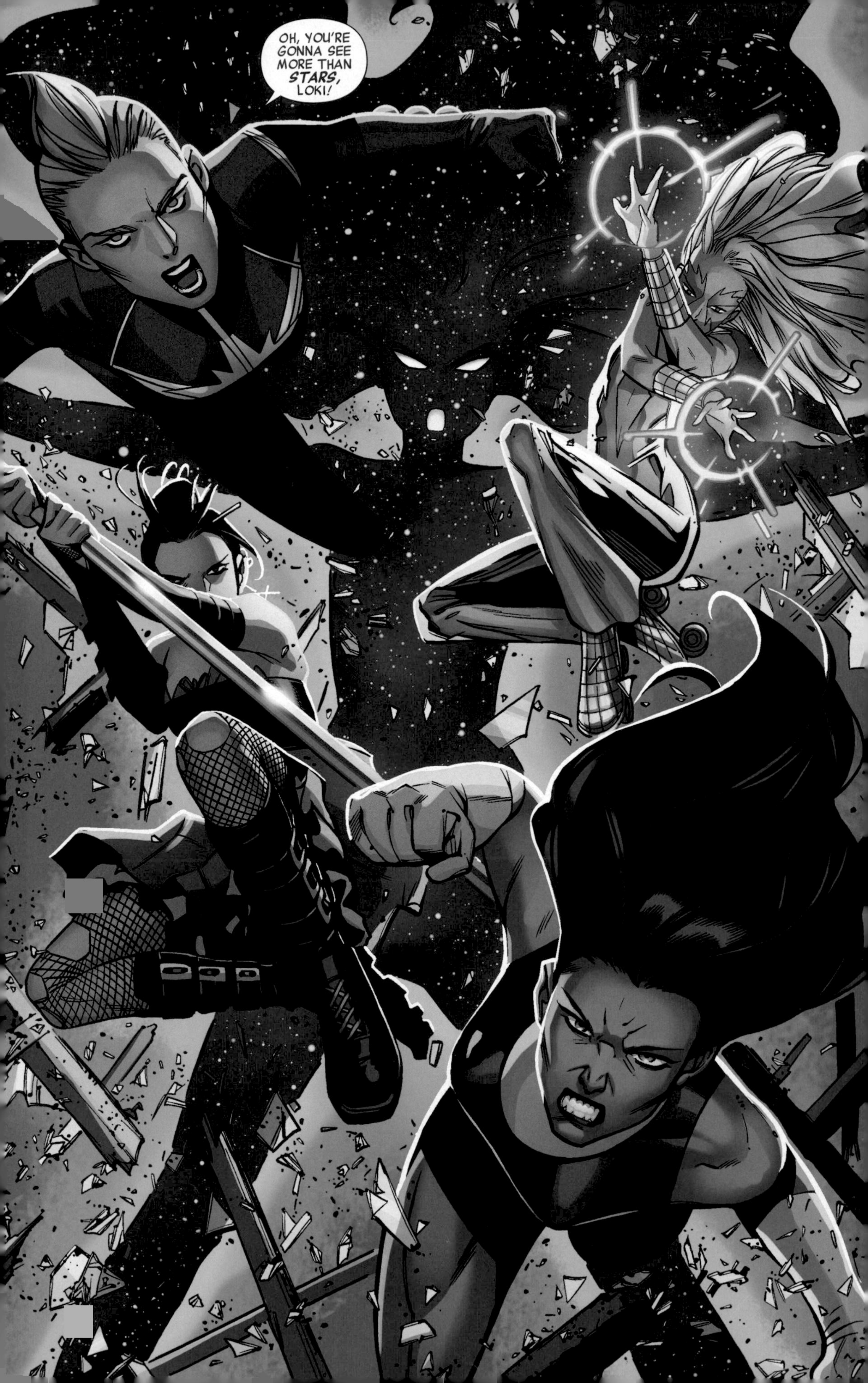
OH, YOU'RE GONNA SEE MORE THAN STARS, LOKI!

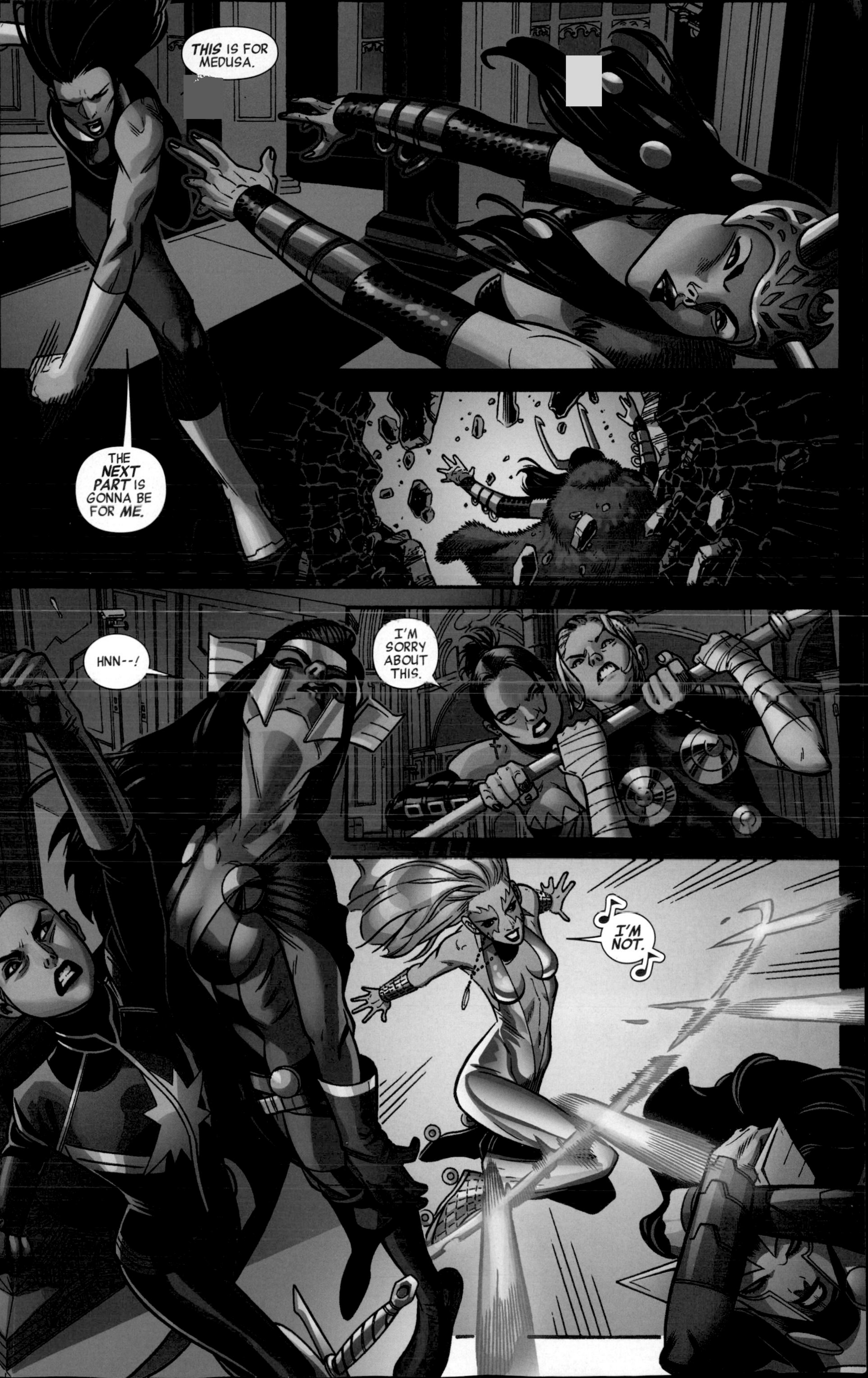
THIS IS FOR MEDUSA.
THE NEXT PART IS GONNA BE FOR ME.
HNN--!
I'M SORRY ABOUT THIS.
I'M NOT.

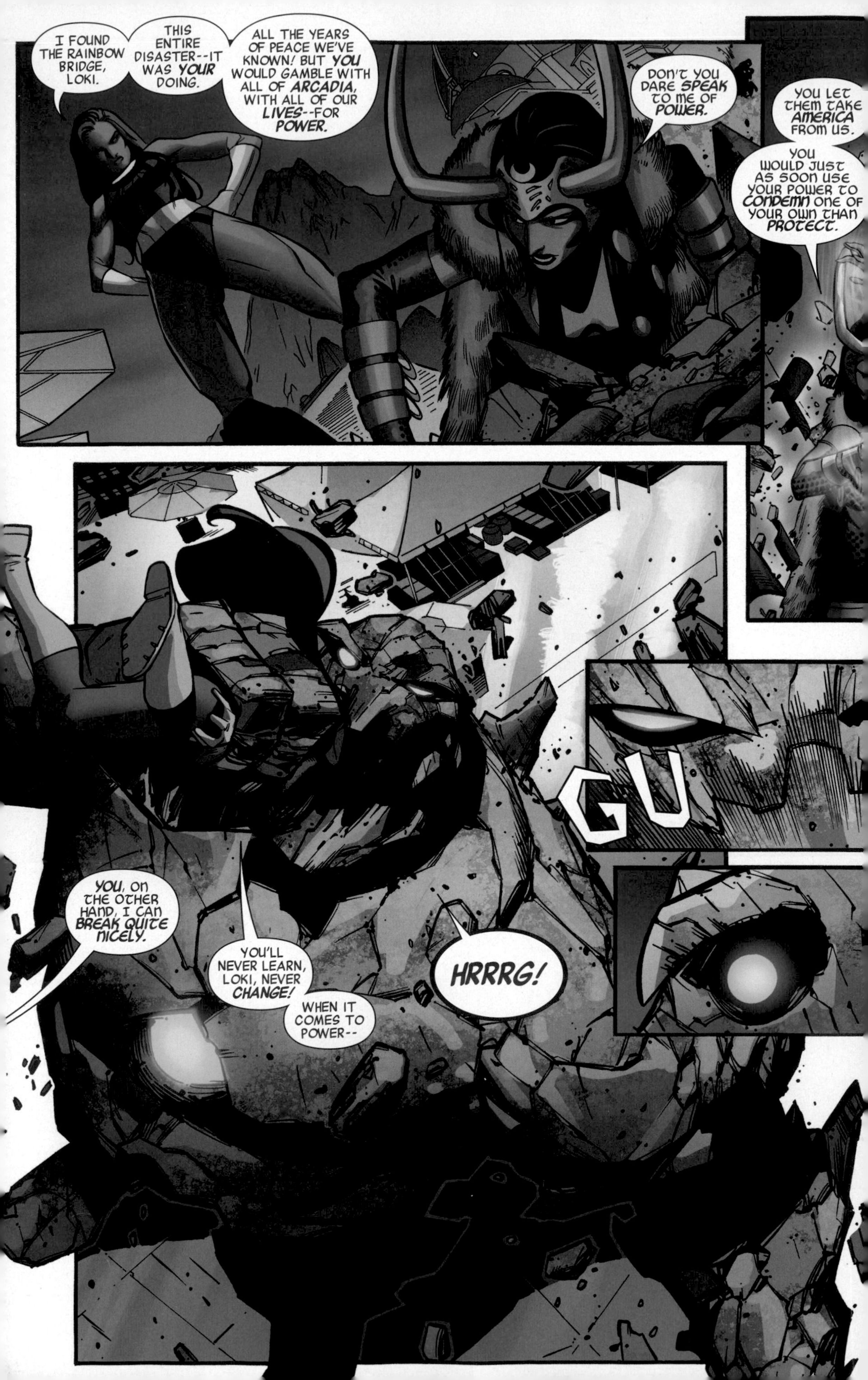
I FOUND THE RAINBOW BRIDGE, LOKI.
THIS ENTIRE DISASTER--IT WAS YOUR DOING.
ALL THE YEARS OF PEACE WE'VE KNOWN! BUT YOU WOULD GAMBLE WITH ALL OF ARCADIA, WITH ALL OF OUR LIVES--FOR POWER.
DON'T YOU DARE SPEAK TO ME OF POWER.
YOU LET THEM TAKE AMERICA FROM US.
YOU WOULD JUST AS SOON USE YOUR POWER TO CONDEMN ONE OF YOUR OWN THAN PROTECT.
GU
YOU, ON THE OTHER HAND, I CAN BREAK QUITE NICELY.
YOU'LL NEVER LEARN, LOKI, NEVER CHANGE!
WHEN IT COMES TO POWER--
HRRRG!

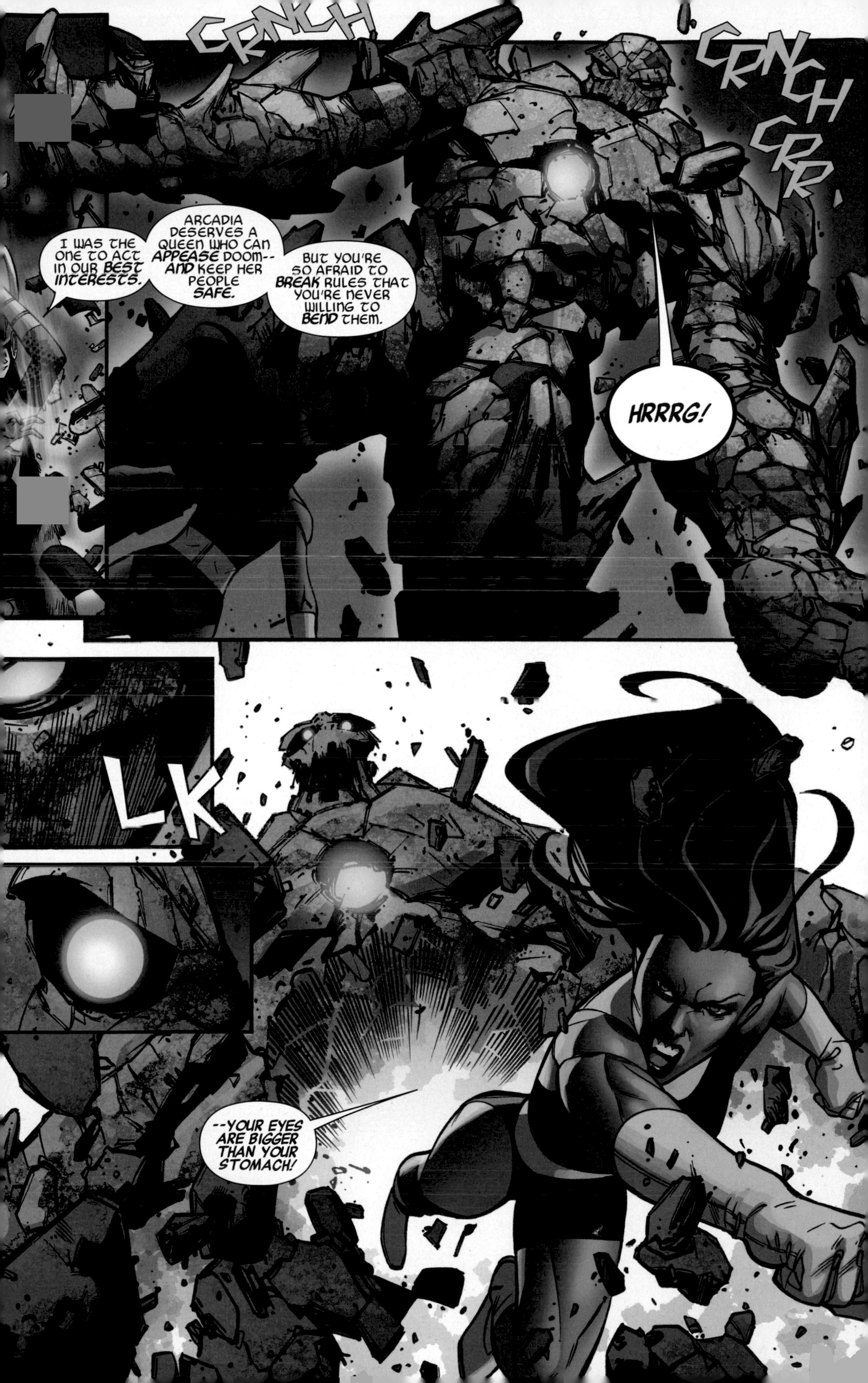
CRNCH
CRNCH CRR
I WAS THE ONE TO ACT IN OUR BEST INTERESTS.
ARCADIA DESERVES A QUEEN WHO CAN APPEASE DOOM-- AND KEEP HER PEOPLE SAFE.
BUT YOU'RE SO AFRAID TO BREAK RULES THAT YOU'RE NEVER WILLING TO BEND THEM.
HRRRG!
LK
--YOUR EYES ARE BIGGER THAN YOUR STOMACH!

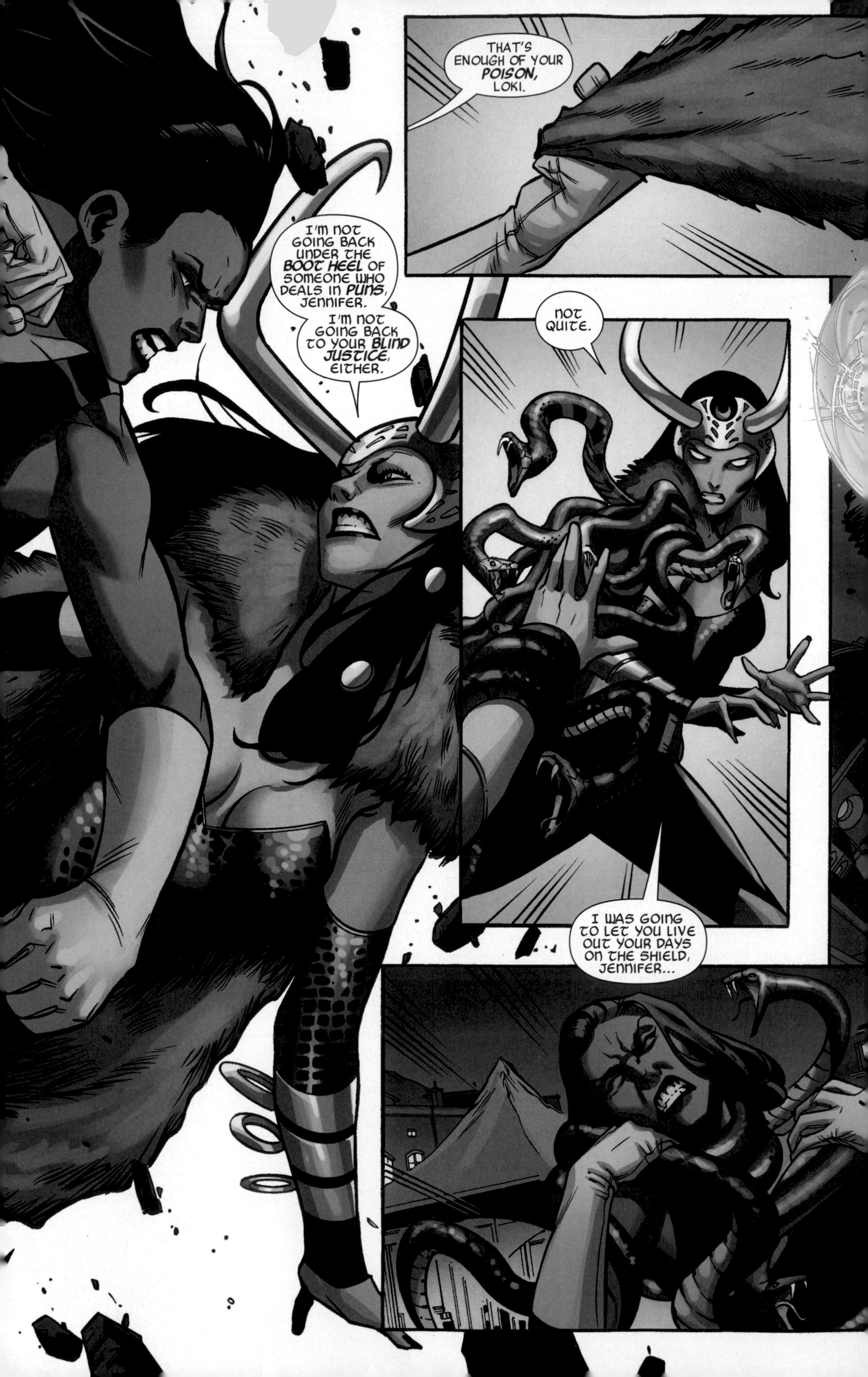
THAT'S ENOUGH OF YOUR POISON, LOKI.
I'M NOT GOING BACK UNDER THE BOOT HEEL OF SOMEONE WHO DEALS IN PUNS, JENNIFER.
I'M NOT GOING BACK TO YOUR BLIND JUSTICE, EITHER.
NOT QUITE.
I WAS GOING TO LET YOU LIVE OUT YOUR DAYS ON THE SHIELD, JENNIFER...

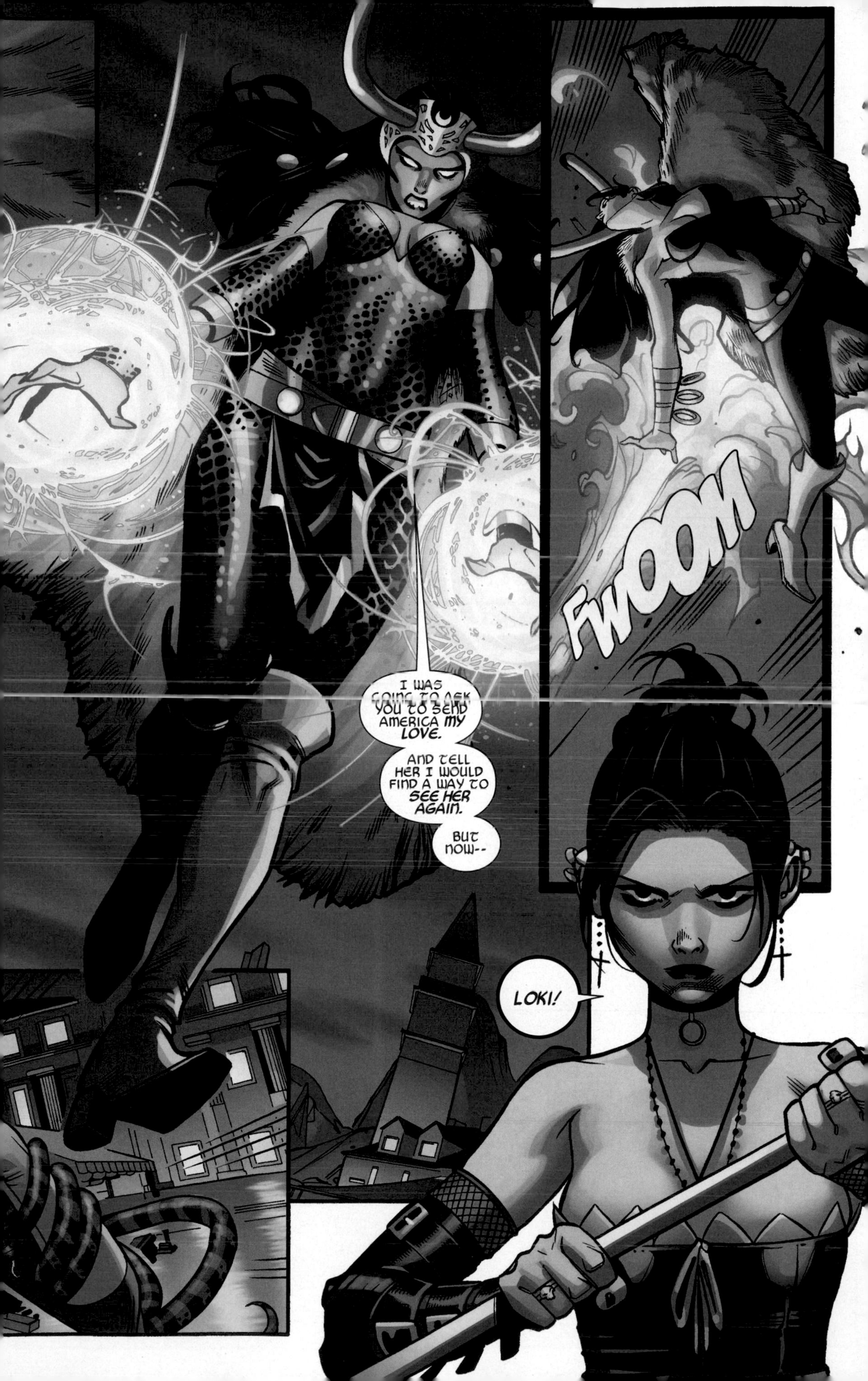
FWOOM
I WAS GOING TO ASK YOU TO SEND AMERICA MY LOVE.
AND TELL HER I WOULD FIND A WAY TO SEE HER AGAIN.
BUT NOW--
LOKI!

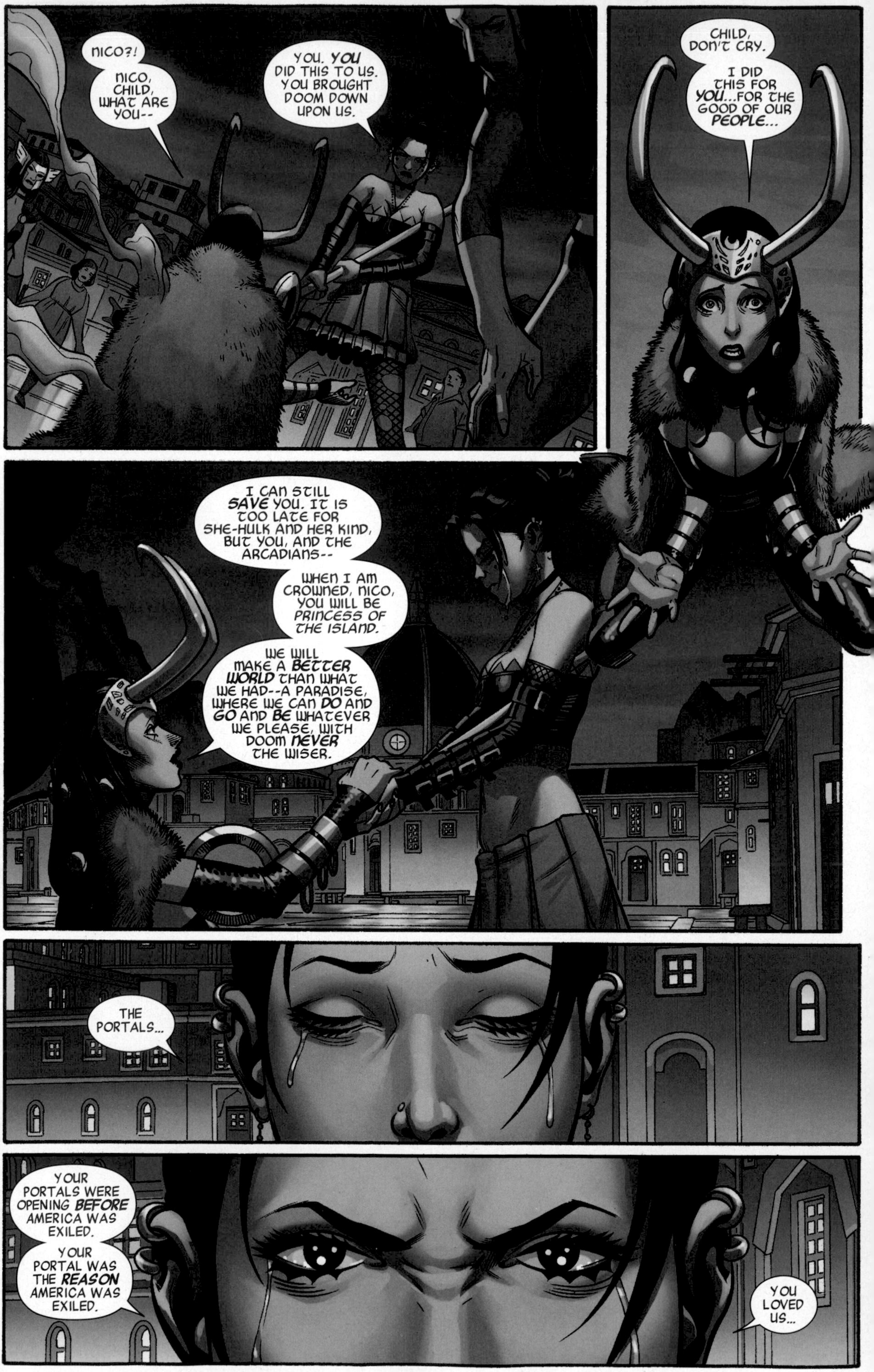
NICO?!
NICO, CHILD, WHAT ARE YOU--
YOU. YOU DID THIS TO US. YOU BROUGHT DOOM DOWN UPON US.
CHILD, DON'T CRY.
I DID THIS FOR YOU...FOR THE GOOD OF OUR PEOPLE...
I CAN STILL SAVE YOU. IT IS TOO LATE FOR SHE-HULK AND HER KIND, BUT YOU, AND THE ARCADIANS--
WHEN I AM CROWNED, NICO, YOU WILL BE PRINCESS OF THE ISLAND.
WE WILL MAKE A BETTER WORLD THAN WHAT WE HAD--A PARADISE, WHERE WE CAN DO AND GO AND BE WHATEVER WE PLEASE, WITH DOOM NEVER THE WISER.
THE PORTALS...
YOUR PORTALS WERE OPENING BEFORE AMERICA WAS EXILED.
YOUR PORTAL WAS THE REASON AMERICA WAS EXILED.
YOU LOVED US...

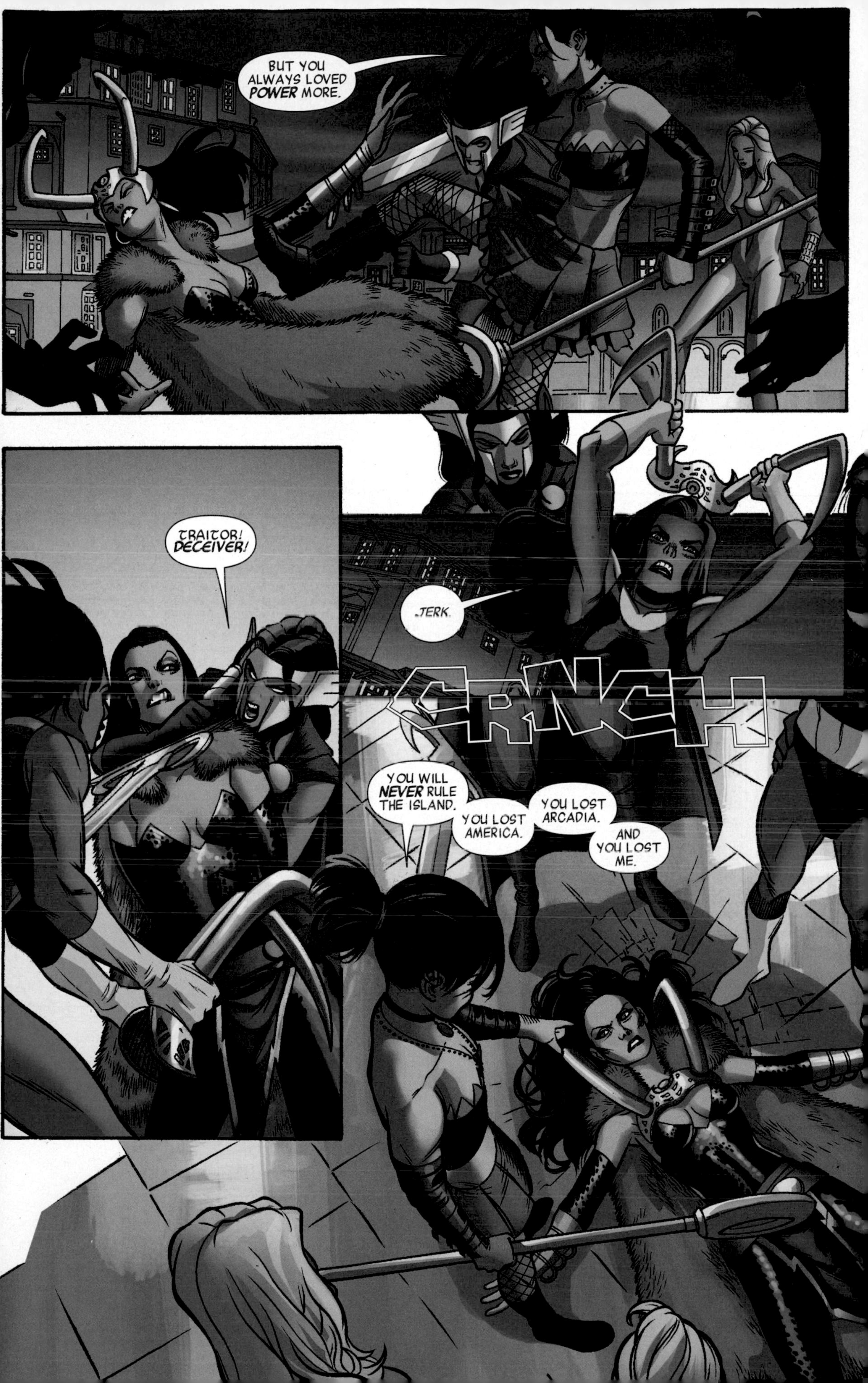
BUT YOU ALWAYS LOVED POWER MORE.
TRAITOR! DECEIVER!
JERK.
CRNCH
YOU WILL NEVER RULE THE ISLAND.
YOU LOST AMERICA.
YOU LOST ARCADIA.
AND YOU LOST ME.

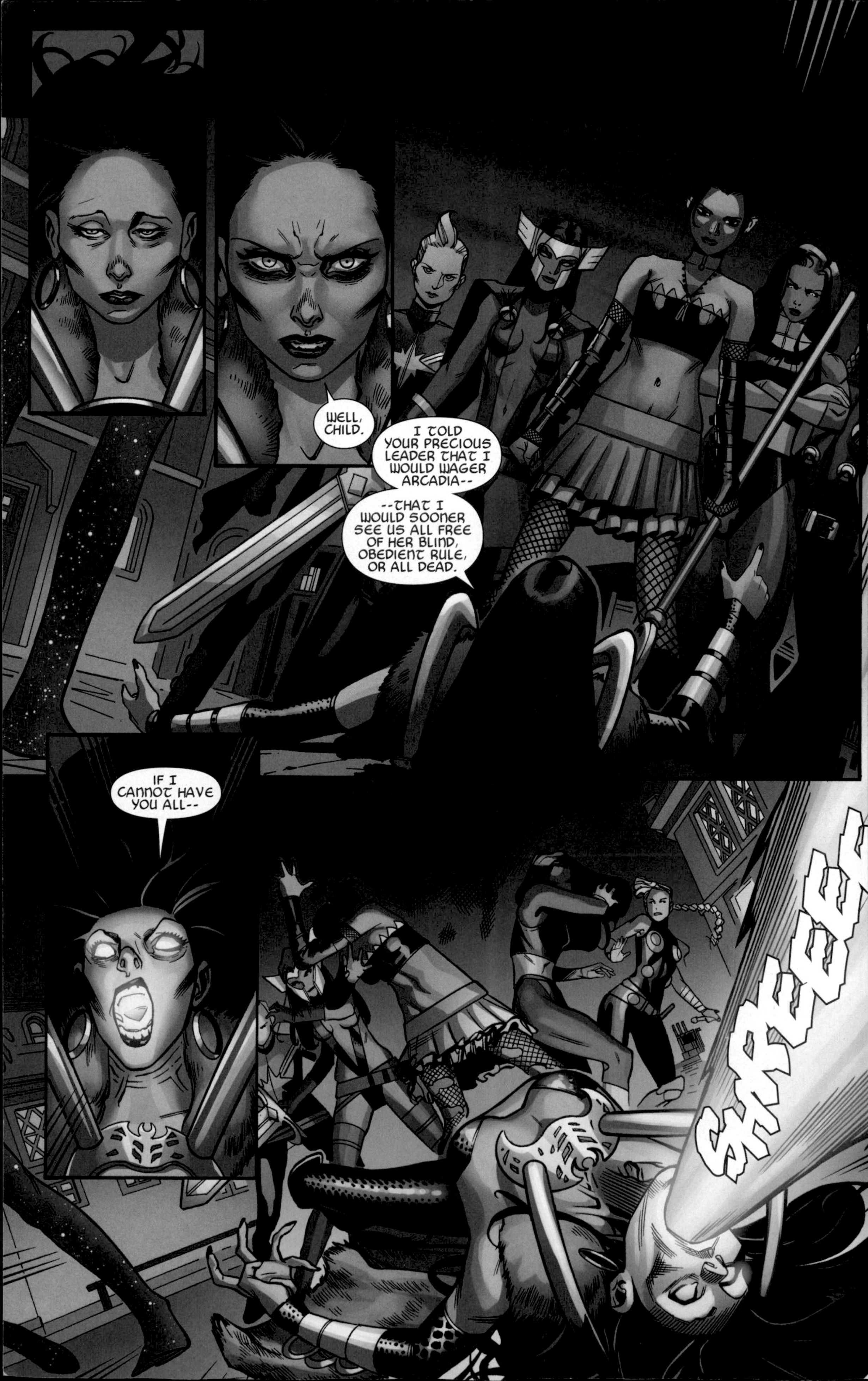
WELL, CHILD.
I TOLD YOUR PRECIOUS LEADER THAT I WOULD WAGER ARCADIA--
--THAT I WOULD SOONER SEE US ALL FREE OF HER BLIND, OBEDIENT RULE, OR ALL DEAD.
IF I CANNOT HAVE YOU ALL--
SHREEE

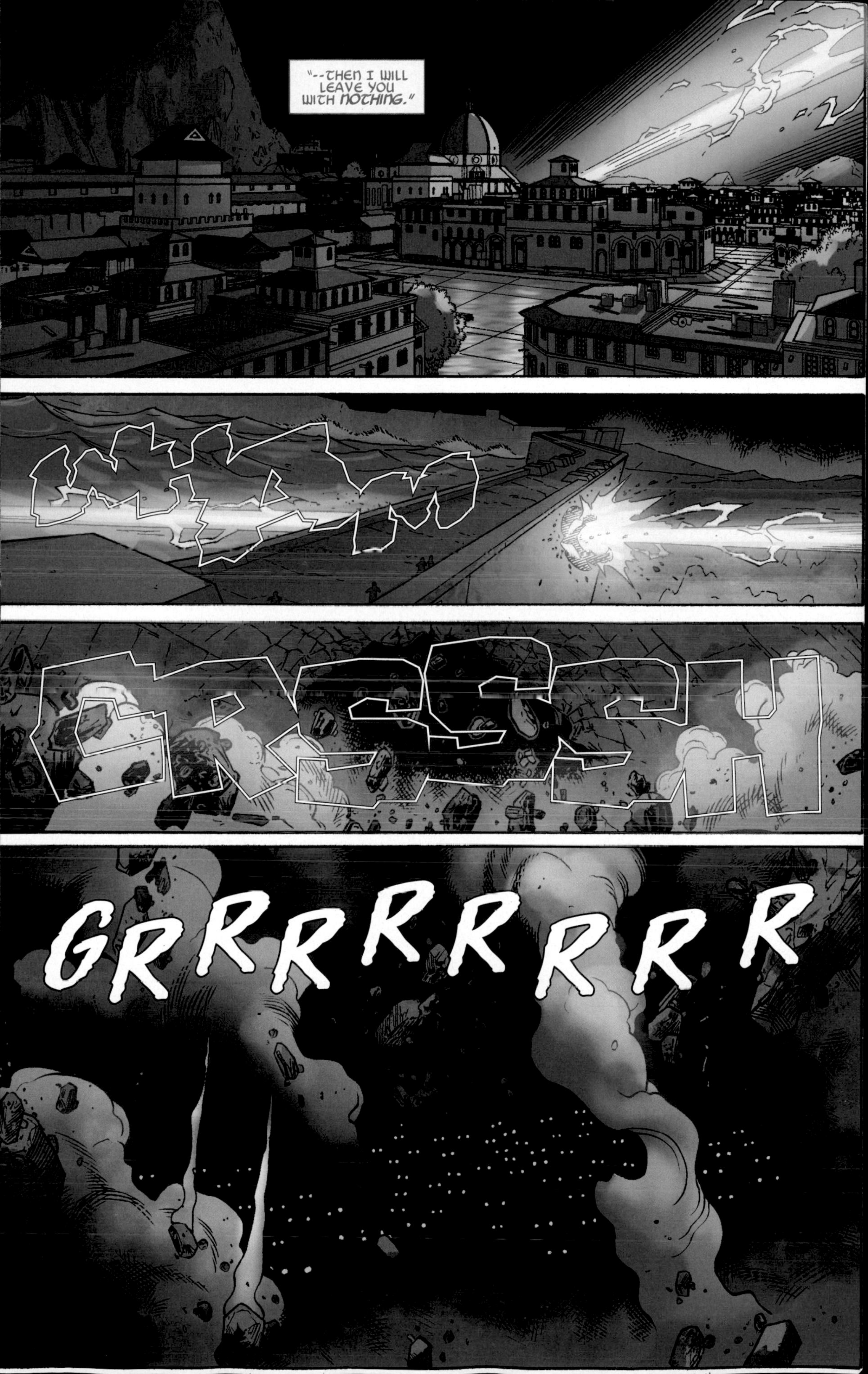
"--THEN I WILL LEAVE YOU WITH NOTHING."
GRRRRRRRR

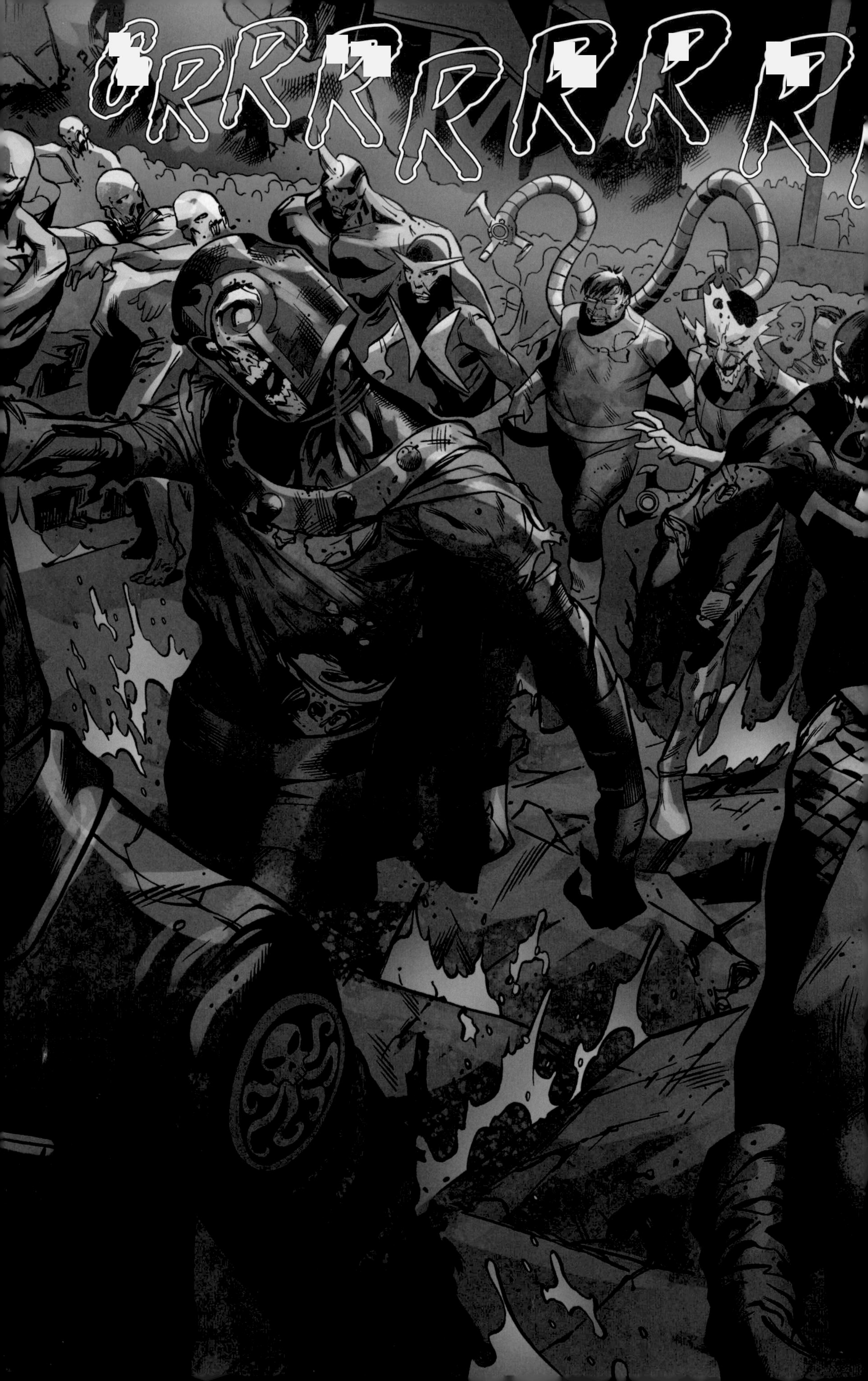
GRRRRRR

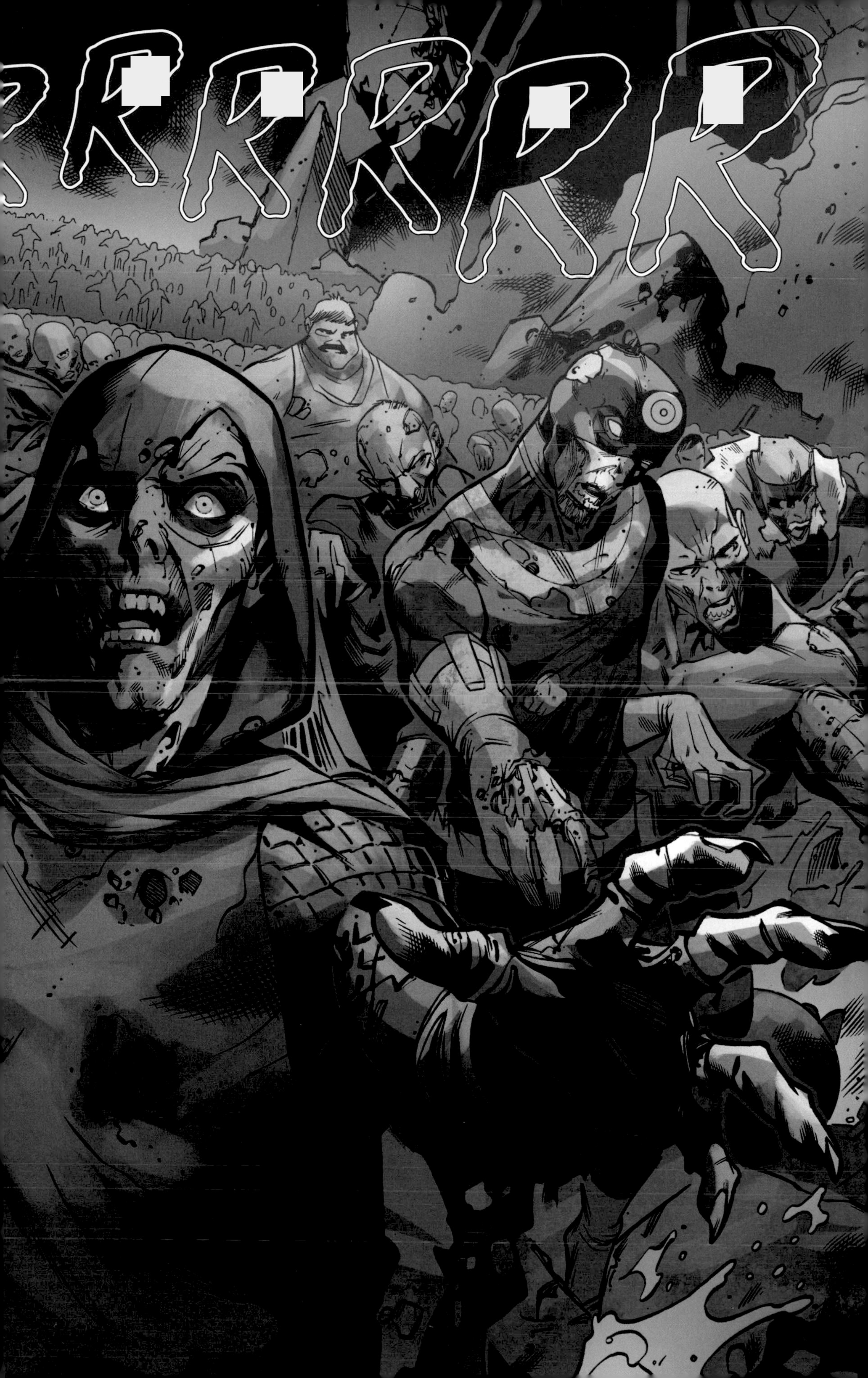
RRRRRR

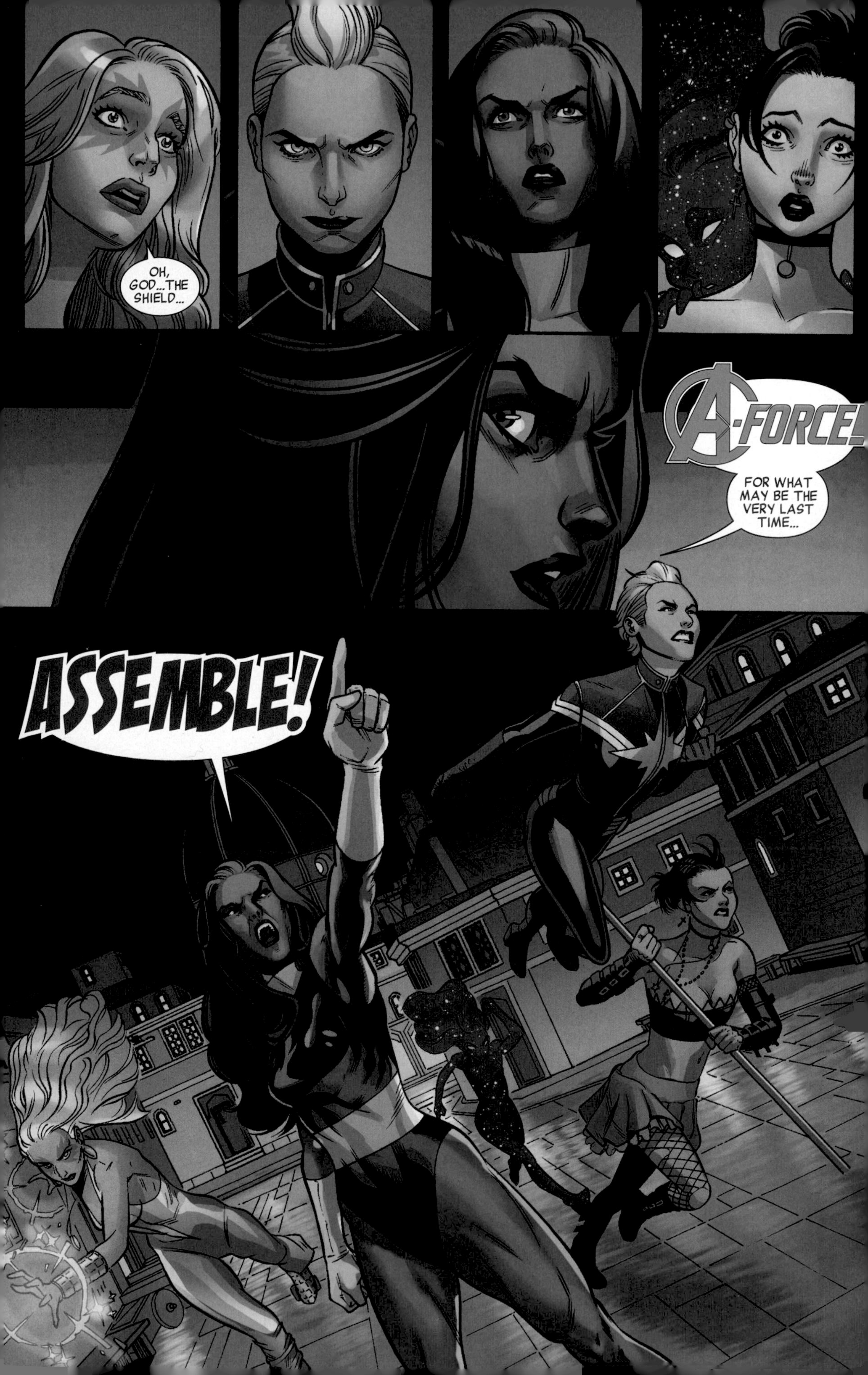
OH, GOD... THE SHIELD...
A-FORCE!
FOR WHAT MAY BE THE VERY LAST TIME...
ASSEMBLE!

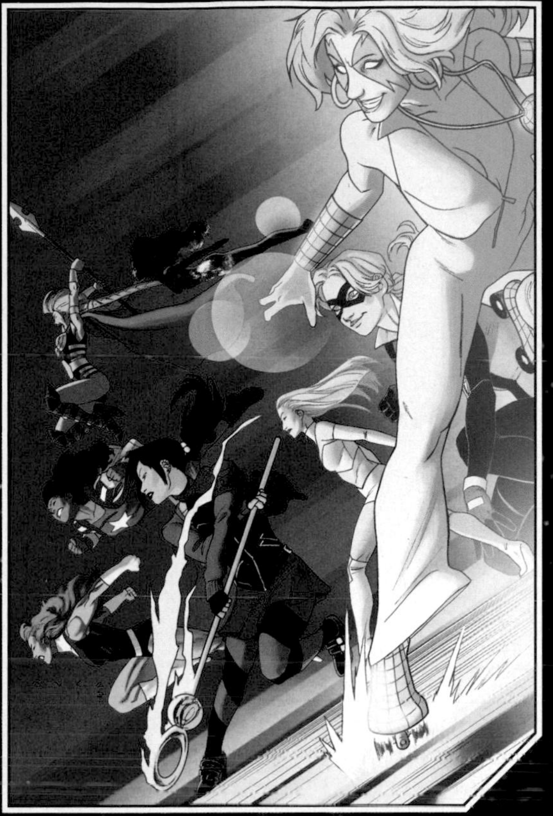

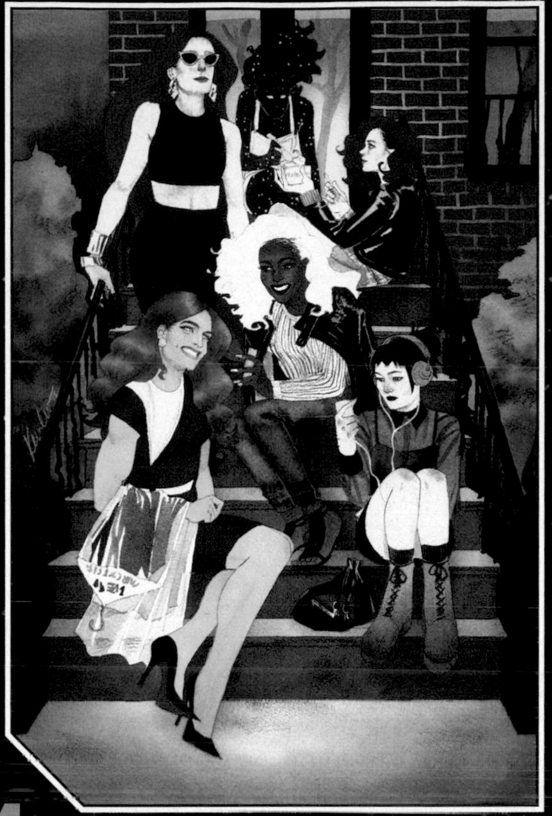

#2 VARIANT
BY **KRIS ANKA**

#3 VARIANT
BY **KEVIN WADA**

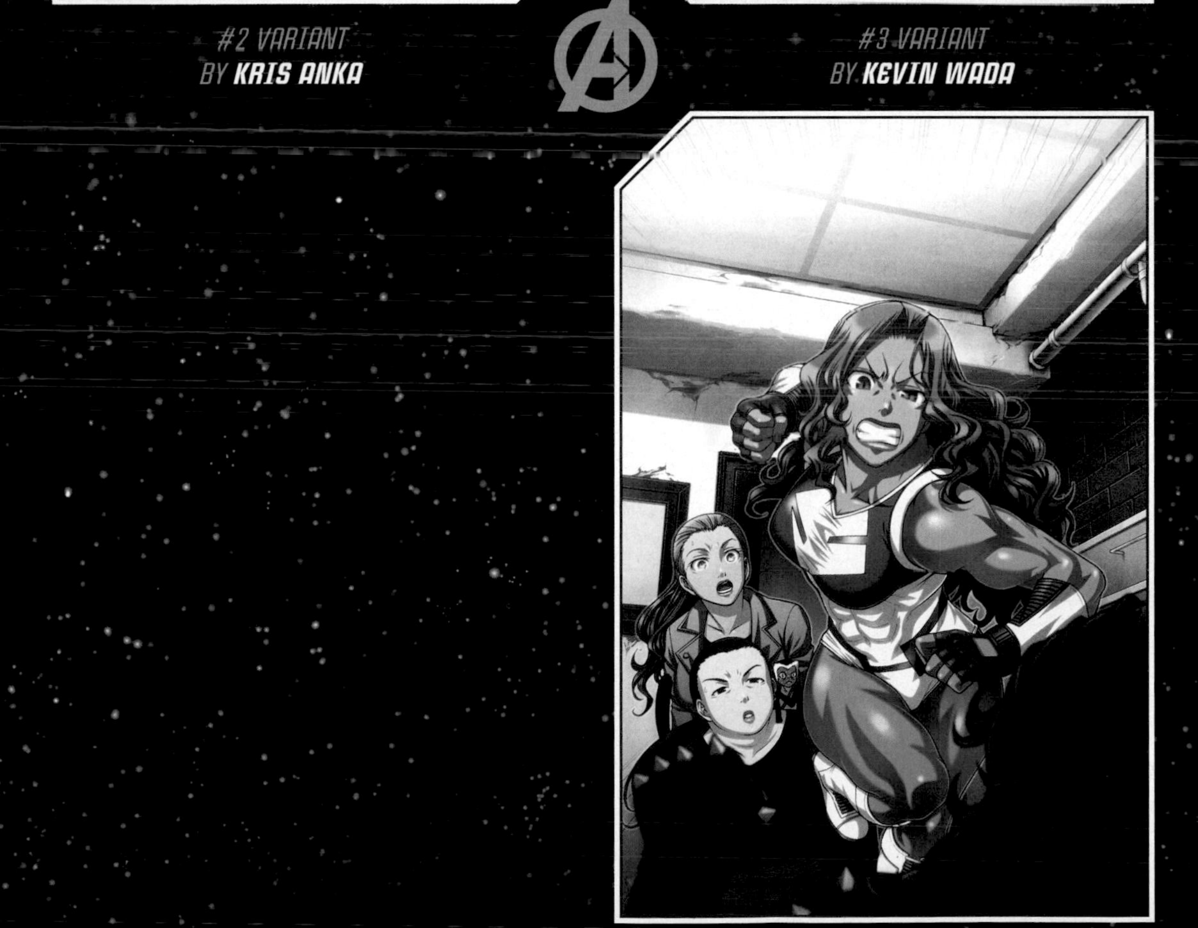

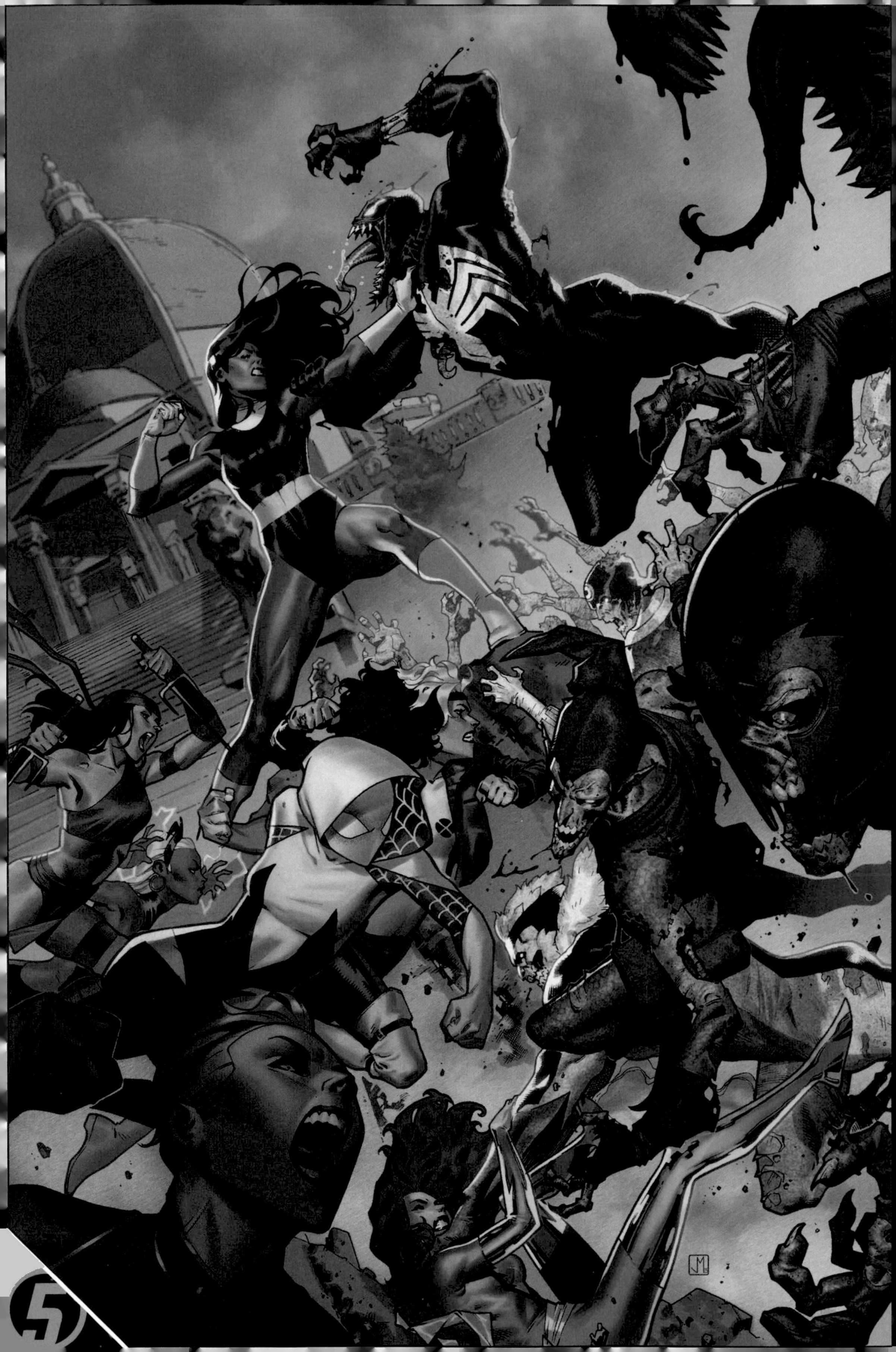

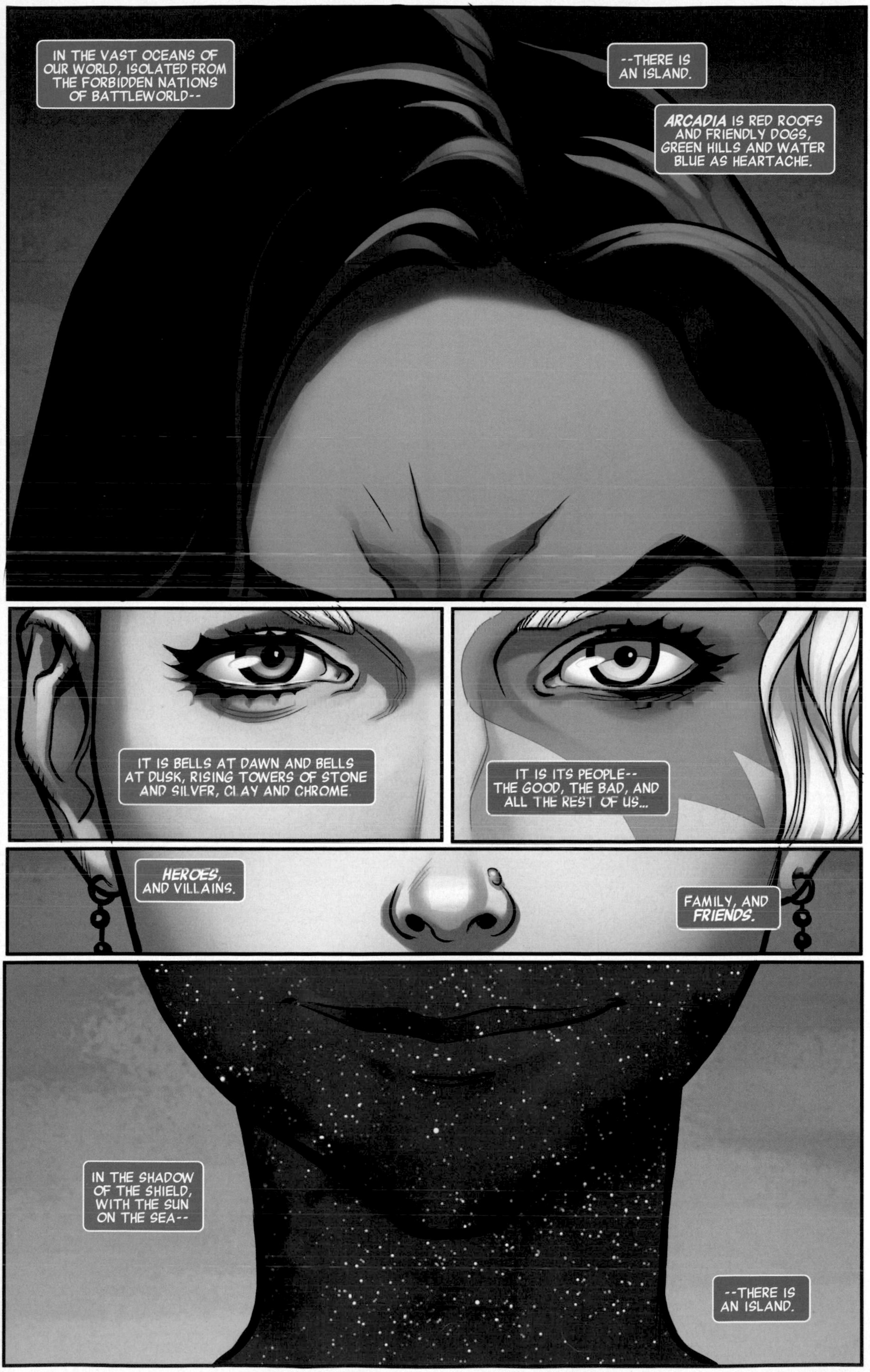

IN THE VAST OCEANS OF OUR WORLD, ISOLATED FROM THE FORBIDDEN NATIONS OF BATTLEWORLD--
--THERE IS AN ISLAND.
ARCADIA IS RED ROOFS AND FRIENDLY DOGS, GREEN HILLS AND WATER BLUE AS HEARTACHE.
IT IS BELLS AT DAWN AND BELLS AT DUSK, RISING TOWERS OF STONE AND SILVER, CLAY AND CHROME.
IT IS ITS PEOPLE-- THE GOOD, THE BAD, AND ALL THE REST OF US...
HEROES, AND VILLAINS.
FAMILY, AND FRIENDS.
IN THE SHADOW OF THE SHIELD, WITH THE SUN ON THE SEA--
--THERE IS AN ISLAND.

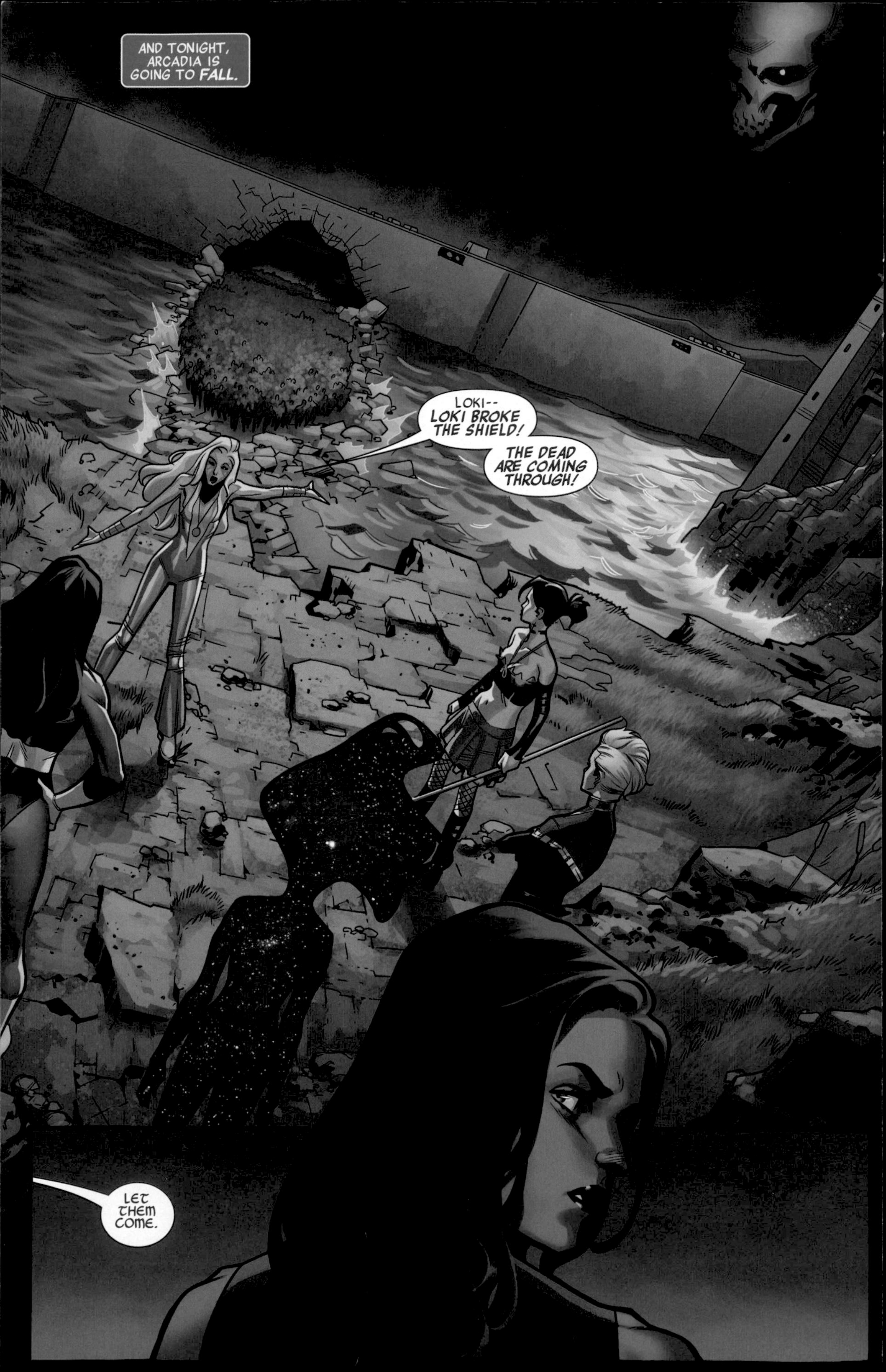
AND TONIGHT, ARCADIA IS GOING TO FALL.
LOKI-- LOKI BROKE THE SHIELD!
THE DEAD ARE COMING THROUGH!
LET THEM COME.

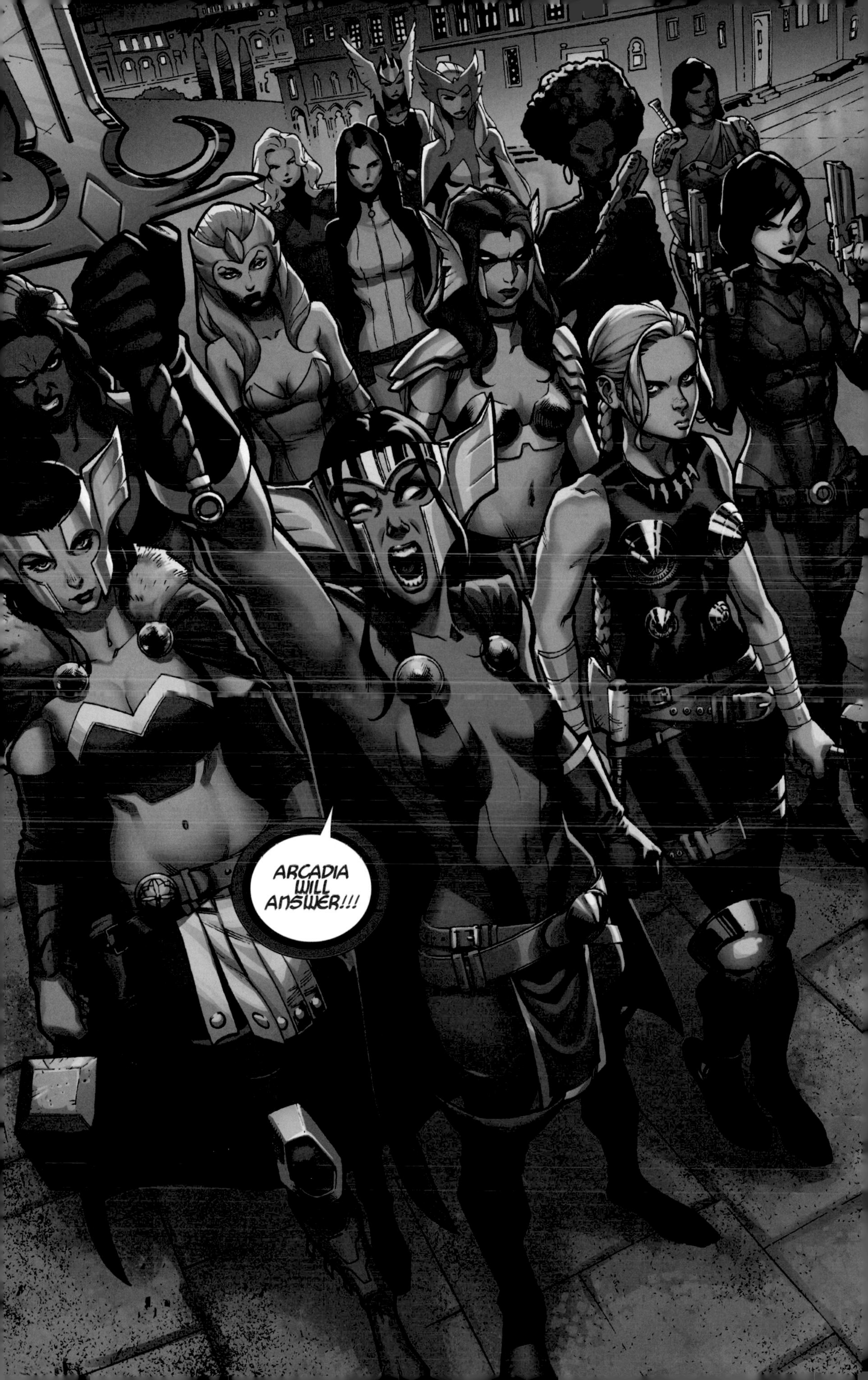
ARCADIA WILL ANSWER!!!

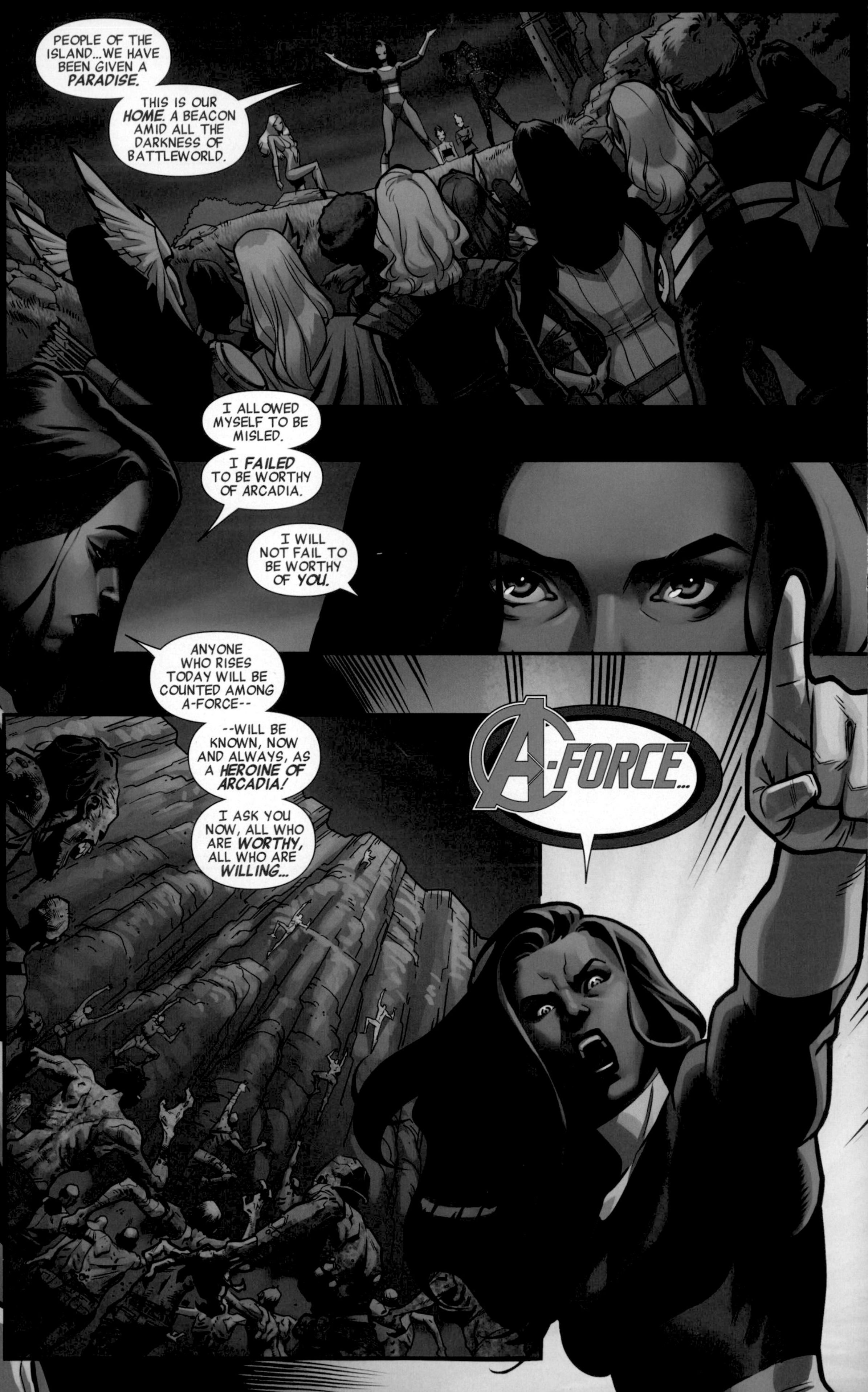

PEOPLE OF THE ISLAND...WE HAVE BEEN GIVEN A PARADISE.
THIS IS OUR HOME. A BEACON AMID ALL THE DARKNESS OF BATTLEWORLD.
I ALLOWED MYSELF TO BE MISLED.
I FAILED TO BE WORTHY OF ARCADIA.
I WILL NOT FAIL TO BE WORTHY OF YOU.
ANYONE WHO RISES TODAY WILL BE COUNTED AMONG A-FORCE--
--WILL BE KNOWN, NOW AND ALWAYS, AS A HEROINE OF ARCADIA!
I ASK YOU NOW, ALL WHO ARE WORTHY, ALL WHO ARE WILLING...
A-FORCE...

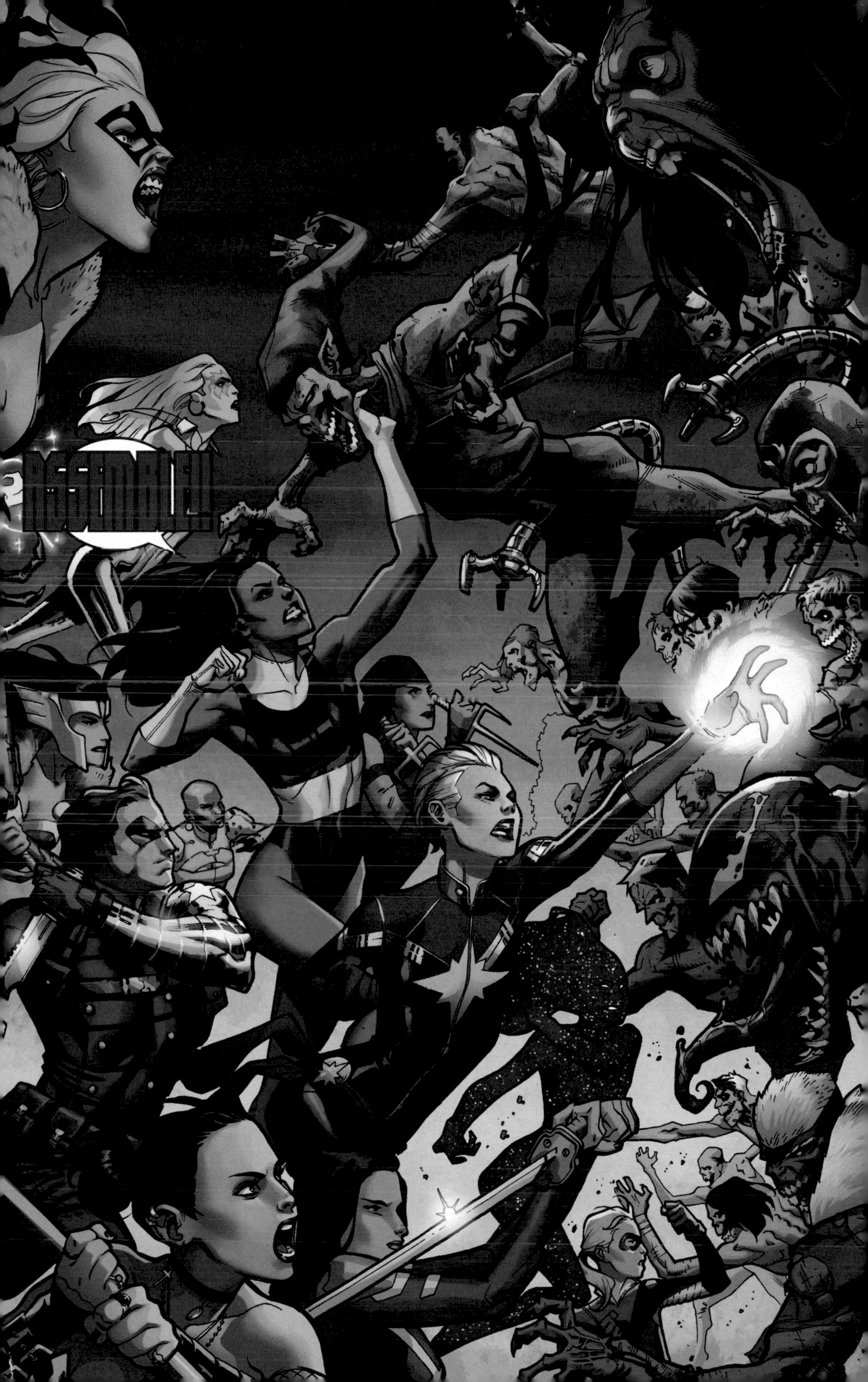
ASSEMBLE!!

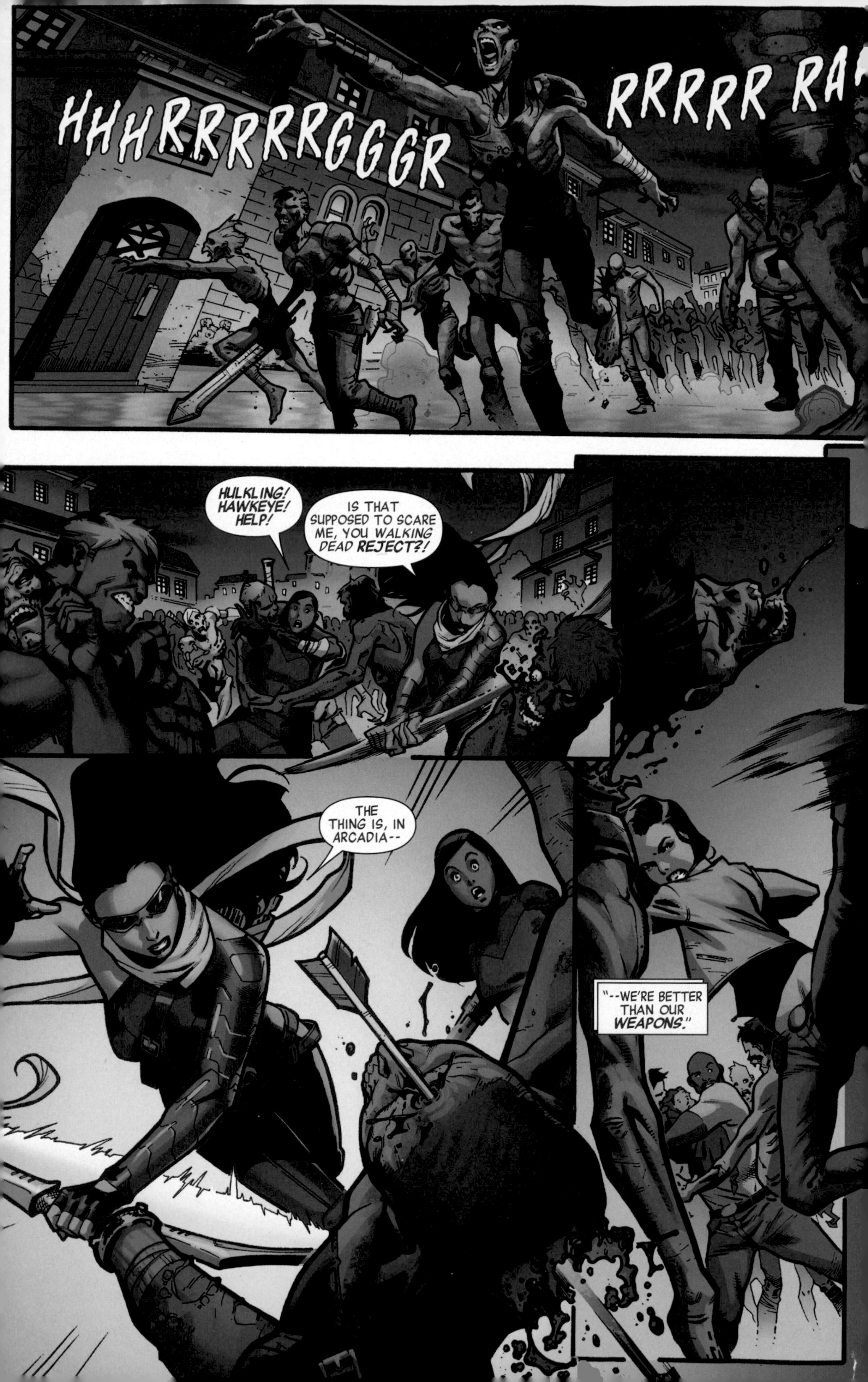
HHHRRRRRRGGGR
RRRRRR RA
HULKLING! HAWKEYE! HELP!
IS THAT SUPPOSED TO SCARE ME, YOU WALKING DEAD REJECT?!
THE THING IS, IN ARCADIA--
"--WE'RE BETTER THAN OUR WEAPONS."

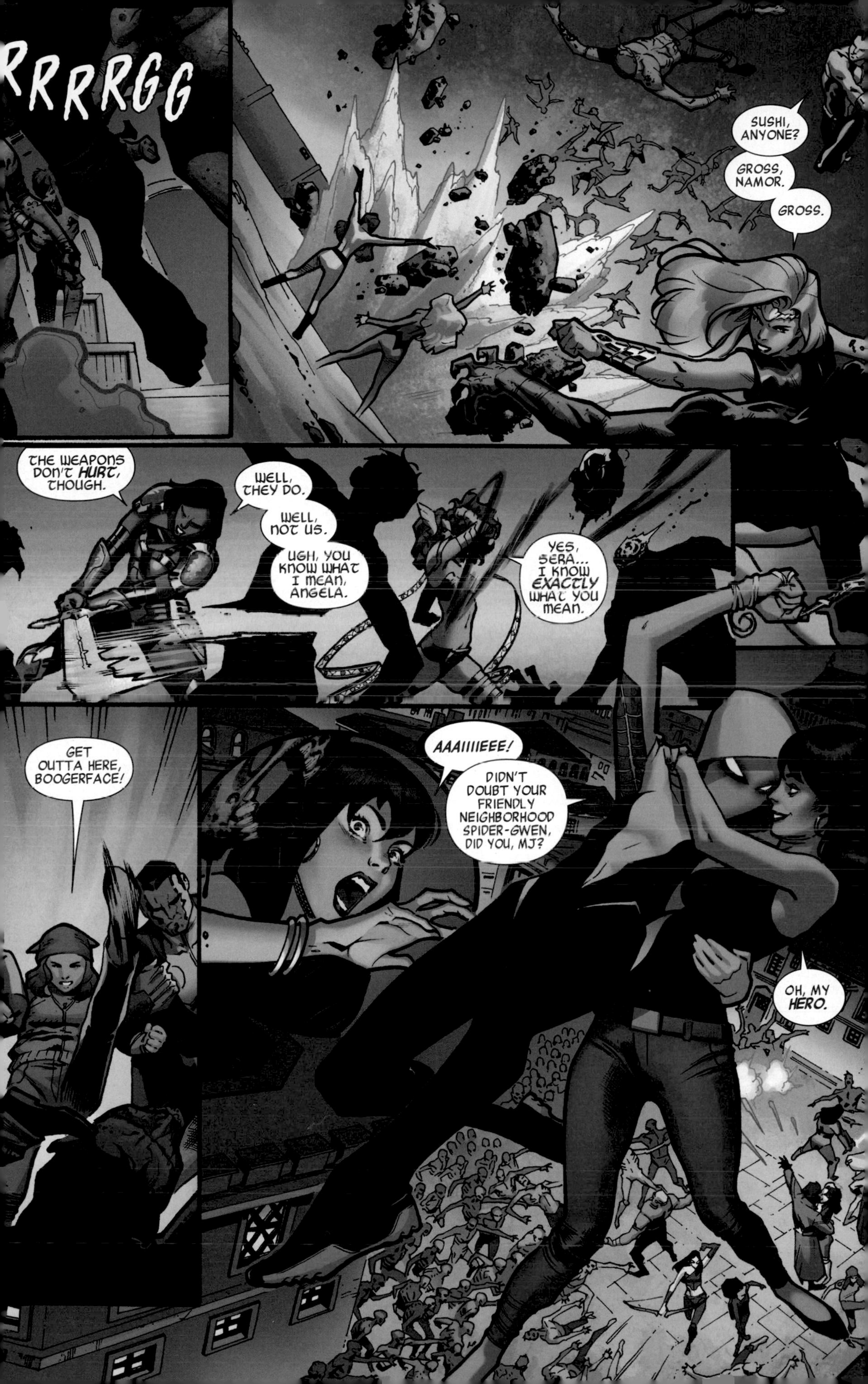
RRRRGG
SUSHI, ANYONE?
GROSS, NAMOR.
GROSS.
THE WEAPONS DON'T HURT, THOUGH.
WELL, THEY DO.
WELL, NOT US.
UGH, YOU KNOW WHAT I MEAN, ANGELA.
YES, SERA... I KNOW EXACTLY WHAT YOU MEAN.
GET OUTTA HERE, BOOGERFACE!
AAAIIIIEEE!
DIDN'T DOUBT YOUR FRIENDLY NEIGHBORHOOD SPIDER-GWEN, DID YOU, MJ?
OH, MY HERO.

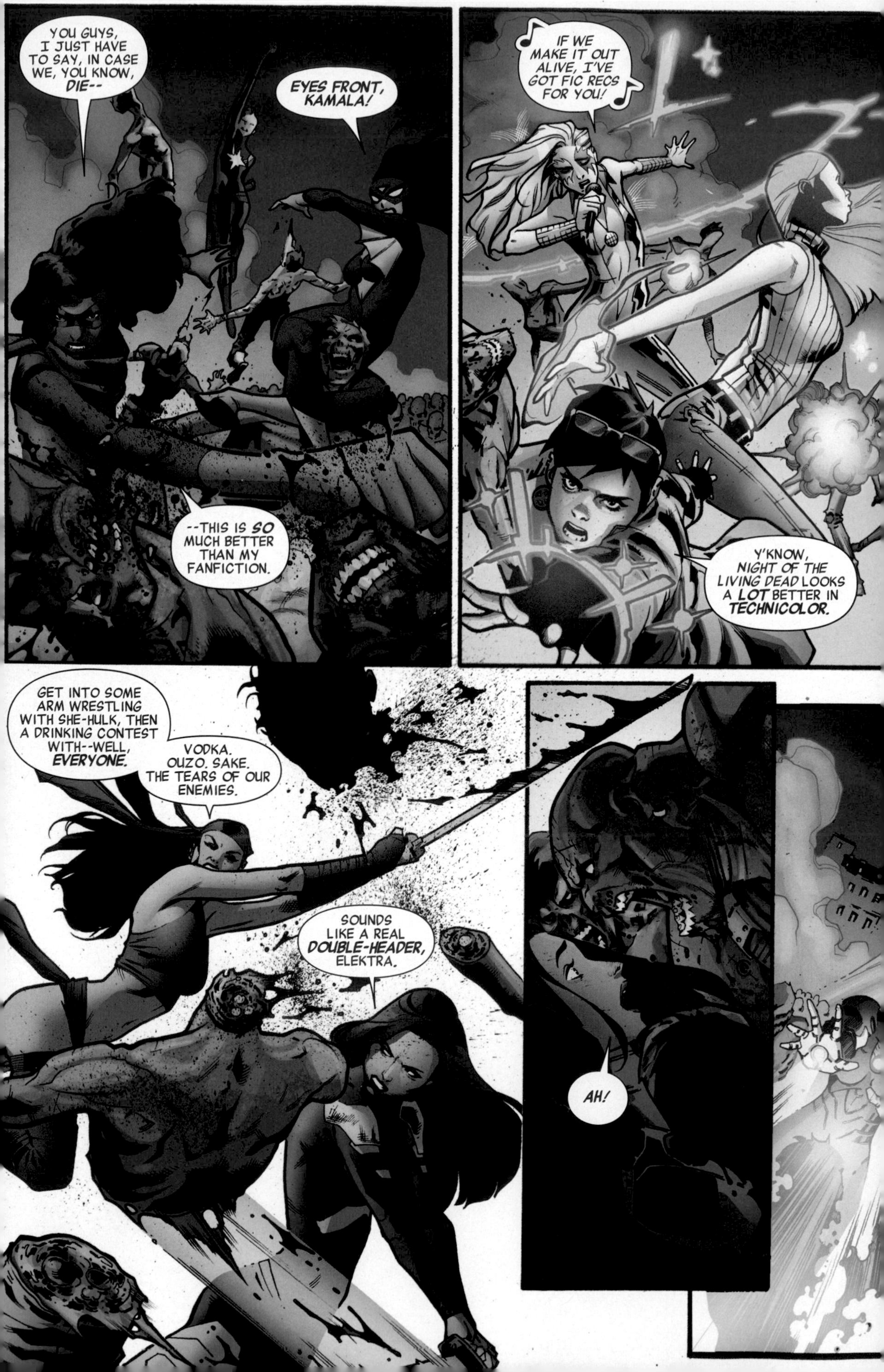
YOU GUYS, I JUST HAVE TO SAY, IN CASE WE, YOU KNOW, DIE--
EYES FRONT, KAMALA!
--THIS IS SO MUCH BETTER THAN MY FANFICTION.
IF WE MAKE IT OUT ALIVE, I'VE GOT FIC RECS FOR YOU!
Y'KNOW, NIGHT OF THE LIVING DEAD LOOKS A LOT BETTER IN TECHNICOLOR.
GET INTO SOME ARM WRESTLING WITH SHE-HULK, THEN A DRINKING CONTEST WITH--WELL, EVERYONE.
VODKA. OUZO. SAKE. THE TEARS OF OUR ENEMIES.
SOUNDS LIKE A REAL DOUBLE-HEADER, ELEKTRA.
AH!

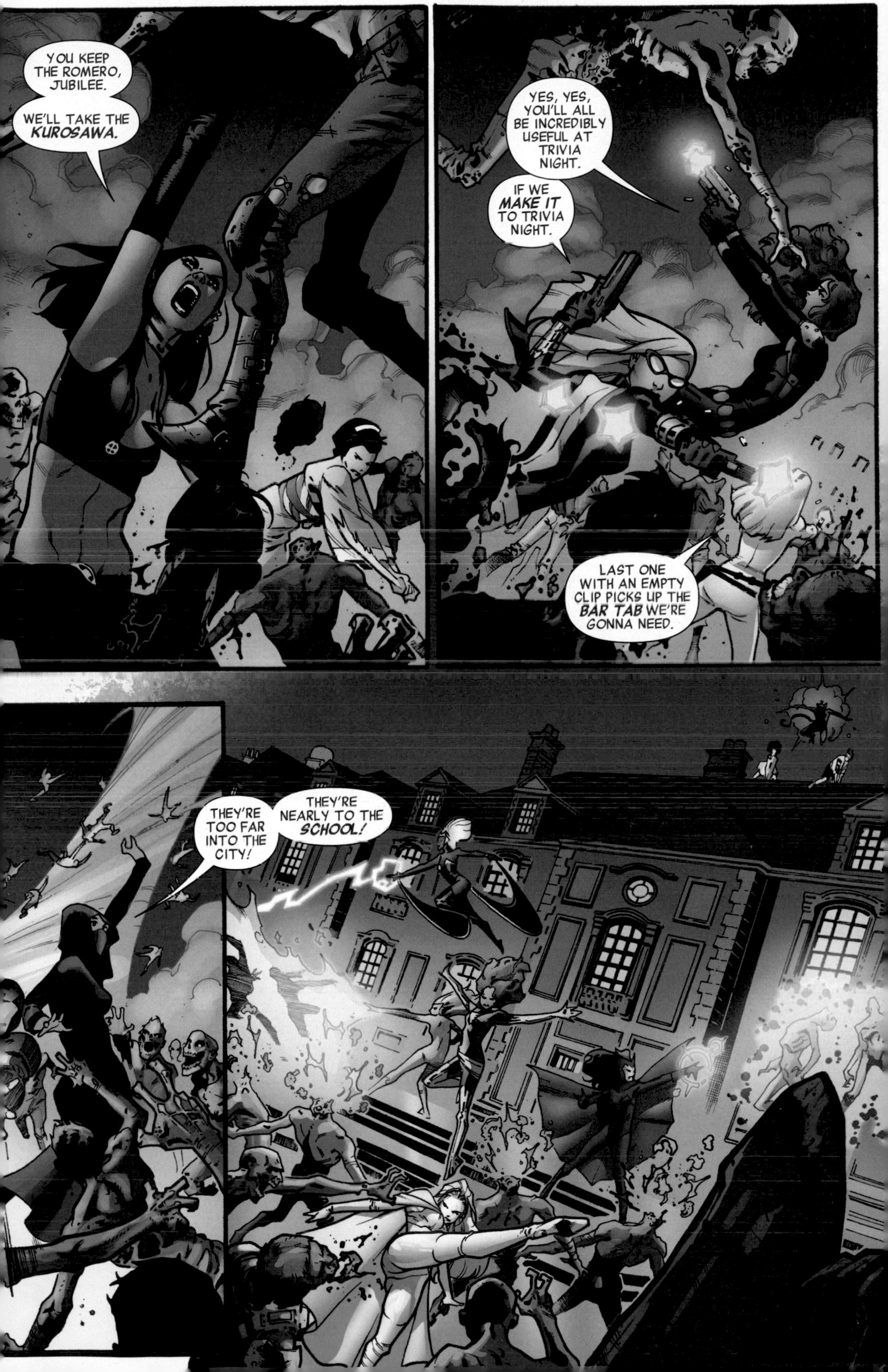
YOU KEEP THE ROMERO, JUBILEE.
WE'LL TAKE THE KUROSAWA.
YES, YES, YOU'LL ALL BE INCREDIBLY USEFUL AT TRIVIA NIGHT.
IF WE MAKE IT TO TRIVIA NIGHT.
LAST ONE WITH AN EMPTY CLIP PICKS UP THE BAR TAB WE'RE GONNA NEED.
THEY'RE TOO FAR INTO THE CITY!
THEY'RE NEARLY TO THE SCHOOL!

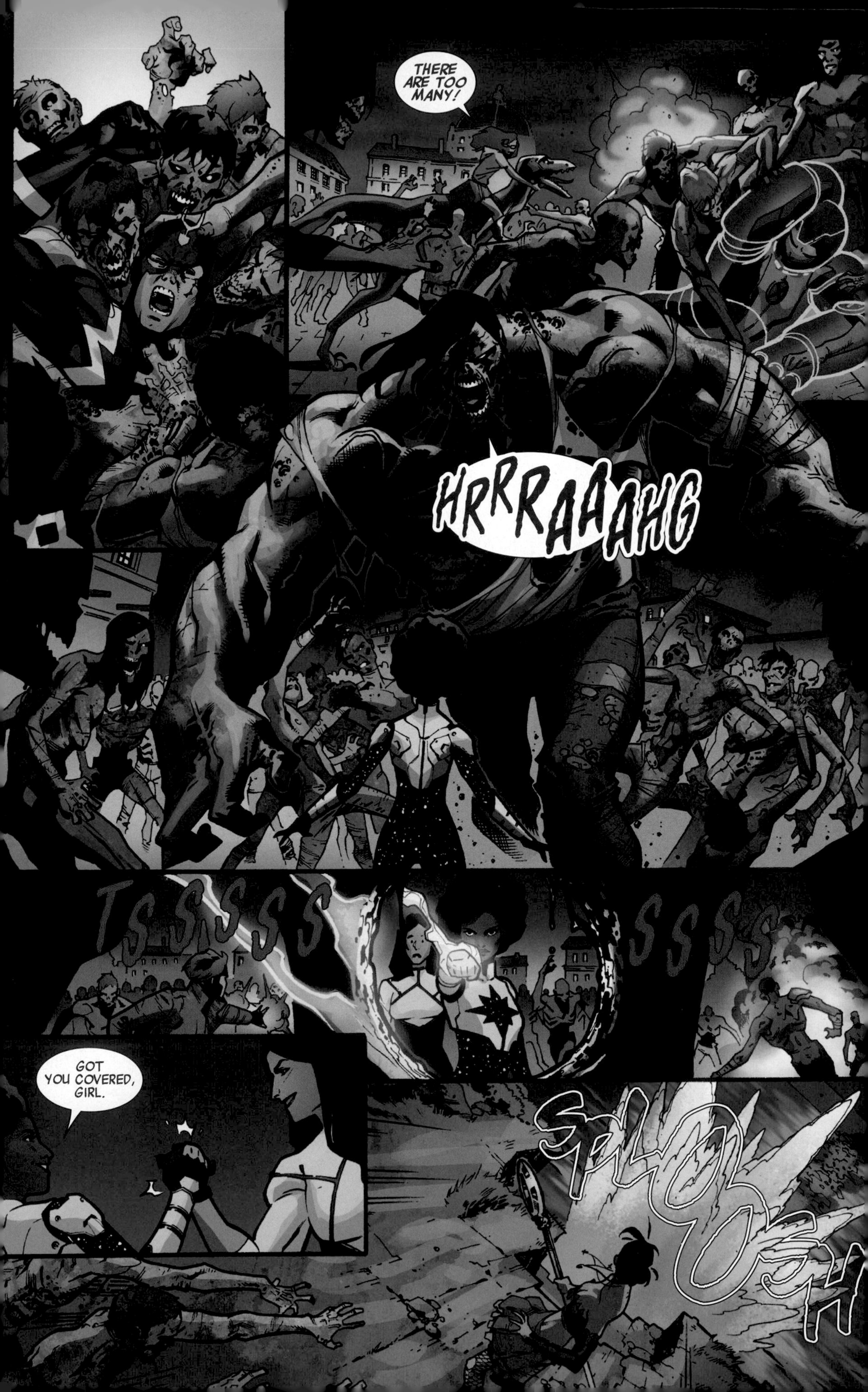
THERE ARE TOO MANY!
HRRRAAAHG
TSSSSS
TSSSSS
GOT YOU COVERED, GIRL.
SPLOOOSH

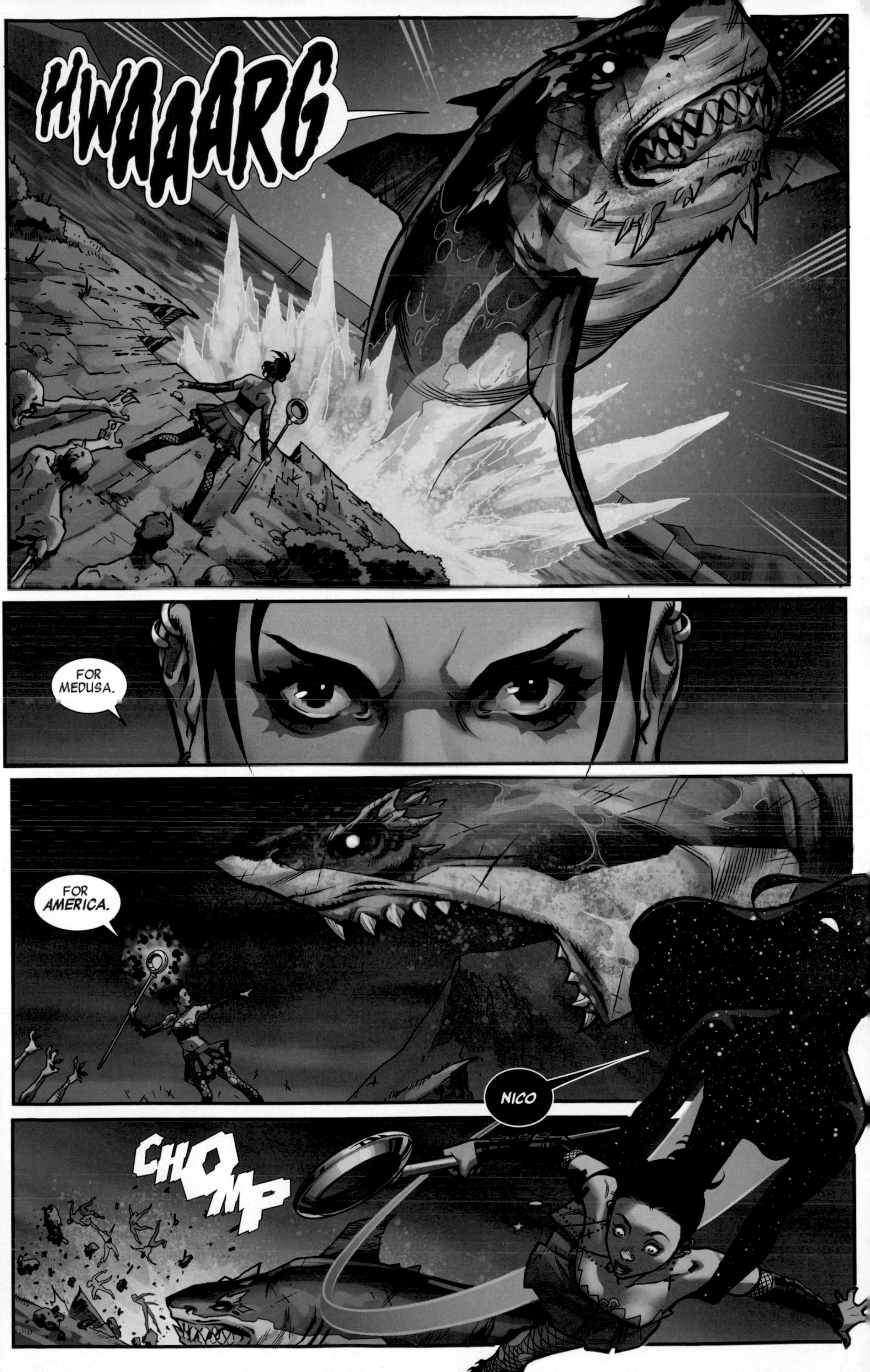
HWAAARG
FOR MEDUSA.
FOR AMERICA.
NICO
CHOMP

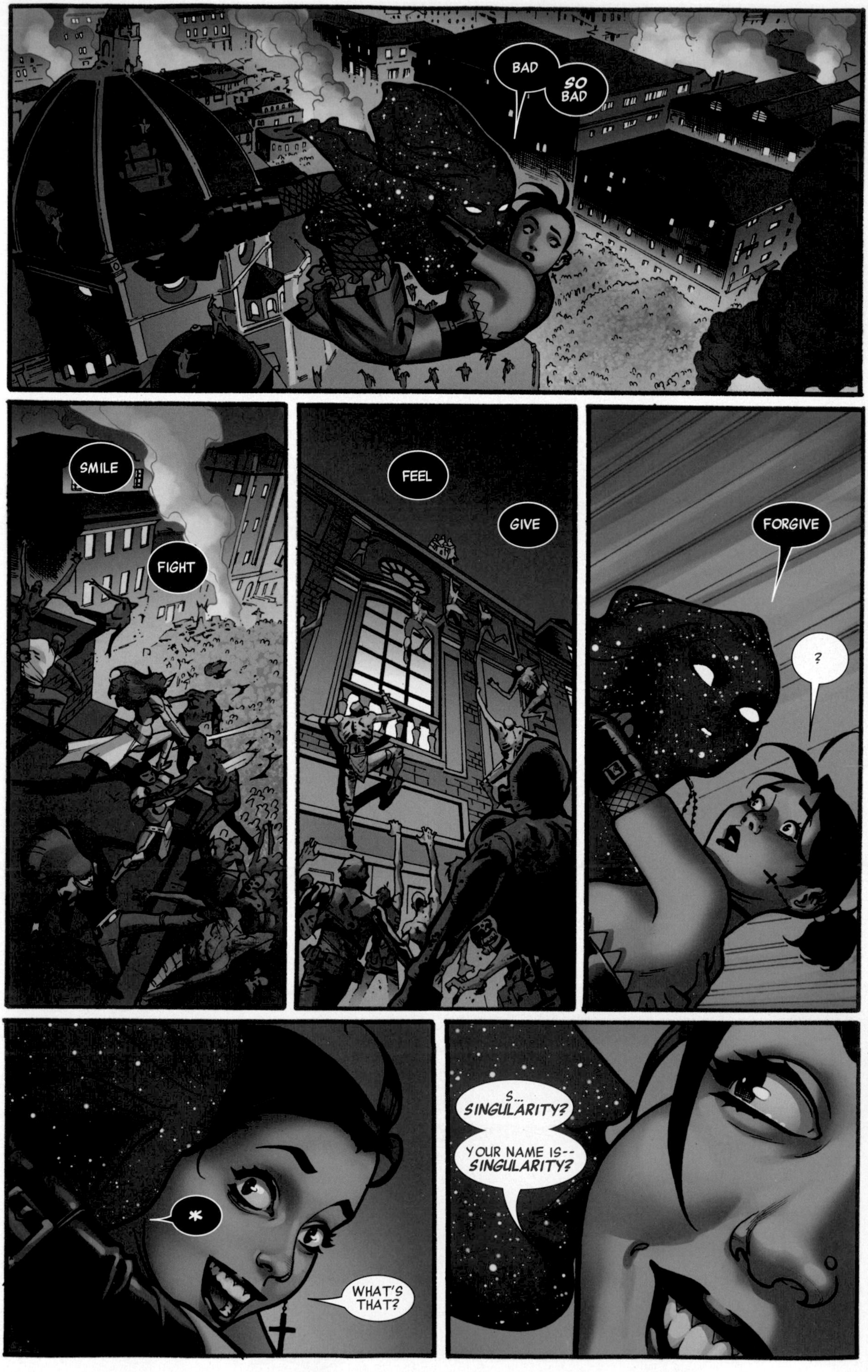
BAD
SO BAD
SMILE
FIGHT
FEEL
GIVE
FORGIVE
?
*
WHAT'S THAT?
S... SINGULARITY?
YOUR NAME IS-- SINGULARITY?

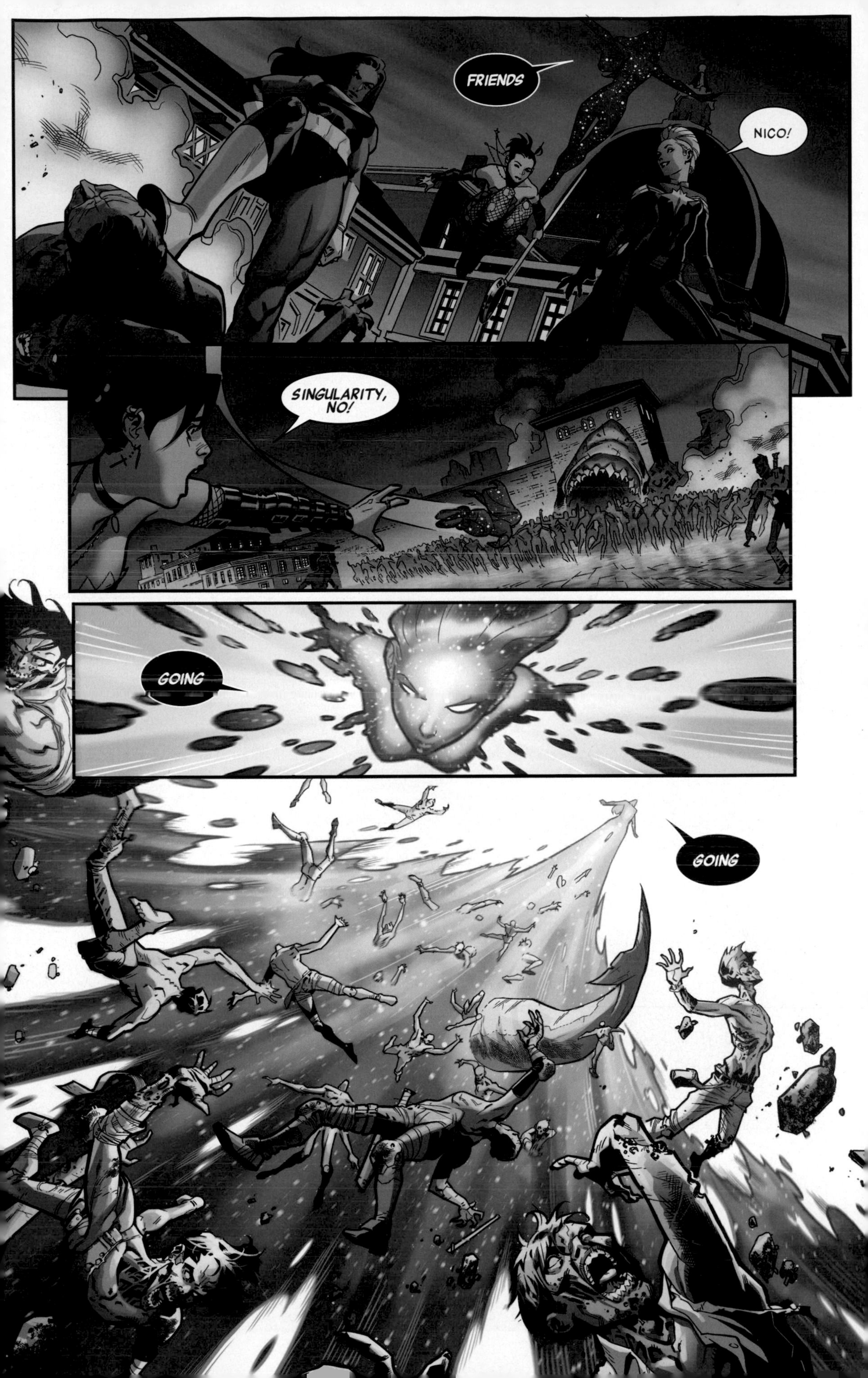
FRIENDS
NICO!
SINGULARITY, NO!
GOING
GOING

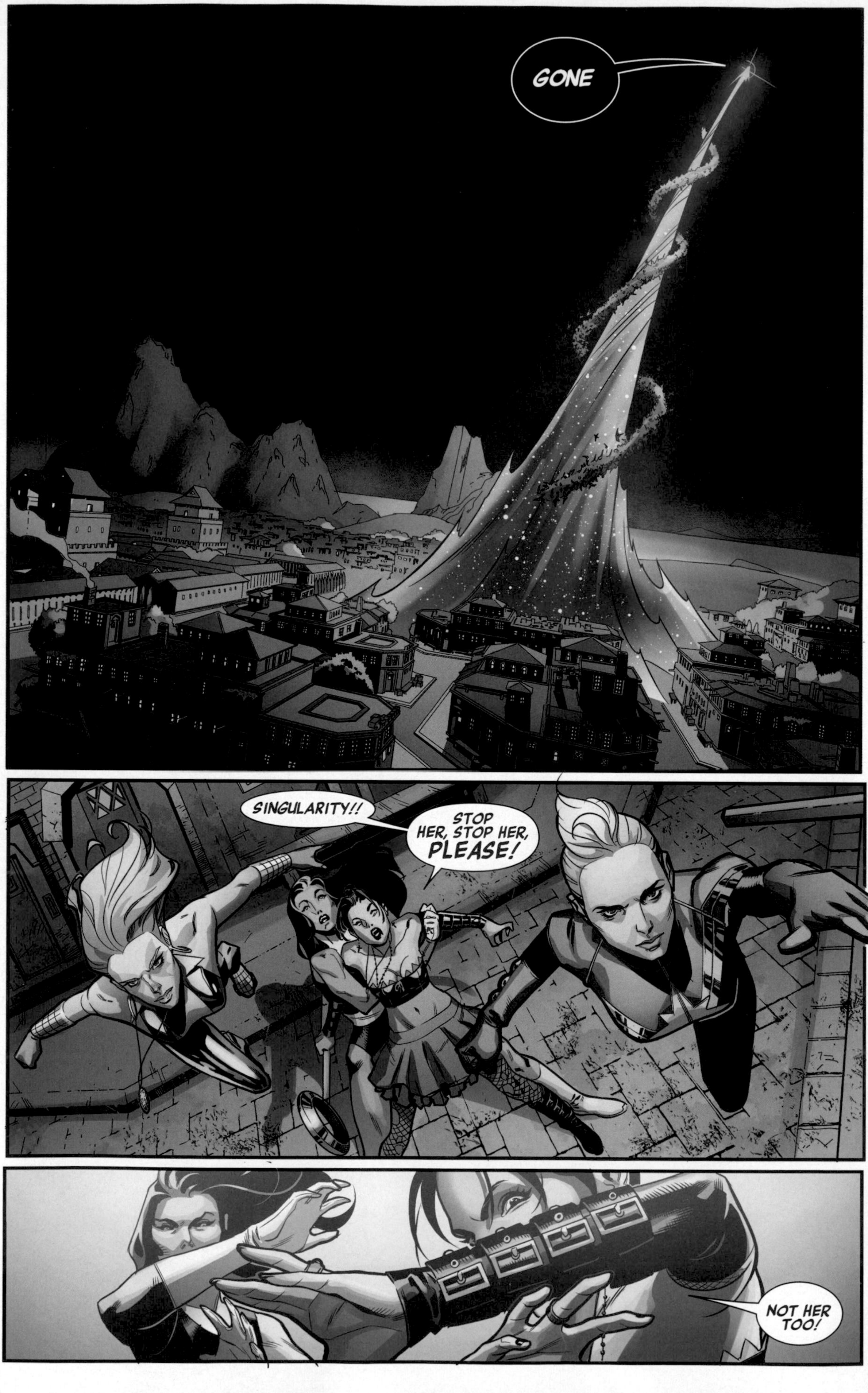
GONE
SINGULARITY!!
STOP HER, STOP HER, PLEASE!
NOT HER TOO!

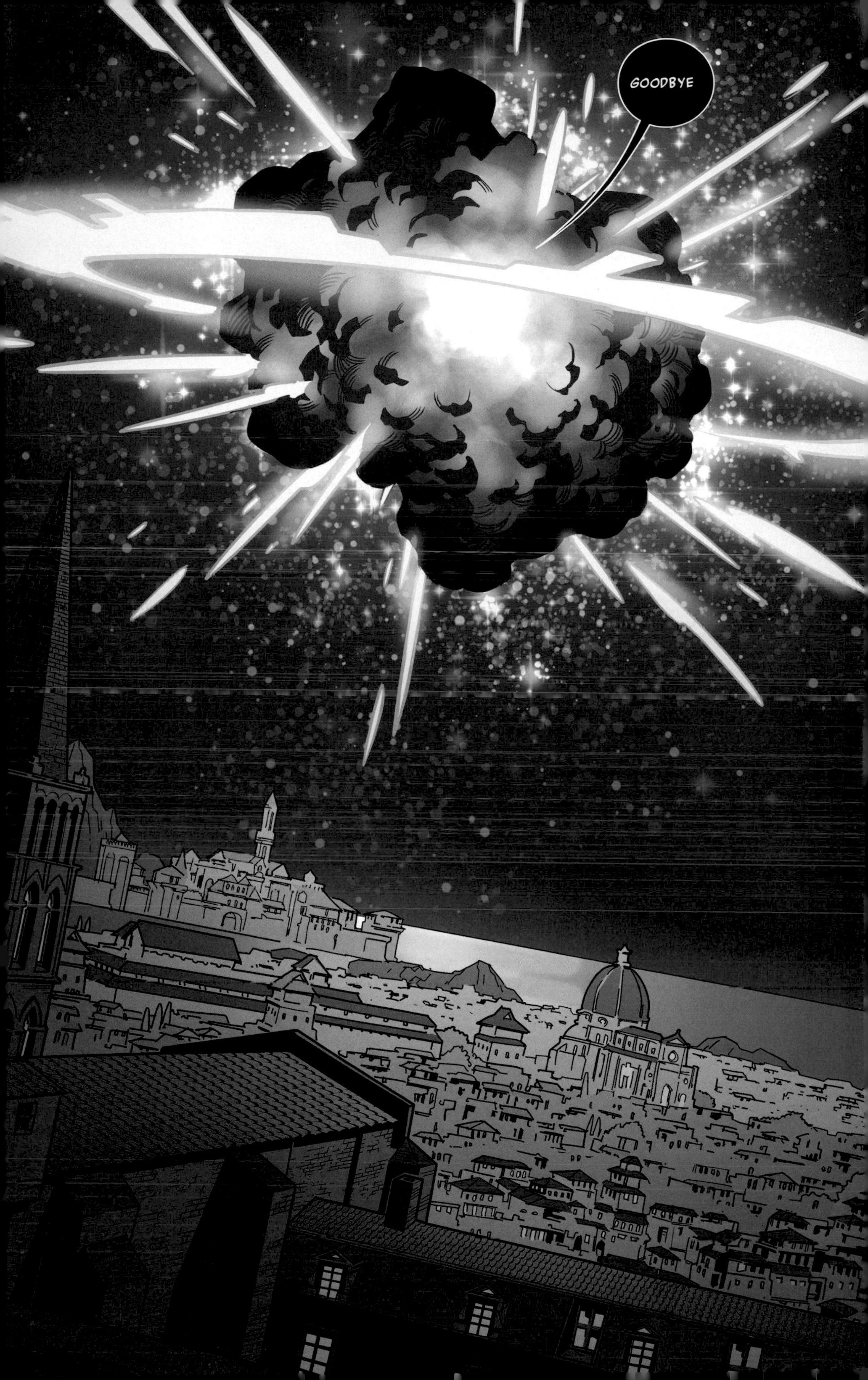
GOODBYE

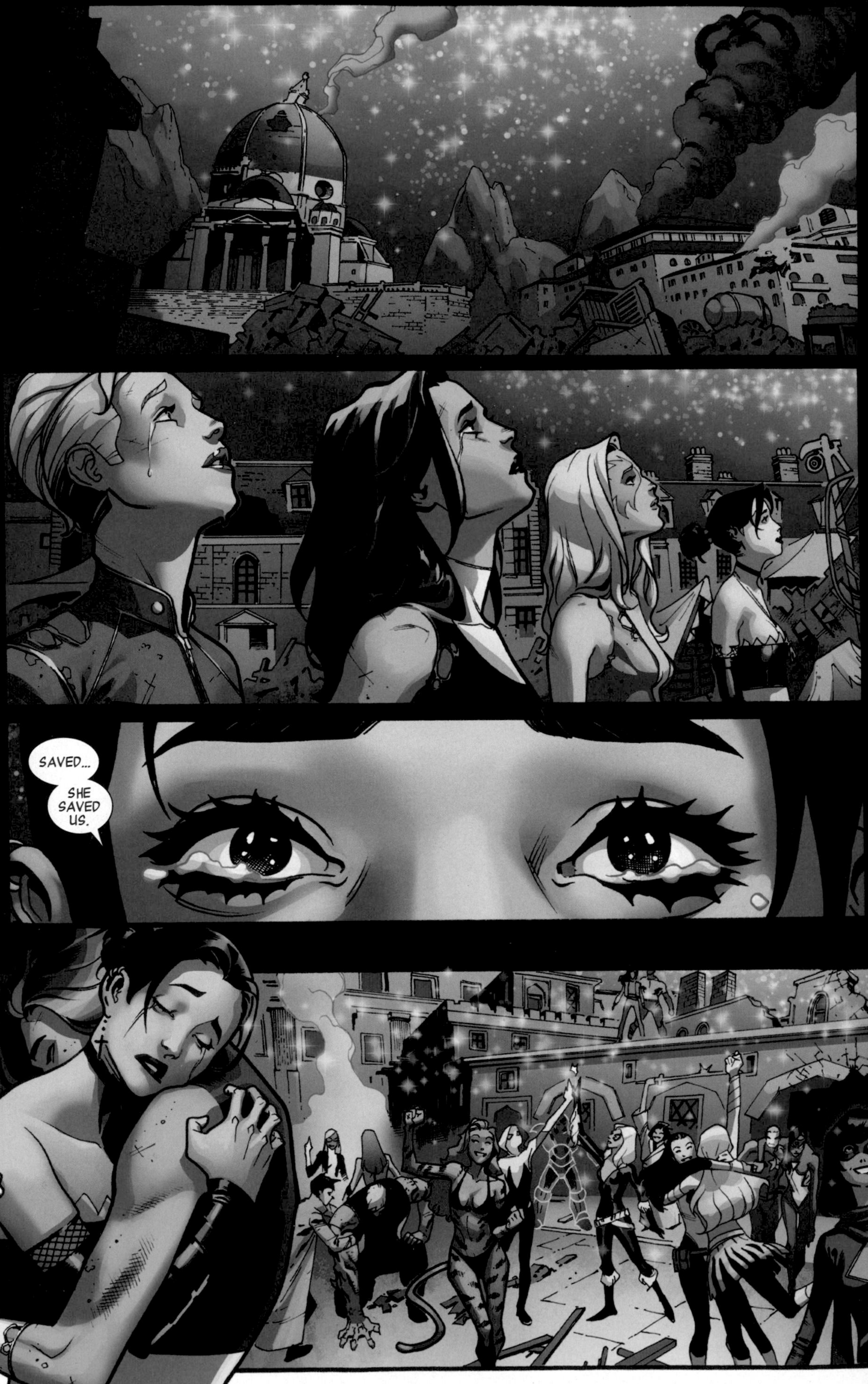
SAVED... SHE SAVED US.

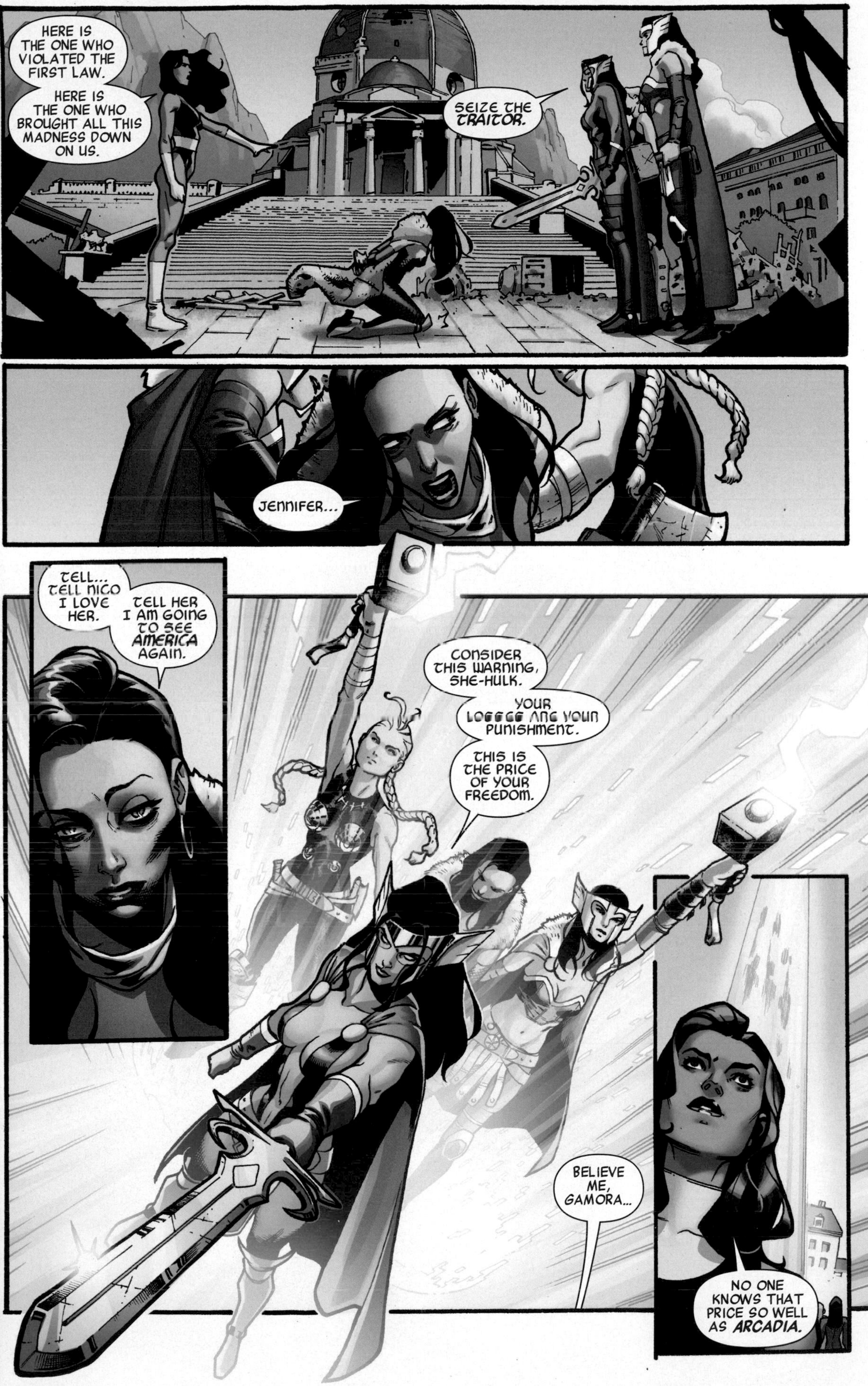
HERE IS THE ONE WHO VIOLATED THE FIRST LAW.
HERE IS THE ONE WHO BROUGHT ALL THIS MADNESS DOWN ON US.
SEIZE THE TRAITOR.
JENNIFER...
TELL... TELL NICO I LOVE HER.
TELL HER I AM GOING TO SEE AMERICA AGAIN.
CONSIDER THIS WARNING, SHE-HULK.
YOUR LOSSES ARE YOUR PUNISHMENT.
THIS IS THE PRICE OF YOUR FREEDOM.
BELIEVE ME, GAMORA...
NO ONE KNOWS THAT PRICE SO WELL AS ARCADIA.

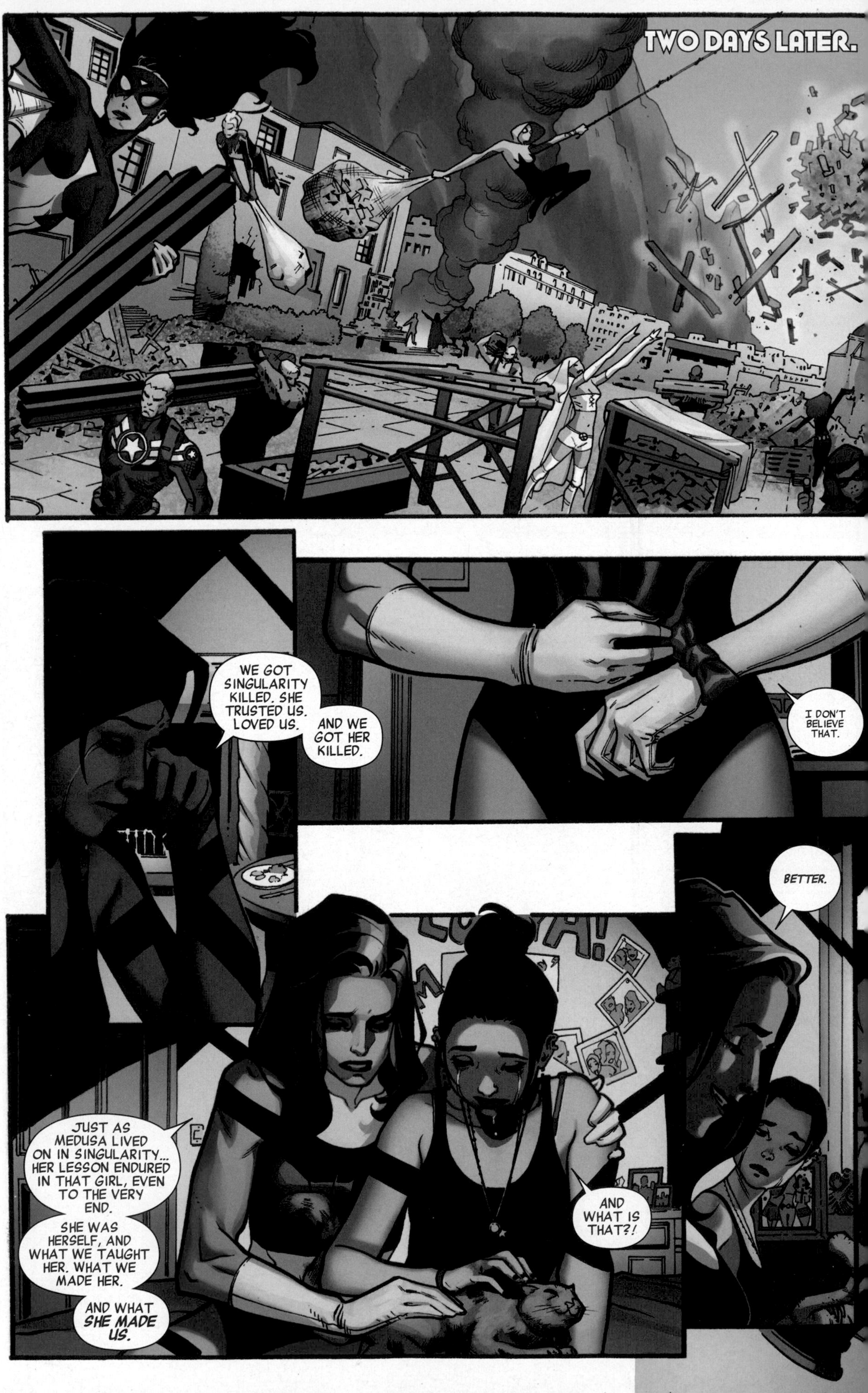

TWO DAYS LATER.
WE GOT SINGULARITY KILLED. SHE TRUSTED US. LOVED US.
AND WE GOT HER KILLED.
I DON'T BELIEVE THAT.
BETTER.
AND WHAT IS THAT?!
JUST AS MEDUSA LIVED ON IN SINGULARITY... HER LESSON ENDURED IN THAT GIRL, EVEN TO THE VERY END.
SHE WAS HERSELF, AND WHAT WE TAUGHT HER. WHAT WE MADE HER.
AND WHAT SHE MADE US.

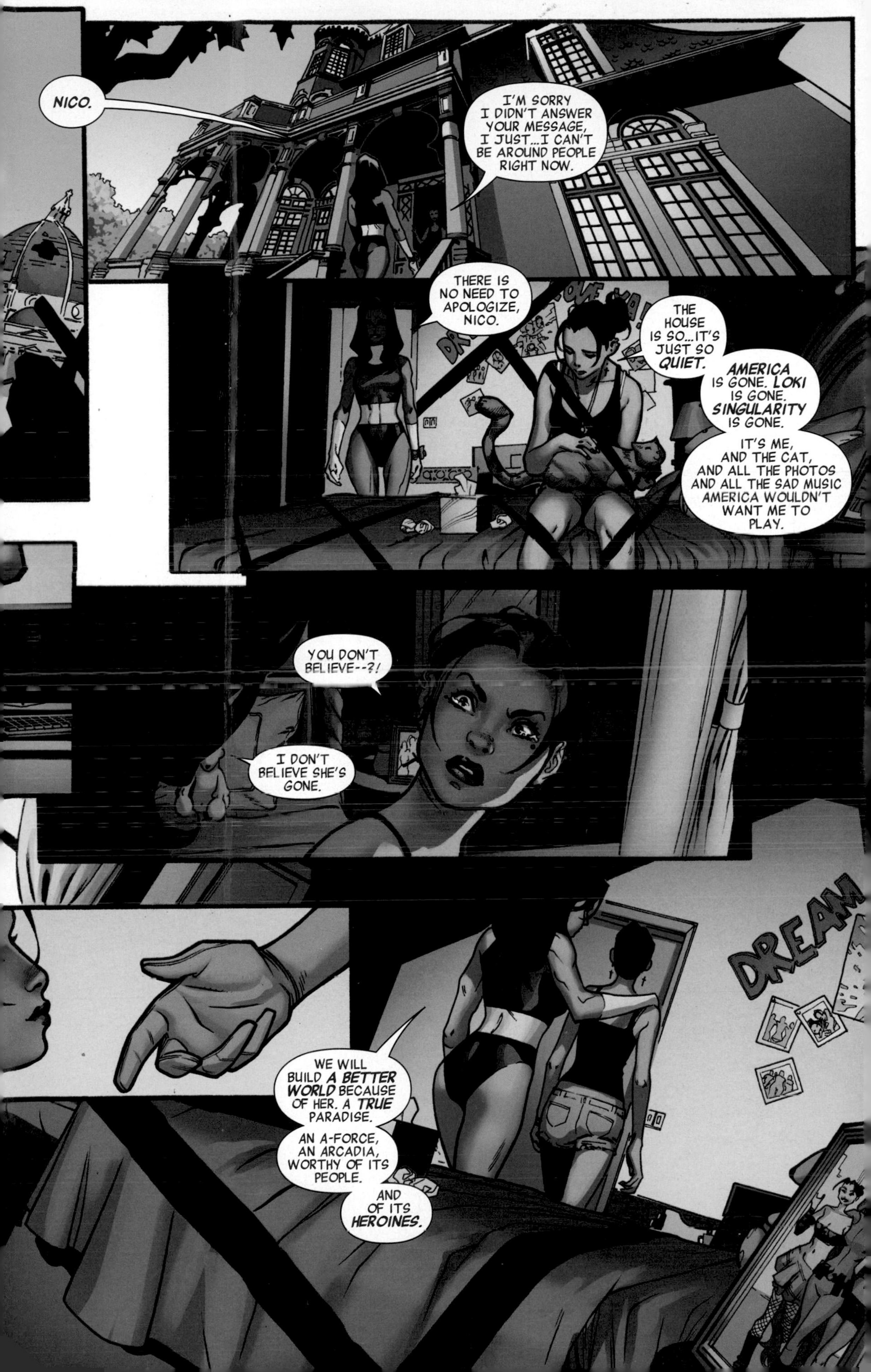
NICO.
I'M SORRY I DIDN'T ANSWER YOUR MESSAGE, I JUST...I CAN'T BE AROUND PEOPLE RIGHT NOW.
THERE IS NO NEED TO APOLOGIZE, NICO.
THE HOUSE IS SO...IT'S JUST SO QUIET.
AMERICA IS GONE. LOKI IS GONE. SINGULARITY IS GONE.
IT'S ME, AND THE CAT, AND ALL THE PHOTOS AND ALL THE SAD MUSIC AMERICA WOULDN'T WANT ME TO PLAY.
YOU DON'T BELIEVE--?!
I DON'T BELIEVE SHE'S GONE.
WE WILL BUILD A BETTER WORLD BECAUSE OF HER. A TRUE PARADISE.
AN A-FORCE, AN ARCADIA, WORTHY OF ITS PEOPLE.
AND OF ITS HEROINES.
DREAM

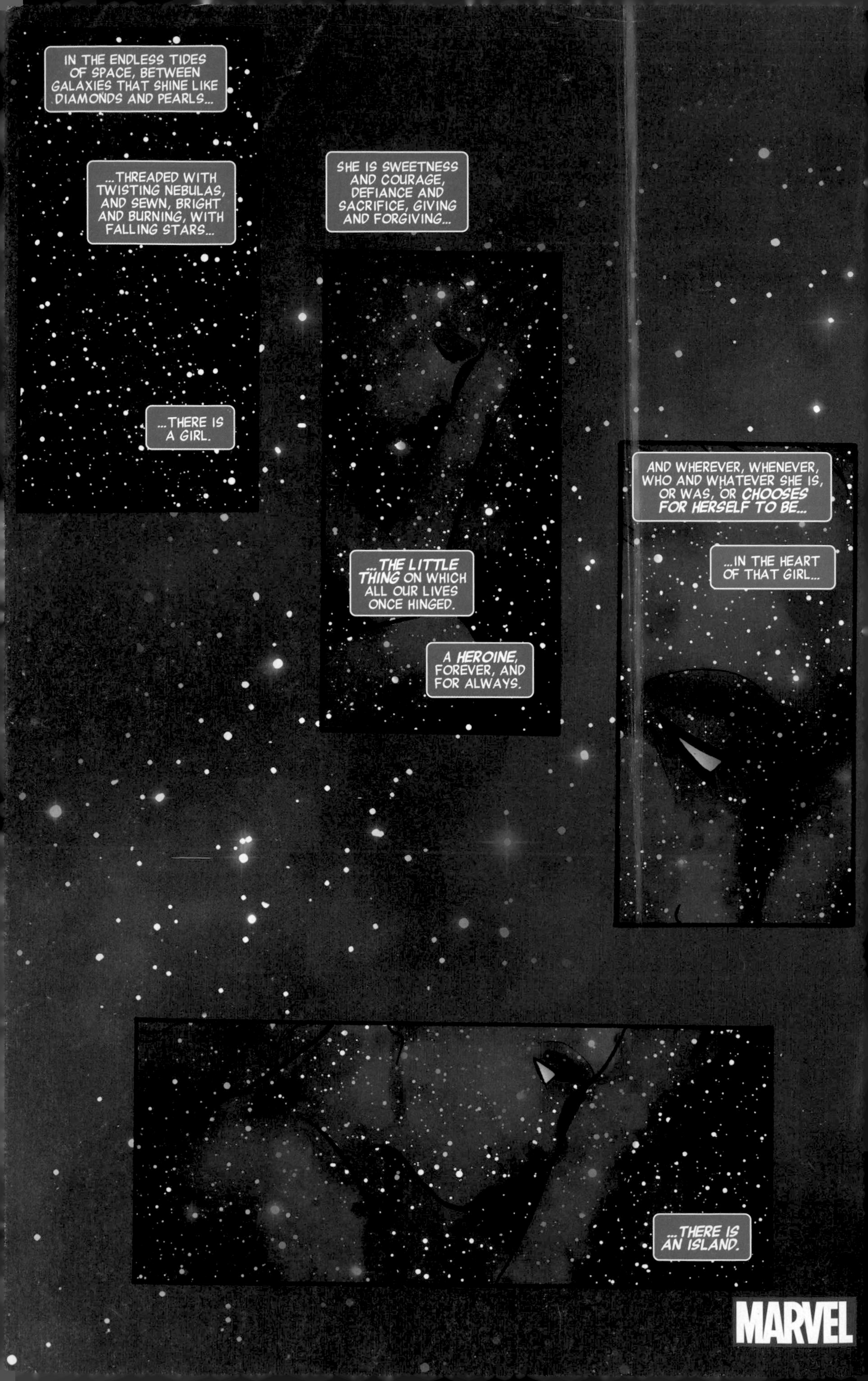
IN THE ENDLESS TIDES OF SPACE, BETWEEN GALAXIES THAT SHINE LIKE DIAMONDS AND PEARLS...
...THREADED WITH TWISTING NEBULAS, AND SEWN, BRIGHT AND BURNING, WITH FALLING STARS...
...THERE IS A GIRL.
SHE IS SWEETNESS AND COURAGE, DEFIANCE AND SACRIFICE, GIVING AND FORGIVING...
...THE LITTLE THING ON WHICH ALL OUR LIVES ONCE HINGED.
A HEROINE, FOREVER, AND FOR ALWAYS.
AND WHEREVER, WHENEVER, WHO AND WHATEVER SHE IS, OR WAS, OR CHOOSES FOR HERSELF TO BE...
...IN THE HEART OF THAT GIRL...
...THERE IS AN ISLAND.
MARVEL